Interpreting American History:

Reconstruction

INTERPRETING AMERICAN HISTORY SERIES

Brian D. McKnight and James S. Humphreys, series editors

THE AGE OF ANDREW JACKSON
Edited by Brian D. McKnight and James S. Humphreys

THE NEW DEAL AND THE GREAT DEPRESSION
Edited by Aaron D. Purcell

RECONSTRUCTION
Edited by John David Smith

INTERPRETING AMERICAN HISTORY

RECONSTRUCTION

Edited by
JOHN DAVID SMITH

The Kent State University Press
Kent, Ohio

© 2016 by The Kent State University Press, Kent, Ohio 44242
ALL RIGHTS RESERVED
Library of Congress Catalog Card Number 2015036113
ISBN 978-1-60635-292-2
Manufactured in the United States of America

LIBRARY OF CONGRESS CATALOGING-IN-PUBLICATION DATA
Names: Smith, John David, 1949- editor.
Title: Interpreting American history : Reconstruction / edited by John David Smith.
Description: Kent, Ohio : The Kent State University Press, [2016] | Series: Interpreting American history series | Includes bibliographical references and index.
Identifiers: LCCN 2015036113 | ISBN 9781606352922 (paperback : alkaline paper)
Subjects: LCSH: Reconstruction (U.S. history, 1865-1877) | Southern States--Politics and government--1865-1950. | Southern States--History--1865-1951.
Classification: LCC E668 .I58 2016 | DDC 973.8--dc23
LC record available at http://lccn.loc.gov/2015036113

Once again for Randall M. Miller—

teacher and friend

Contents

	Foreword	ix
	Acknowledgments	xi
	Introduction	1
1	Reconstruction Historiography: An Overview *John David Smith*	12
2	Presidential Reconstruction *Kevin Adams*	46
3	Radical Reconstruction *Shepherd W. McKinley*	69
4	Reconstruction: Emancipation and Race *R. Blakeslee Gilpin*	91
5	Reconstruction: National Politics, 1865-1877 *Edward O. Frantz*	112
6	Reconstruction: Gender and Labor *J. Vincent Lowery*	130
7	Reconstruction: Intellectual Life and Historical Memory *K. Stephen Prince*	151
8	Reconstruction: Transnational History *Andrew Zimmerman*	171
	Bibliography	197
	Contributors	225
	Index	227

Foreword
Interpreting American History Series

Of all the history courses taught on college campuses, historiography is one of the most challenging. The historiographic essays most often available are frequently too specialized for broad teaching and sometimes too rigorous for the average undergraduate student. Every day, frustrated scholars and students search for writings that offer both breadth and depth in their approach to the historiography of different eras and movements. As young scholars grow more intellectually mature, they search for literature, sometimes in vain, that will clarify historiographical points. As graduate students prepare for seminar presentations, comprehensive examinations, and dissertation work, they continue to search for works that will help to place their work within the broader study. Then, when they complete their studies and enter the professoriat, they find themselves less intellectually connected to the ideas that they once showed a mastery of, and they again ask about the lack of meaningful and succinct studies of historiography . . . and the circle continues.

Within the pages of this series, innovative scholars discuss the different interpretations of the important eras and events of history, focusing not only on the intellectual shifts that have taken place but also on the various catalysts that drove these shifts. It is the hope of the series editors that these volumes fill the aforementioned intellectual voids and speak to young scholars in a way that will supplement their other learning, that the same pages that speak to undergraduate students will also remind the established scholar of his or her historiographic roots, that a difficult subject will be made more accessible to curious minds, and that these ideas are not lost among the details offered within the classroom.

Brian D. McKnight, University of Virginia's College at Wise
James S. Humphreys, Murray State University

Acknowledgments

I thank Brian D. McKnight and James S. Humphreys for asking me to contribute this book to their series, so too to editor Joyce Harrison at Kent State University Press. Joyce also did a superb job preparing the bibliography. The contributors to the book responded thoughtfully to my requests for revisions, and I hope that they agree that their hard work contributed to a better book. Jeffrey J. Crow kindly critiqued sections of the manuscript and Michael Levine expertly copyedited the manuscript. As always, I thank Sylvia A. Smith for her unwavering love and patience.

Introduction

Writing in 1935 in his brilliant and brooding *Black Reconstruction,* the African American historian, sociologist, and propagandist W. E. B. Du Bois lamented America's post-Civil War Era as a missed opportunity to reconstruct the war-torn nation in deed as well as in word. "If the Reconstruction of the Southern states, from slavery to free labor, and from aristocracy to industrial democracy, had been conceived as a major national program of America, whose accomplishment at any price was well worth the effort," Du Bois complained, "we should be living today in a different world." Seven decades following the end of America's bloodiest war, Du Bois judged Reconstruction not just "a failure, but a splendid failure."[1]

Like Du Bois, historians have largely defined Reconstruction as a failed effort in what the historian Eric J. Hobsbawm termed "forced democratization."[2] In his recent *The Wars of Reconstruction: The Brief, Violent History of America's Most Progressive Era,* historian Douglas R. Egerton rejects the notion that Reconstruction was a failure, instead interpreting the period as "a noble attempt to create a more democratic America." "Too often the central question becomes why Reconstruction *failed,*" Egerton notes, "as opposed to *ended,* which hints that the process itself was somehow flawed and contributed to its own passing." In his book, Egerton underscores the various ways that white violence, what he terms "the wars of Reconstruction," cut short "the nation's first meaningful campaign for racial equality."[3]

Most historians, however, who have plowed what historian Bernard A. Weisberger termed "The Dark and Bloody Ground of

Reconstruction Historiography," have judged the dozen years following the Civil War a disastrous moment in U.S. history—an unequivocal failure.[4] Those, including neoabolitonists and later racial liberals, who found President Abraham Lincoln's promised "new birth of freedom" unfulfilled during the postwar years, regarded Reconstruction as both a missed opportunity and a travesty of justice for black southerners and white Unionists. In contrast, those who identified with white southerners and the Lost Cause mentalité condemned Reconstruction as a usurpation of federal power and the imposition of "Negro rule." According to Egerton, by the late nineteenth century "the wars of Reconstruction had entered a new campaign, as writers, activists, and intellectuals sought to impose their vision of the period on American readers."[5]

The first generation of professional, "scientific" scholars, immersed in Jim Crow-era legal definitions of race and Social Darwinist understandings of human progress, sympathized unabashedly with the Lost Cause perspective. These scholars attacked Reconstruction as a proverbial "chamber of horrors," populated by venal carpetbaggers, treasonous scalawags, and ignorant freedmen—all manipulated by unscrupulous Republicans who wreaked vengeance against former Confederates. The early historians described Reconstruction as a period characterized by "unrelieved sordidness in political and social life."[6] In 1910 William Archer, a British observer of America's so-called race problem, captured the tone of contemporary American historians by referring to "the bad old days of Reconstruction."[7]

Led by Columbia University's William A. Dunning and his doctoral students (the so-called Dunning School of historians), early-twentieth-century scholars denounced Reconstruction because the period exemplified what they considered the imposition by the federal government of punitive, vengeful interference in the affairs of the former Confederate states and an unwise experiment in racial democracy.[8] As historian Eric Foner explains,

> The villains of the piece were vindictive Radical Republicans, who sabotaged [President] Andrew Johnson's lenient plan for bringing the South back into the Union, and instead fastened black su-

premacy upon the defeated Confederacy. An orgy of corruption and misgovernment allegedly followed, only brought to a close when the South's white communities banded together to restore "home rule" (a polite euphemism for white supremacy). Resting on the assumption that black suffrage was the gravest error of the entire Civil War period, this interpretation survived for decades because it accorded with and legitimated firmly entrenched political and social realities.[9]

According to historian Glenda Gilmore, the Dunningites in their writings "completely rewrote the history of the conflict." They interpreted the Civil War as "a tragic misunderstanding and that Reconstruction had been a scurrilous punishment foisted upon helpless white southerners by arrogant Yankees who exploited African Americans by giving them citizenship rights."[10]

Despite attempts by Du Bois and other black and white scholars to rehabilitate Reconstruction's reputation, and consequently to "sustain the black counter-memory" of the Civil War and Reconstruction Eras, the Dunning interpretation generally dominated representations of the period in American popular culture and historiography from the turn of the century until after World War II.[11] White supremacy and its concomitants, including racial segregation, disfranchisement of black southerners, and racial violence held sway in these years. Throughout the period, films, novels, popular histories, and textbooks perpetuated beyond the academy the Dunning School's version of Reconstruction as a nightmare.

Decades earlier, the liberal white historian John Spencer Bassett (who famously incurred the ire of whites for ranking Booker T. Washington second only to Robert E. Lee among southerners) urged African Americans to revise the history of Reconstruction, what he termed "this much misunderstood portion of our past." Bassett believed "it will be a great thing for the Negroes themselves to show them [white scholars] that the period of reconstruction was less a failure than has been said in the histories. If they can see in what respect the best representative of the race served well and unselfishly, it will be an incentive to the best they can do in the future. It will have a good effect on the whites."[12] Later revisionist scholars, including Francis B. Simkins, Howard K. Beale, and John Hope Franklin, followed Bassett in calling for Reconstruction scholarship that transcended the traditional failure paradigm.[13]

The sustained revision of the Dunning School began during the Civil Rights Era of the 1960s, the so-called Second Reconstruction, when racial hierarchies and proscription in American life came under heavy fire. In influential syntheses published in 1961 and 1965, respectively, historians John Hope Franklin and Kenneth M. Stampp mapped out the contours of the next two decades of historical scholarship on Reconstruction.[14] Professional historians refer to these scholars and those whom they influenced as the "revisionists" and to their interpretation of Reconstruction as "revisionist."

No longer writing from the assumption of inherent black inferiority, from the 1960s onward the revisionists accentuated Reconstruction's successes, the positive, realistic changes it wrought, not just its failures and missed opportunities for long-term social change. "The new work recast Radical Republicans as well-meaning progressives who sought to reconstruct the United States on the best possible basis, were fair to the white South, and believed in the promises of equality outlined in the Declaration of Independence."[15] In doing so, the revisionists corrected what they considered several false arguments espoused by the Dunning School historians.

Those scholars, for example, had exaggerated the domination of blacks in and the amount of corruption committed by the "black and tan" Reconstruction governments. By 1877, few federal troops occupied the South; the region never experienced "bayonet rule." Freedmen's Bureau officers provided valuable humanitarian relief to the freedpeople as well as to poor, indigent whites. Accentuating the positive, the revisionists celebrated the Thirteenth, Fourteenth, and Fifteenth Amendments, as well as the Civil Rights Acts of 1866 and 1875, as precursors of later legislation that also revolutionized racial change. Revisionists also argued that the Radical Republicans acted with genuine concern for the welfare of the freedpeople, not merely out of vindictiveness against the former Confederates.

Denouncing the Dunningites, the revisionists emphasized that whites, including many former southern Unionists, joined blacks in the Reconstruction state governments. The new southern state constitutions they drafted enacted overdue reforms in education, public policy, and taxation. The revisionists also examined many hitherto ignored aspects of black life during Reconstruction, including African American political and religious activity, the freedpeoples' economic hopes and dreams, and intraracial conflict within black communities. Whether "liberal-integrationist," "neo-Du Boisian," or "proto-black separatist" in their specific interpretations, the revisionists positioned the freedpeople at the center of the Reconstruction story, interpreting them as active, autonomous agents of political and social change, not as mere victims of white racism, neoslavery, and Ku Klux Klan, Red Shirt, and White League terrorism.[16]

The revisionists credited the freedpeople, Freedmen's Bureau agents, northern missionaries, and teachers with fashioning an incipient interracial democracy from the crucible of emancipation. According to historian Michael W. Fitzgerald, they interpreted Reconstruction as "basically a demand for equality before the law and for black political inclusion."[17] Reconstruction failed, revisionists agreed, but not because of the extremes of Radical Republicans, but rather due to the intransigence of reactionary and obstructionist white southerners. Thanks to the revisionists, historian David W. Blight writes, "no field of American historiography became so active and explosive, and no traditional interpretation was so fundamentally overturned as that of Reconstruction."[18]

Despite the importance of the revisionists' arguments, a number of scholars found Reconstruction more limited and decidedly less revolutionary than the revisionists had maintained. Writing during the late 1960s and the 1970s, the so-called postrevisionists, including William S. McFeely, Michael Les Benedict, William Gillette, Leon F. Litwack, and Michael Perman, "insisted the impact of the Civil War upon American life was less pervasive than had once been believed."[19] Commenting on the revisionists, Perman stated that the postrevisionists' work "demonstrated that few possibilities existed for a Reconstruction policy capable of changing the South's political attitudes and structures." He regretted that their scholarship "confirms the suspicion that the problem was, in all likelihood, intractable. The Reconstruction episode was, therefore, not a failure. Rather it was a tragedy." Perman also explained that "perhaps the problems" wrought by Reconstruction "were so far-reaching and so complex that they defied solution."[20]

Whereas the revisionists, "living in the throes of the civil rights movement tended to understand ex-slaves and Republicans as actors in an early chapter from a sweeping and ongoing drama about the making of a more democratic America," the postrevisionists, "dwelling during the Viet Nam War era and sharing the weariness and mistrust of the federal government typically questioned the intent and radicalism of political transformation during Reconstruction."[21] Stressing continuity between the Old and New Souths, postrevisionists judged congressional Republicans too cautious, more conservative than radical, more disappointing than inspiring. They pointed, for example, to the absence of serious land reform of the plantation South. As Fitzgerald has explained, the postrevisionists emphasized "the half-hearted character of Reconstruction," approaching the topic with a "jaundiced view of American institutions." "In a sense," he explains, "this interpretation parallels the revisionists, in that it stressed the essential moderation of the Reconstruction project. The difference is the moral evaluation, and the sense that stronger remedies [to achieve legal equality] were essential."[22]

Foner's landmark *Reconstruction: America's Unfinished Revolution, 1863–1877* (1988) synthesized extant revisionist scholarship while integrating rich social history and postrevisionist insights into his narrative. At its core, Foner interpreted Reconstruction as "a revolutionary challenge to white supremacy."[23] After a quarter century, his book remains the standard treatment of the subject. "Reconstruction is one of the most misunderstood periods of American history," he recalled in 2013, "and I hoped my work would put the final nail in the Dunning School."[24]

Foner successfully hammered home the point that Reconstruction accomplished much good in the postwar South, redefining Americans' understanding of freedom and setting in motion many positive changes in American life, including black voting and the drafting of new southern state constitutions. Empowered by the vote, blacks organized politically, built churches and fraternal organizations, and established public schools, newspapers, and other institutions. In initiating individual and group autonomy, blacks did much to establish Reconstruction's political and economic agenda, Foner said. Although thwarted in their bid for land (he positioned contests over the plantation system as the key political question of the period), blacks seized the opportunity created by emancipation to establish as much independence as possible in their working lives, consolidate their families and communities, and stake a claim to equal citizenship. He wrote, "Black participation in Southern public life after 1867 was the most radical development of the Reconstruction years, a massive experiment in interracial democracy without precedent in the history of this or any other country that abolished slavery in the nineteenth century."[25]

But Foner also made clear that Reconstruction had severe limitations. Because most former slaves failed to obtain their own land to farm, the freedmen remained largely a peasant class—wage laborers, sharecroppers, or farm tenants with limited freedom. Others, trapped by debt peonage or the convict lease system, lived under slave-like conditions. According to Foner, then, Reconstruction, signified not a tragic era as the Dunningites had maintained; rather, it achieved short-terms gains, especially in terms of degrees of racial equality. Looking ahead to the mid-twentieth century, Foner dubbed Reconstruction an "unfinished revolution." Expanding upon Foner's interpretation, historian Mark Wahlgren Summers notes "that the end of Reconstruction was not so much the end of a long fight as the end of one round in a fight that for many of the participants would last lifelong."[26]

Assessing the historical literature on Reconstruction in 2006, Fitzgerald remarked that recent scholarship had abandoned the postrevisionsists' argument "that more radical measures [by Republicans] would have worked better" in achieving more revolutionary outcomes, especially for the freedpeople. "More common now," he added, "is the grim suspicion that nothing would have yielded a decent outcome."[27] Though cognizant of Reconstruction's failures, the historian David Brion Davis nevertheless recently framed its successes comparatively. In his opinion, "few emancipations in history have been followed by anything equivalent to America's first civil rights legislation and the constitutional amendments that for a limited time in the Reconstruction Era led to a significant number of African Americans to vote, to serve in state legislatures, and even to serve in the U.S. Senate . . . (two) and House of Representatives (twenty)."[28]

Interpreting American History: Reconstruction provides advanced undergraduate and graduate students with a primer on the burgeoning historical literature on the post–Civil War years that, according to Summers, has become "something of a growth industry" among historians.[29] In their historiographic essays, the contributors have focused principally on recent scholarship, much of which has followed Foner's lead in critiquing the postrevisionists and examining Reconstruction's achievements and limitations. But contemporary writings also have filled in the interstices in Foner's magnum opus, paying more attention to gender and relationships between class, labor, power, and work both North and South. Contemporary historians have surpassed Foner in determining "what Reconstruction meant in practice."[30]

Today's best work on Reconstruction focuses on integrating Reconstruction in the South into larger national and international contexts. It tends to examine social and economic questions more so than political ones. For example, scholars have studied Reconstruction in the northern and western states and how northern Republicans abandoned black southerners at the onset of southern "redemption." Economic and social changes in northern society and politics during Reconstruction, especially the triumph of postwar industrial capitalism, also continue to attract attention from historians. Many contemporary scholars are investigating gender broadly defined, including understandings of women, men, families, and households. Class, especially divisions in the postemancipation South and the plight of northern workers, preoccupies students, as do questions pertaining to historical memory, education, religion, and Reconstruction in a global and comparative context. These topics and numerous others preoccupy historians as Americans commemorate the sesquicentennial of the Civil War and Reconstruction.

John David Smith opens the book with an overview of Reconstruction historiography, including the pre-Dunning historical literature. Essays by Kevin Adams and Shepherd W. McKinley treat the scholarship on the two principal chronological periods of the era, Presidential and Radical Reconstruction, respectively. R. Blakeslee Gilpin examines writings on emancipation and race and Edward O. Franz considers national politics. More recent scholarship has focused on gender and labor and intellectual life and historical memory, topics assessed in articles by J. Vincent Lowery and K. Stephen Prince, respectively. The collection concludes with an essay on the international, transnational, and comparative history of Reconstruction by Andrew Zimmerman.

Readers of *Interpreting American History: Reconstruction* will find confirmed Foner's 2000 observation on the future of Reconstruction scholarship. "So long," he explained, "as the issues central to Reconstruction remain unresolved—the balance of power in the federal system, the place of black Americans in national life, and the relationship between economic and political democracy—the era seems certain to attract the attention of new generations of historians."[31] Or, as historian Adam Rothman explained more recently, "as long as we continue to ask new questions and question old answers, the historiography of slavery, the Civil War, and Reconstruction will remain fascinating and controversial because it unearths the struggles at the root of American national identity."[32]

INTRODUCTION

Notes

1. W. E. B. Du Bois, *Black Reconstruction in America: An Essay Towards a History of the Part Which Black Folk Played in the Attempt to Reconstruct Democracy in America, 1860-1880* (1935; repr., New York: Atheneum, 1973), 708.
2. Eric J. Hobsbawm, *The Age of Capital, 1848-1875* (New York: Scribner, 1975), 143.
3. Douglas R. Egerton, *The Wars of Reconstruction: The Brief, Violent History of America's Most Progressive Era* (New York: Bloomsbury Press, 2014), 15, 16 (emphases in original).
4. Bernard A. Weisberger, "The Dark and Bloody Ground of Reconstruction Historiography," *Journal of Southern History* 25 (Nov. 1959): 427-47.
5. Egerton, *Wars of Reconstruction*, 319-20.
6. Eric Foner, "Foreword," in *Reconstruction in the United States: An Annotated Bibliography*, comp. David Lincove (Westport, Conn.: Greenwood Press, 2000), xiii.
7. William Archer, *Through Afro-America: An English Reading of the Race Problem* (New York: E. P. Dutton, 1910), 240.
8. On the Dunning School, see John David Smith and J. Vincent Lowery, eds., *The Dunning School: Historians, Race, and the Meaning of Reconstruction* (Lexington: Univ. Press of Kentucky, 2013). Historian Michael Perman terms the Dunningites "the 'New South school' because of their regional mindset." See Perman, "The Politics of Reconstruction," in *A Companion to the Civil War and Reconstruction*, ed. Lacy K. Ford (Malden, Mass.: Blackwell Publishing, 2005), 324.
9. Foner, "Foreword," xiii-xiv.
10. Glenda Gilmore, "Which Southerners? Which Southern Historians? A Century of Southern History at Yale," *Yale Review* 99 (Jan. 2011): 60.
11. Robert J. Cook, *Troubled Commemoration: The American Civil War Centennial, 1961-1965* (Baton Rouge: Louisiana State Univ. Press, 2007), 257.
12. John Spencer Bassett to Carter G. Woodson, October 20, 1917, Carter Godwin Woodson Papers, Manuscript Division, Library of Congress, Washington, D.C.
13. See Francis B. Simkins, "New Viewpoints of Southern Reconstruction," *Journal of Southern History* 5 (Feb. 1939): 49-61; Howard K. Beale, "On Rewriting Reconstruction History," *American Historical Review* 45 (July 1940): 807-27; and John Hope Franklin, "Whither Reconstruction Historiography?" *Journal of Negro Education* 17 (Autumn 1948): 446-61.
14. See John Hope Franklin, *Reconstruction: After the Civil War* (Chicago: Univ. of Chicago Press, 1961), and Kenneth M. Stampp, *The Era of Reconstruction, 1865-1877* (New York: Vintage Books, 1965).
15. Kate Masur, review of *Reconstructions: New Perspectives on the Postbellum United States*, ed. Thomas J. Brown, in H-CivWar (Oct. 2007), http://www.h-net.org/reviews/showrev.php?id=13650 (accessed July 3, 2013).

16. John C. Rodrigue, "Black Agency after Slavery," in *Reconstructions: New Perspectives on the Postbellum United States,* ed. Thomas J. Brown (New York: Oxford Univ. Press, 2006), 43n6.

17. Michael W. Fitzgerald, "Reconstruction Politics and the Politics of Reconstruction," in ibid., 92.

18. David W. Blight, "W. E. B. Du Bois and the Struggle for American Historical Memory," in *History and Memory in African-American Culture,* ed. Geneviève Fabre and Robert O'Meally (New York: Oxford Univ. Press, 1994), 71n48.

19. Eric Foner, "Reconstruction Revisited," *Reviews in American History* 10 (Dec. 1982): 84.

20. Perman, "Politics of Reconstruction," 339; Michael Perman, *Emancipation and Reconstruction,* 2nd ed. (Wheeling, Ill.: Harlan Davidson, 2003), 3.

21. John M. Giggie, "Rethinking Reconstruction," *Reviews in American History* 35 (Dec. 2007): 554.

22. Michael Fitzgerald, "Political Reconstruction, 1865-1877," in *A Companion to the American South,* ed. John B. Boles (Malden, Mass.: Blackwell Publishers, 2002), 289; Fitzgerald, "Reconstruction Politics and the Politics of Reconstruction," 93. Fitzgerald also identifies a "post-postrevisionist" interpretation of Reconstruction in historian Mark W. Summers's *Railroads, Reconstruction, and the Gospel of Prosperity* (1984). Summers considers Republican malfeasance so heinous during Reconstruction that the party "deserved to lose power." See Fitzgerald, "Political Reconstruction, 1865-1877," 292.

23. Michael W. Fitzgerald, review of *The Bloody Shirt: Terror after Appomattox,* by Stephen Budiansky, in H-Law (June 2008), http://www.h-net.org/reviews/showrev.php?id=14581 (accessed July 1, 2008).

24. Eric Foner, interview with Catherine Clinton, *Civil War Times* 52 (June 2013): 25.

25. Eric Foner, *Reconstruction: America's Unfinished Revolution, 1863-1877* (New York: Harper and Row, 1988), xxv.

26. Marl Wahlgren Summers, "What Fresh Hell Is This? Revisiting Reconstruction," *Register of the Kentucky Historical Society* 110 (Summer/Autumn 2012): 568n2.

27. Fitzgerald, "Reconstruction Politics," 108.

28. David Brion Davis, *The Problem of Slavery in the Age of Emancipation* (New York: Alfred A. Knopf, 2014), 335, 388n26, 332.

29. Summers, "What Fresh Hell Is This?" 560.

30. Fitzgerald, "Reconstruction Politics," 114.

31. Foner, "Foreword," xiv.

32. Adam Rothman, *Slavery, the Civil War, and Reconstruction* (Washington, D.C.: American Historical Association, 2012), 18.

CHAPTER ONE

Reconstruction Historiography

An Overview

JOHN DAVID SMITH

In 1901 Woodrow Wilson, then teaching political science at Princeton University, commented that after thirty years, the time was ripe to study the period of Reconstruction following the Civil War, "not as partisans, but as historians." Although Reconstruction still remained an incendiary subject for many Americans, "like a banked fire, still hot and fiery within," historians nonetheless were up to the task. Reconstruction was "a period too little studied as yet," Wilson noted, but one that could "be judged fairly enough, with but a little tolerance, breadth, and moderation added to the just modicum of knowledge." The topic was essential, he insisted, for understanding constitutional change between 1860 and 1876 but, more importantly, for grasping the implications for American life in the twentieth century. "The national government which came out of Reconstruction was not the national government which went into it."[1]

The following year David Yancey Thomas, a Kentuckian then working on his doctorate at Columbia University, surveyed what he termed "The South and Her History." Paraphrasing one of his professors, John W. Burgess, the Tennessee-born, German-educated founder and dean of Columbia's School of Political Science, Thomas wrote that because the North won the Civil War, northerners were entitled to write the history of the antebellum period. Burgess reasoned that generally, "the victor can and will be more literal, generous, and sympathetic than the vanquished." Conversely, Thomas explained, "the history of reconstruction must be written by Southerners, who were the ultimate victors in that life-and-death struggle." Thomas went on to explain that Reconstruction constituted one of the most attractive areas of research for his generation of graduate students. "The scientific spirit of the universities," he wrote, "has largely divested them of inherited passions and prejudices, and they are going at the task of writing history with a simple desire to discover and tell the truth." He cited as an example James W. Garner's revised Columbia doctoral dissertation, published as *The Reconstruction of Mississippi* (1901), which was welcomed by reviewers North and South. "Doctors' theses dealing with such subjects are appearing every year," Thomas explained.[2]

In 1908, Thomas praised Peter Joseph Hamilton's *The Reconstruction Period: The History of North America,* stating that "it is refreshing to find at last a southern historian who has the courage to say that slavery was the cause of the war. It is still more refreshing to find one who does not burden his pages with recriminations, hurling back at those who love to dwell on the enormities of slavery and the heinousness of secession a double return for the immorality and criminality of reconstruction. However, this is already growing rare."[3] Eighteen years later, however, Thomas set forth his own view of Reconstruction in chauvinistic terms. After recounting Reconstruction's overthrow in Arkansas, he wrote that "the nightmare of carpet-bag rule was over and Arkansas breathed the air of freedom once more."[4] Thomas's point underscores the correctness of Wilson's observation: post-Civil War writings on Reconstruction smacked of intense partisanship.

Maine's James G. Blaine, one of the leading Republican politicians of the period, best exemplifies the northern perspective. In *Twenty Years of Congress* (1893), Blaine unabashedly blamed white southerners during Reconstruction for failing to show good faith toward the freedman, refusing to guarantee him "the inherent rights of human nature," and thereby alienating northerners. Blaine took pains to condemn the Black Codes of the various former Confederate states, laws that he believed whites passed in order to restore slavery "in a modified form." This "objectionable and cruel legislation" signified a slap in the face to the "liberal and magnanimous tenders of sympathy from the National Administration." Blaine also criticized Andrew Johnson's lenient policies toward the former Confederate states. The president, Blaine asserted, "quietly ignored the facts of secession, the crime of rebellion, the ruthless sundering of Constitutional bonds which these States had attempted." Blaine charged Johnson with ignoring "the immense losses both of life and property which they had inflicted upon the Nation, and gave no consideration to the suffering which they had causelessly brought upon the people." "History and just judgment of mankind will vindicate the wisdom and the righteousness of the Republican policy," he stated, "and that vindication will always carry the condemnation of Andrew Johnson."[5]

Blaine praised the Republicans for restoring the Union on a firm foundation and for recognizing the humanity of the freedpeople. It took bravery, commitment, and focus to overcome slavery's shadow. The Republicans "gave hope to the hopeless, help to the helpless, liberty to the downtrodden," and all the while they raised "the character and enlightened the conscience of the oppressing race." "In every step taken after the simple article of emancipation was decreed," he explained, "the Republicans who controlled the Government met with obstacles from without and within. There were thousands in their own ranks who did not wish the negro advanced to citizenship; there were tens of thousands who were unwilling to see him advanced to the elective franchise. But happily there were hundreds of thousands who plainly saw that only in name, and that without the elective franchise his citizenship would have no legitimate and . . . no automatic protection."[6]

Blaine defended military occupation of the southern states and praised President Ulysses S. Grant's stewardship. Without U.S. troops, the freedmen would have lost the vote. Former Rebels, Blaine wrote, worked to concentrate power in their hands and to prevent blacks from voting. They allowed such "vicious organizations" as the Ku Klux Klan to form "for the express purpose of depriving the negro of the political rights conferred upon him by law."

Klansmen, supported by whites who feared reprisals against them if they served as witnesses as to Klan treachery, "whipped, maimed, or murdered the victims of their wrath." Southern Democrats fashioned a united region of sixteen states predicated on "a tyranny of opinion which threatens timid dissentients with social ostracism and suppresses the bolder form of opposition by force." But, Blaine maintained, southern whites were shortsighted. Blacks were rapidly gaining in population. "Ceasing to be a slave the colored man must be a citizen. He cannot be permanently held in a condition between the two. He cannot be remanded to slavery. His numbers will ultimately command what should now be yielded on the ground of simple justice and wise policy." In the end, Blaine praised his Republican colleagues for ending slavery, restoring the Union, bringing prosperity to the nation, and asserting national authority.[7]

Perhaps not surprisingly, white southerners who wrote during the Jim Crow era interpreted Reconstruction differently. In 1900, for example, the Reverend John W. Stagg of Charlotte, North Carolina, an ardent segregationist who favored abrogating the Fifteenth Amendment, wrote that for white southerners, Reconstruction "was Hell come upon the earth. No people, since the day that man was created upon the earth, ever endured such outrages and indignities." He added, "Had they not been starved out during four years of fighting, they would have taken up arms after '65, in an attempt to throw off the yoke of the conqueror."[8]

That year, Columbia University's William P. Trent, a native Virginian, similarly proclaimed Reconstruction a disastrous tragedy both for the South and the nation. The Radical Republicans, he charged, "by opposing [President Andrew] Johnson, by advocating negro suffrage, by talking about conquered provinces, by insisting upon the presence of troops in the South, by affiliating with the carpetbaggers and the scalawags, filled the Southern whites with a rage which the victories of Grant and Sherman had not caused and which the vindictive eloquence of [Robert] Toombs and other irreconcilables would have been powerless to inspire." Trent further accused congressional Republicans of drawing upon "the docility of the freedmen" and initiating "a saturnalia of misrule" that established "the greatest tyranny this country has ever known." "Is it any wonder," he asked, "that the memory of such outrages has been slow to fade in the South, that old men and women look upon the hardships suffered during the war as almost trivial in comparison with the degradation and oppression they underwent at the hands not of soldiers but of rascals and renegades and misguided negroes?" Confronted by what Trent described as a "drastic reconstruction," southerners not surprisingly responded by erecting undemocratic governments and maintaining white supremacy at any cost, including the brutal murder of blacks. "As Anglo-Saxons," he explained, "they were determined to escape from both military rule and negro domination . . . hence, wisely or not, they threw themselves into the arms of the Democratic party and began to intimidate and cheat the negro."[9]

In 1902, another southerner compared the Civil War to the Spanish American War. Both conflicts, the writer explained in the *Southern History Association Publications,* had unintended, even undesired results. "The logic of events drove the conquerors into what was not foreseen, but from which it was apparently impossible to recede. The absurdity or arrogance is in claiming wisdom, foresight, virtue, for what was not contemplated, and in being seers and prophets after the achievements of evolution, which was hardly dependent on human sagacity, and certainly was not provided for the initial stages." According to the anonymous writer, the Civil War unleashed the "Pandora's box of reconstruction," most egregiously Radical Reconstruction, "a period unsurpassed in passion, hate, cruelty, rapine, fraud, by anything that ever occurred on this continent." President Abraham Lincoln never intended black suffrage, the disfranchisement of former Rebels, and the substitution of white supremacy by Negro rule. "That fearful Saturnalia of wrong and political corruption . . . unparalleled by any other treatment of the subjugated by civilized nations . . . was continued in its savagery until relief came to the Southern States largely through the firm and patriotic intervention of President Hayes."[10] Reconstruction's demise, like the war with Spain, thus served to reunite the nation.

Mainstream historians also shared such reconciliationist views. For example, in 1920 William E. Dodd, the distinguished University of Chicago historian and later U.S. ambassador to Germany, remarked that once "set free," southern blacks "were almost as much of a social menace as they had been in bondage. If they did not have the vote, they would probably become the peons of the white people of the south. If they were given the right to vote, they would become at once the objects of the most corrupting of sectional competitions."[11] That same year Ellis P. Oberholtzer, a leading historian and editor of the period, wrote unabashedly of "the havoc wrought in the mess by negro suffrage, Loyal Leagues, carpet-baggers, scalawags, and their props and stays, the radical hierarchy at Washington." He referred to "that whole lurid panorama that we call Reconstruction. The more we know of this era in our history the gladder we can be that it is now far behind us."[12] A reviewer agreed with Oberholtzer's interpretation of Reconstruction, describing the period as one "unsavory mess."[13]

Two historians, James Ford Rhodes, the talented industrialist-turned-historian, and William A. Dunning, Burgess's former prize student at Columbia, dominated Reconstruction historiography between 1890 and 1920. They concurred in interpreting the postwar years as a "tragic era"—a national tragedy that challenged white civilization. By the turn of the century most historians, following Rhodes and Dunning, portrayed the Radical Republicans as vindictive villains, political opportunists who used the freedpeople "as an instrument of power over the white South."[14] Rhodes made his mark in his influential multivolume *History of the United States from the Compromise of 1850* (1892-1906), while Dunning wrote two seminal books, *Essays on the Civil War and Reconstruction* (1898) and *Reconstruction, Political and Economic, 1865-1877* (1907). More importantly, Dunning trained generations of doctoral students whose generally like-minded dissertations, consisting of detailed state studies on Reconstruction, shaped much later scholarship. Historians deem these students and their disciples to be members of the Dunning School. Their interpretations of Reconstruction in turn sparked revisionist cycles that vigorously challenged the findings of Rhodes, Dunning, and the Dunningites.

Rhodes, a self-taught historian from Ohio, generally identified with white southerners and defended the South during the postwar years, charging that Radical Reconstruction was a mistaken policy. He argued that the former Confederate states could have reentered the Union smoothly without federal interference. While Rhodes criticized slavery harshly (in doing so Burgess charged "the abolitionist assumes again the historian's place") and held the "peculiar institution" accountable for the Civil War, judging the northern cause one of morality and civilization, he nevertheless condemned Reconstruction as "a sickening tale of extravagance, waste, corruption, and fraud." Rhodes judged the freedmen mentally and morally unqualified for citizenship and hence unprepared to vote. In his opinion, the blacks "almost always voted wrong." Rhodes blamed scalawags ("knavish native white natives"), carpetbaggers ("the vulturous adventurers who flocked from the North"), and northern reformers who foisted black suffrage on the South, unmindful of what Rhodes termed "the great fact of race." He condemned the Military Reconstruction Acts of 1867 as unjust, predicated on "misguided humanitarianism, a desire to punish the South, and a design to maintain Republican supremacy in government." Rhodes charged Thaddeus Stevens with hating the South and manifesting that feeling through malicious legislation, alleged that the Radicals erred in considering the freedmen capable of citizenship, and asserted that conveying suffrage upon the blacks was an egregious blunder. Reconstruction's overthrow, according to Rhodes, constituted "a victory for righteousness," one that "all lovers of good government must rejoice."[15]

Dunning, a New Jersey native who studied in Berlin after earning his doctorate at Columbia in 1885, interpreted Reconstruction as a dangerous, volatile period in American history, a political and social revolution whereby blacks and radical white northerners and southerners overthrew orthodox white southern racial control and political power. In *Essays on the Civil War and Reconstruction,* Dunning decried Reconstruction as the nadir of American history because during the postwar years Radical Republicans stood "the social pyramid on its apex" by positioning the freedpeople "on the necks of their former masters." Dunning complained that during Reconstruction, blacks "exercised an influence in political affairs out of all relation to their intelligence or property." Those who assumed power, Dunning complained, "were very frequently of a type which acquired and practiced the tricks and knavery rather than the usual arts of politics, and the vicious courses of these negroes strongly confirmed the prejudices of the whites."[16]

Dunning's *Reconstruction, Political and Economic, 1865-1877,* the first scholarly synthesis of Reconstruction on the national level, drew heavily on Rhodes's scholarship. Dunning viewed the restoration plans of Lincoln and Johnson favorably and considered their redirection by the Radicals, especially under Thaddeus Stevens ("truculent, vindictive, and cynical") and Charles Sumner ("the perfect type of that narrow fanaticism which erudition and egotism combine to produce"), pernicious. The Radical Republicans, supported by so-called scalawags and carpetbaggers, condemned the South to a period that Dunning described as a carnival of misrule and corruption led by ignorant freedmen and the venal government leadership of President Grant. Assessing what he considered the black American's behavior and abilities during Reconstruction, Dunning wrote, "The negro had no pride of race and no aspiration save to be like the whites." Gradually, he said, domination by freedpeople succumbed to a coalition of right-minded white northerners and oppressed white southerners. The overthrow of Reconstruction ushered in so-called home rule, a euphemism conservatives of Dunning's day used for white supremacy.[17] As a reviewer remarked, Dunning's monograph "recognizes the patience, patriotism and, in the main, wisdom shown by the Southern people proper in the terrible and to a great extent, needless sufferings through which they were made to pass."[18]

Dunning directed eight dissertations on Reconstruction in individual states. Most of these theses were the first scholarly discussions of their topics, especially on the state level. The most important members of the Dunning School were William W. Davis (Florida), Walter Lynwood Fleming (Alabama), James W. Garner (Mississippi), J. G. de Roulhac Hamilton (North Carolina), Charles

W. Ramsdell (Texas), and C. Mildred Thompson (Georgia). Paul L. Haworth, the least known and most politically and socially progressive of Dunning's protégés, wrote his Columbia dissertation on the disputed presidential election of 1876 and also wrote a general work, *Reconstruction and Union, 1865-1912* (1912). With the exception of Haworth, Dunning's students generally described Reconstruction as a twelve-year-long nightmare of debauchery, exploitation, and plunder of native white southerners by dishonest and greedy outsiders, shiftless insiders, corrupt Washington bureaucrats, despotic U.S. Army officers, and brutal freedmen bent on revenge and social and political equality. Commenting on the state of American historiography in 1908, Dunning found it gratifying that "the time is fully come when a Southern point of view can contribute most effectively to the clarification of our traditions and our ideals."[19] According to historian Eric Foner, for the "Dunning School" historians, "Reconstruction was the darkest page in the saga of American History."[20] They justified the Black Codes, denounced the Civil Rights Act of 1866, criticized the military governments established in 1867, and condemned the Radical governments as controlled by self-interested politicians who manipulated the South's former slaves.[21]

Dunning's negative view of Reconstruction found its way into the first blockbuster film, *The Birth of a Nation* (1915), and two widely popular works by journalists, Claude G. Bowers's *The Tragic Era: The Revolution after Lincoln* (1929) and George Fort Milton's *The Age of Hate: Andrew Johnson and the Radicals* (1930). All three judged Reconstruction a direful moment in the history of American democracy. The Dunning School's long-standing influence on Reconstruction historiography, as Vernon L. Wharton explained in 1965, "may be attributed to the fact that it was compatible with the practices, principles, beliefs, and prejudices that justified domination of the world by people whose origins were in northern and western Europe."[22] Beyond this, as Carl N. Degler reminded historians in 1973, "Dunning's views provided the framework against which much of modern historical study directs itself. Yet Dunning repays study, if his pro-South and anti-Negro biases are recognized."[23]

Though the Rhodes-Dunning interpretation of Reconstruction as a "chamber of horrors" found its way into scholarship as late as the 1960s, it came under fire by revisionists many decades earlier. As early as 1905, Harvard's Albert Bushnell Hart insisted that white southerners had a distorted impression of Reconstruction. "Some good things were done by these Reconstruction legislatures," Hart wrote, "particularly the founding of systems of common schools throughout the South."[24] Four years later Hart's former student, the African American historian W. E. B. Du Bois, presented "Some Actual Benefits of Reconstruction" before the annual meeting of the American Historical Association. While Du Bois acknowledged corruption among some black politicians and admitted that many of the freedmen were ignorant and easily deceived, he maintained that previous historians had ignored that the former slaves generally learned quickly, acted responsibly, and received pitifully little support from the U.S. government. Du Bois defended the freedpeople from allegations of misrule and responsibility for Reconstruction's failure. He underscored three long-term contributions black voters and black legislators had made by enacting landmark legislation and reforming southern state constitutions: "1. Democratic Government. 2. Free public schools. 3. New social legislation." "Practically the whole new growth of the South has been accomplished under the laws which black men helped to frame thirty years ago," Du Bois affirmed. "I know of no greater compliment to negro suffrage."[25]

Later, in 1935, in his Marxist-inspired *Black Reconstruction: An Essay Towards a History of the Part Which Black Folk Played in the Attempt to Reconstruct Democracy in America, 1860–1880,* Du Bois charged previous historians with intellectual dishonesty and lamented that he worked "in a field devastated by passion and belief."[26] Du Bois described the freedpeople as active players in the Civil War and Reconstruction story, not mere bystanders caught in or manipulated by the path of social and political change. According to historian Christopher Phelps, in *Black Reconstruction* Du Bois was "testing his Marxist wings" and "called Reconstruction a proto-typical or embryonic 'dictatorship of the proletariat.'"[27] Du Bois assumed "that the Negro in America and in general is an average and ordinary human being, who under given environment develops like other human beings," not an inferior, an outcast from evolution and human development. In a chapter titled "The Propaganda of History," Du Bois wrote that partisan historians, including Rhodes, Burgess, Dunning, and his students characterized the freedpeople as ignorant, lazy, dishonest, extravagant, and responsible for Reconstruction-era "bad government." To counter this, Du Bois wrote creatively, passionately, and powerfully that during the Civil War Era, African Americans worked to tear down the edifice of slavery in order to build a new structure on the foundation of democracy. "The legislation of this period was not bad," Du Bois explained in response to those who debunked Reconstruction, "as is proven by the fact that it was retained for long periods after 1876 and much of it still stands."[28]

For all its rhetorical power, Du Bois's *Black Reconstruction* failed, as black critic A. A. Taylor remarked in 1935, to show that during Reconstruction "Negroes constituted an organized breaking-away from work on the plantations with a view to forcing immediate economic or political concessions either from planters or from the government of the Confederacy." Beyond this, Taylor faulted Du Bois for falling short of proving that the freedpeople "dictated 'the forms and methods of government' in those states in which the black population exceeded the white. Sufficient evidence is not presented to show that the masses attempted to control the state and to socialize industry."[29] Another African American historian, Charles H. Wesley, was more favorable, lauding Du Bois as "the lyric historian, stringing his lyre. He is the literary knight with the plumed pen." Wesley found special meaning in *Black Reconstruction* for people of color. Du Bois proved that the Negro was not to blame for Reconstruction's failure: "It was not his lack of capacity. There was no connection between race and corruption.... So timely a volume cannot fail to have influence in a period when American Democracy reluctantly seems almost on the verge of granting to the Negro population some of its citizenship privileges."[30]

Du Bois's *Black Reconstruction* signaled the opening salvo in what became a steady stream of revisionist works on Reconstruction from the World War II period to the Civil Rights Era.[31] In 1939

Francis Butler Simkins, a white southerner and a former graduate student of Dunning's, explained how "the successful historian of Reconstruction, by revealing early phases of the still burning race question, arouses more attention among the reading public than is usually accorded historical works." Simkins charged that "conservative scholars have described the follies and rascalities of Negro politicians and their Carpetbagger friends so as to make the reader thankful that such knavery cannot be repeated in his time" and explained that what he considered the "extremely partisan," "biased," "one-sided and unhistorical" interpretation of Reconstruction remained alive and, "like Banquo's ghost it will not down." He drew a direct relationship between white southerners' interpretation of Reconstruction and the disfranchisement of blacks. "White Southerners will argue the issues of the Civil War and even the merits of the Democratic party," Simkins added, "but there is scarcely one in a position of authority who will debate Negro suffrage and the related issues of Reconstruction."[32]

The following year, historian Howard Kennedy Beale, who had faulted Du Bois for overvaluing class at the expense of culture, also challenged previous partisan scholars of Reconstruction.[33] Beale asked, "Is it not time that we studied the history of Reconstruction without first assuming, at least subconsciously, that carpetbaggers and Southern white Republicans were wicked, that Negroes were illiterate incompetents, and the whole white South owed a debt of gratitude to the restoration of 'white supremacy?'"[34] Responding to E. Merton Coulter's reactionary *The South during Reconstruction* (1947), a work that many historians consider to be the last major Dunningite study in spirit if not in direct influence, the African American scholar John Hope Franklin charged that Coulter, like Dunning, interpreted Radical Reconstruction as "a social and political system in which all the forces that made for civilization were dominated by a mass of barbarous freedmen."[35] In his landmark historiographical essay of 1959, "The Dark and Bloody Ground of Reconstruction Historiography," Bernard A. Weisberger pointed out that despite the surge of critical, revisionist writings on Reconstruction on the local level, the era's positive qualities, including black suffrage, had yet to enter either general histories or textbooks. The traditional "Carpetbag-bayonet rule-Negro domination" myth continued to reign.³⁶

Franklin sought to fill this void in his revisionist *Reconstruction: After the Civil War* (1961), arguing that Reconstruction was less protracted, less corrupt, and generally more positive than white southerners and previous historians had charged. Franklin's book constituted the first full-scale, mainstream (non-Marxist and hence acceptable to scholars) work since Dunning's *Reconstruction, Political and Economic*.³⁷ In Franklin's accounting, President Johnson was an incompetent and the Ku Klux Klan consisted of terrorist white supremacists. Military rule was a myth. The Radicals promoted racial justice and extended democracy. That said, Franklin regretted that "in the postwar years the Union had not made the achievements of the war a foundation for the healthy advancement of the political, social, and economic life of the United States."³⁸

With the start of the 1960s Civil Rights Era, the revisionist historians began to dismiss, if not vilify, the Dunningites as outright racists, condemning their work as relics of the segregation era, a time when elite whites dominated southern historical scholarship and Jim Crow defined the status of black Americans. According to historian Fletcher M. Green, a new "Revisionist School" of historians "conducted a veritable crusade for the cause" of repudiating the "Dunning School."³⁹ As Eric Foner has explained, "Not until the 1960s, when the civil rights revolution altered historians' views of race and destroyed the assumptions of black incapacity . . . did a revisionist wave sweep over the field."⁴⁰ Not surprisingly, then, in his *Reconstruction: After the Civil War* Franklin underscored the importance of constitutional questions and the political meaning of federal intervention in the South. As historian Michael Fitzgerald has observed, Franklin in his book "strove for a balanced tone suited to the interracial, legally focused, integrationist northern constituency for civil rights" of the 1960s.⁴¹

In his revisionist *The Era of Reconstruction, 1865–1877* (1965), Kenneth M. Stampp put another nail in the Dunningites' historiographical coffin. His synthesis emphasized the political triumphs of the

South's Radical governments. According to Stampp, they "were by far the most democratic the South has ever known. They were the only governments in southern history to extend to Negroes complete civil and political equality, and to try to protect them in the enjoyment of the rights they were granted." Contrary to the legend of Reconstruction, Stampp explained, the downfall of the Radical governments "was hardly a victory for political democracy." Rather, those who "'redeemed' the South tried to relegate poor men, Negro and white, once more to political obscurity."[42]

Over time "the victory of revisionism," popularized by Franklin and Stampp, became the consensus.[43] In 1969, historian Richard N. Current identified essentially different attitudes toward race as separating the work of the revisionists from that of their forebears. "The recent historians," Current wrote, "assume that the freedmen of the 1860's and 1870's, despite handicaps of their previous servitude, were by nature quite capable of participating in self-government. The revisionists differ most fundamentally from their predecessors in a relative lack of race bias."[44]

That same year, Stampp and Leon F. Litwack proclaimed that after three decades of research and changed ideas about race and society, "revisionism has won the day and bids fair to become the new orthodoxy." After noting remaining gaps in the scholarship (works on the carpetbaggers and scalawags, southern blacks after Reconstruction, Lincoln's role in Reconstruction, and biographies of key Radicals remained to be written), Stampp and Litwack acknowledged "it would be folly to assume that the revisionism of today will altogether satisfy the historians of tomorrow." Nevertheless, they defined late 1960s Reconstruction revisionism as including "humanitarianism, ideals and ideology." In their opinion, "The appreciation of the complexity of motivation and a more sophisticated approach to problems of human behavior are the very essence of Reconstruction revisionism."[45] As Foner explains, "By the end of the 1960s, the old interpretation [of Reconstruction] had been completely reversed. Southern freedmen were the heroes, Redeemers the villains, and if the era was 'tragic,' it was because change did not go far enough."[46]

Despite the revisionists' grip on Reconstruction scholarship, during the 1960s and 1970s a school of so-called postrevisionists emerged that raised doubts about the depth and breadth of change during the dozen postwar years.[47] Historian Herman Belz described the revisionism of the late 1960s and early 1970s as "a new orthodoxy," one that maintained "not only that Reconstruction failed, but that it was fatally flawed from the very outset because it did not revolutionize landholding in the South." He added that "as the conservative southern view no longer finds serious expression, a new line of conflict appears to be emerging between a liberal political interpretation which argues that substantial though short-lived gains were made by blacks during Reconstruction, and a more radical economic interpretation which holds that very little of significance was accomplished, or at least very little relative to what was possible."[48] Race, emphasis on black agency and "political engagement," what historian Michael Fitzgerald terms "the dramatic backdrop of the 1960s," provided "an implicit analogy with the civil rights struggle" that "animated writing on Reconstruction" during that tumultuous decade. By the 1970s, "Radical Republicans were primarily criticized for not being radical enough."[49]

"Instead of seeing the Civil War and its aftermath as a . . . revolutionary impulse thwarted," Foner explains, "postrevisionist writers questioned whether much of importance had happened at all."[50] By the 1970s a number of leading scholars, including William S. McFeely, Michael Les Benedict, William Gillette, Leon F. Litwack, and Michael Perman identified continuity between the Old and New South and emphasized Reconstruction's conservatism, its limitations, flaws, and failures.[51] For all its alleged radicalism, Reconstruction in fact had minimal impact on federal-state relations, emphasized cooperation not confrontation, and failed to provide support for the freedpeople in meaningful ways, especially in providing schools, redistributing southern land, providing credit, and protecting the former slaves from white paramilitary violence. In 1979, Gillette described why he considered "the postrevisionist approach . . . the most fruitful one."

Postrevisionism does not reject revisionism; it is certainly not reactionary in the sense of returning to the undeserved abuse and prejudicial condemnation that characterized the views of the Dunningite historians. However, postrevisionism does seek to replace the tendency of certain neorevisionist historians to overestimate the accomplishments of reconstruction and provide apologies for its shortcomings; thus the postrevisionist approach attempts to provide a fresh view with which to analyze the limits of legislation and the manifest failures of reconstruction.[52]

Disillusioned by the Vietnam War and the shortcomings of the civil rights movement, the postrevisionists faulted the Radical Republicans for not going far enough, even in the area of civil rights.[53] As Richard O. Curry put it in 1974, according to the postrevisionists, "The Military Reconstruction Acts, and the Fourteenth and Fifteenth Amendments were rather slender reeds upon which to engineer a social and political revolution."[54]

Reconstruction failed, postrevisionists said, because it was basically nonrevolutionary and too conservative. As Foner notes, by stressing continuity over discontinuity, the postrevisionist paradigm positions Reconstruction as part of southern or national history, "rather than some kind of bizarre aberration." And ironically, postrevisionism returned "blacks to their traditional status as passive victims of white manipulation." That said, Foner wondered in 1982 whether the postrevisionist interpretation lent itself to a modern synthesis of Reconstruction: "Whether a convincing overall portrait of Reconstruction based on postrevisionist premises can be constructed is, indeed, open to question." He proposed an approach that considered "the subtle dialectic of continuity and change in economic, social, and political relations as the nation adjusted to emancipation."[55] In his 1980 presidential address before the American Historical Association, Franklin bemoaned the fact that despite the revisionists' contributions, historians actually knew remarkably little about Reconstruction. He implored historians to contribute "major works with a grand sweep and a bold interpretation."[56]

Responding to his own question and to Franklin's call, eight years later Foner published his magisterial *Reconstruction: America's Unfinished Revolution, 1863-1877* (1988), a work widely accessible and also available in an abridged version, *A Short History of Reconstruction* (1990). Like Du Bois, Foner positioned blacks at center stage of the Reconstruction story, discussing how "their quest for individual and community autonomy did much to establish Reconstruction's political and economic agenda." Foner never loses sight of the importance of black political organization, and especially enfranchisement, on the reshaping of plantation agricultural labor. Although largely denied their own land, the freedmen nonetheless worked hard on the grassroots level to establish their economic independence from whites, consolidated their families and communities, and demanded equal citizenship. Revising the postrevisionists, Foner wrote, "Black participation in Southern public life after 1867 was the most radical development of the Reconstruction years, a massive experiment in interracial democracy without precedent in the history of this or any other country that abolished slavery in the nineteenth century."[57]

Foner treats Reconstruction as a national phenomenon with far-reaching consequences. He focuses closely on how federal Reconstruction policy remodeled the South and strengthened the national state; how race, class, and politics shaped interracial alliances; and how changes in the North's postwar economic and class structure in turn influenced Reconstruction. No longer slaves, the freedpeople negotiated an alternative to gang labor, namely, the new farm tenantry and sharecropping systems. Although Foner interprets Reconstruction as revolutionary experience, socially and politically, he tempers his argument by framing it as a "dialectic of continuity and change." Notwithstanding its transformative effects, most notably the establishment of public schools and the legal rights accorded people of color by the Thirteenth, Fourteenth, and Fifteenth Amendments to the U.S. Constitution, Foner judges Reconstruction a failure—at best "America's unfinished revolution."[58]

Taking stock of the post-Civil War years, Foner stated that "perhaps the remarkable thing about Reconstruction was not that it failed, but that it was attempted at all and survived as long as it did." That said, it was his opinion that "for blacks its failure was a disaster whose magnitude cannot be obscured by the genuine accomplishments that did endure." Well into the next century, conservative white southerners ruled their region, employing "the same violence and fraud that had helped defeat Reconstruction to stifle internal dissent." Although a Marxist critic faulted Foner for identifying "no distinctive class character to" the political mobilization of the freedmen, after more than a quarter century his book remains the definitive work on Reconstruction.[59] In 2005, in *Forever Free: The Story of Emancipation and Reconstruction,* Foner expanded his narrative on Reconstruction to include the modern civil rights movement.[60]

Recent Reconstruction scholarship draws heavily on Foner's *Reconstruction,* which provides a "capstone" of sorts for the revisionist and postrevisionist interpretations.[61] For example, in *The Union League Movement in the Deep South: Politics and Agricultural Change during Reconstruction* (1989), Michael W. Fitzgerald charted the politicization of the freedpeople, underscoring the nexus between grassroots Radical agitation in Alabama and Mississippi and the transition to decentralized tenant farming. Starting in the late 1990s, numerous monographs emphasized the postwar years as a revolutionary era but one circumscribed by white racism, political intransigence, human greed, and weakness. Virtually all of the authors celebrate black agency and credit the freedpeople with playing a significant role in achieving political democracy, albeit limited, depending on time, place, and other contingencies.[62] Although cognizant of significant changes in post-Civil War America, North and South, historians nonetheless expressed disappointment with Reconstruction's limited long-term accomplishments and the return to power of former planters in the South and the rise of a new class of industrialist capitalists in the North. They also noted the emergence of new forms of "slavery," as in the debt peonage and convict lease systems, and the general exploitation of labor in tenancy and sharecropping arrangements in the South and the crushing of unions and the exploitation of immigrant workers in the North. In considering such issues, historians expanded the definition of Reconstruction beyond the usual

1877 cutoff and connected it with civil rights and other "freedom movements" of the late nineteenth and early twentieth centuries.

One noticeable shift in the post-Foner Reconstruction historiography is renewed interest in the old topic of politics and the law of Reconstruction. This resulted in part from a shift from social history to the "new" political history, an approach that integrated cultural, economic, social, and political history. William C. Harris's deeply researched and clearheaded *With Charity for All: Lincoln and the Restoration of the Union* (1997) and *Lincoln's Last Months* (2004) provide long overdue and definitive accounts of Lincoln's heretofore undervalued reconstruction efforts. In *Lincoln and Reconstruction* (2013), John C. Rodrigue adds a tightly argued synthesis and interpretation. Robert R. Dykstra, in *Bright Radical Star: Black Freedom and White Supremacy on the Hawkeye Frontier* (1993), and Xi Wang, in *The Trial of Democracy: Black Suffrage & Northern Republicans, 1860-1910* (1997), examined how northern Republicans joined black activists in protecting black voting rights. Heather Cox Richardson's *The Death of Reconstruction: Race, Labor, and Politics in the Post-Civil War North* (2001) chronicled another story, how northerners' support of the freedpeople waned in direct proportion to the perception that they were dangerous, disaffected workers. *Uncivil War: Five New Orleans Street Battles and the Rise and Fall of Radical Reconstruction* (2006), by James K. Hogue, traces the militarization of politics in the Crescent City and its impact on Reconstruction. In *Roots of Disorder: Race and Criminal Justice in the American South, 1817-1880* (1998), Christopher Waldrep contributed a valuable micro study of race and law in Warren County, Mississippi, unearthing how blacks energetically engaged the legal process to protect their new rights, taking disputes to court and serving on juries and as witnesses, actions that inspired white backlash and, ultimately, "redemption." Others explain how attorneys, law enforcement officers, and judges defined civil and political rights and implemented the Reconstruction amendments, how the freedpeople, wage laborers, and married women embraced contract ideology and adopted it to varied ends, how localized law operated, and how the U.S. Supreme Court's "state action doctrine" served to protect African Americans' civil rights until the 1890s.[63]

Recently, scholars also have finally recognized the importance of southern Republicans, the so-called scalawags, and other Unionists, long vilified by conservative white southerners and never examined closely enough by analytical scholars.[64]

Reconstruction's three constitutional amendments have received excellent analysis by Michael Vorenberg, *Final Freedom: The Civil War, the Abolition of Slavery, and the Thirteenth Amendment* (2001); Alexander Tsesis, *The Thirteenth Amendment and American Freedom: A Legal History* (2004); William E. Nelson, *The Fourteenth Amendment: From Political Principle to Judicial Doctrine* (1988); Pamela Brandwein, *Reconstructing Reconstruction: The Supreme Court and the Production of Historical Truth* (1999); and William Gillette, *The Right to Vote: Politics and the Passage of the Fifteenth Amendment* (1965).[65] For an insightful examination of the 1872 presidential election, see Andrew L. Slap, *The Doom of Reconstruction: The Liberal Republicans in the Civil War Era* (2006). Michael F. Holt chronicles the contested presidential election that signaled Reconstruction's end in *By One Vote: The Disputed Presidential Election of 1876* (2008). Philip Dray's *Capitol Men: The Epic Story of Reconstruction through the Lives of the First Black Congressmen* (2008) is an excellent account of sixteen black southerners elected to the U.S. Congress during Reconstruction, including Robert Smalls, Robert Brown Elliott, Blanche K. Bruce, Pinckney B. S. Pinchback, Richard Cain, Joseph H. Rainey, and Hiram R. Revels. A diverse group, these black leaders were experienced political organizers, literate, competent, and generally honest.

Although now three decades old, Litwack's *Been in the Storm So Long: The Aftermath of Slavery* (1979), remains an immensely valuable social history of how former slaves and former masters responded to the moment of emancipation. In many ways, it has become the template for considering the ways blacks created and sustained their own communities and culture amid, and even in response to, persistent racism and poverty. Litwack and others after him echo Foner in emphasizing black agency as crucial to understanding the dynamics of postwar race relations. More recently, in *Race and Reunion: The Civil War in American Memory* (2001), David W. Blight frames the black narratives of Reconstruction within what he terms the "emancipationist vision" of Civil War memory, a subject revisited by Anne E. Marshall in *Creating a Confederate Kentucky: The Lost Cause and Civil War Memory in a Border State* (2010) and Caroline E. Janney in *Remembering the Civil War: Reunion and the Limits of Reconciliation* (2013). These contemporary scholars join research in collective memory with the social and intellectual history of the postwar years to draw a composite portrait. They also point to the politics and pliability of "memory" as a means used by whites and blacks to place themselves in competing histories of what "freedom" meant.

The current turn toward integrating economic, political, and social history in Reconstruction history appears brilliantly in Steven Hahn's *A Nation under Our Feet: Black Political Struggles in the Rural South from Slavery to the Great Migration* (2003). Hahn emphasizes the freedpeople's collective self-determination. He effectively unveils how their shared experiences as slaves and soldiers and their grassroots folk culture—kinship, labor, school, benevolent society, and religious networks of communication—provided ordinary black men and women with the means to fashion varied political communities that resisted whites resolved to curtail the freedpeoples' hard-fought citizenship during Reconstruction and into the 1890s. Their quest to acquire land and economic independence and their focus on labor relations ran like a leitmotif through communal African American politics from emancipation to World War I.

In her *Out of the House of Bondage: The Transformation of the Plantation Household* (2008), Thavolia Glymph highlights the negotiating between former plantation mistresses and former slave women during the transition from bonded to wage labor in domestic service. Stephen Kantrowitz's important *More Than Freedom: Fighting for Black Citizenship in a White Republic, 1829-1889* (2012) emphasizes the severe limitations, "The Disappointments of Citizenship," experienced by black activists in Boston who sought true racial justice. In his superb synthesis of the new Reconstruction scholarship, *Splendid Failure: Postwar Reconstruction in the American South* (2007), Michael Fitzgerald included recent work on gender, labor, and geography to demonstrate how emancipation affected the everyday lives of southern blacks and whites. Lacking more commitment from northerners to refashion American race relations, Reconstruction was doomed, as Du Bois had proclaimed in 1935, to be a "splendid failure."

As historian Kate Masur maintains, "A focus on gender has been one of the hallmarks of the post-Foner literature."[66] Now, for example, historians routinely identify the varied "political" roles African American women played in the emancipation and Reconstruction stories. And scholars remain ever alert to the ritualized meanings of female and male roles in shaping all manner of power relationships. Laura F. Edwards initiated the trend of combining Reconstruction women's history, gender history, and the household in *Gendered Strife and Confusion: The Political Culture of Reconstruction* (1997), followed by Leslie A. Schwalm, *A Hard Fight for We: Women's Transition from Slavery to Freedom in South Carolina* (1997), and Noralee Frankel, *Freedom's Women: Black Women and Families in Civil War Era Mississippi* (1999).[67] Hannah Rosen's *Terror in the Heart of Freedom: Citizenship, Sexual Violence, and the Meaning of Race in the Postemancipation South* (2009) powerfully reveals how sexual violence—white-on-black rape—became a critical element in hammering out African American citizenship. In *Fighting Chance: The Struggle over Woman Suffrage and Black Suffrage in Reconstruction America* (2011), Faye E. Dutton clarifies the clash between woman suffragists and the champions of the enfranchisement of black men. Significantly, these and other studies follow the trend of emphasizing the importance of gender while expanding not only Reconstruction's chronology (from early in the Civil War until 1900, not 1877), but also its geography (the North, the Midwest, the West, and Appalachia, not just the South).

The works of Heather Cox Richardson and Hugh Davis suggest how recent historians are widening the geography of Reconstruction studies. In *West from Appomattox: The Reconstruction of America after the Civil War* (2007), Richardson interprets Reconstruction more broadly and analytically than most scholars. "This pivotal era," she writes, "defined modern America as southerners, northerners, and westerners gradually hammered out a national identity that united three regions into a country that could become a world power." Richardson argues that a new ideology of individualism, one that transcended region, evolved between the Civil War and the Spanish American War. According to Richardson, the idea of the American West in general, and cowboys in particular, contributed significantly to the worldview of middle-class Americans. She concluded that "regardless of the harsh realities of the late nineteenth century West, the peculiarities of the postwar years made it represent economic opportunity, political purity, and social equality."[68] In *We Will Be Satisfied with Nothing Less: The African American Struggle for Equal Rights in the North during Reconstruction* (2011), Davis centers on the varied roles African American northerners played in campaigning for male suffrage rights and equal access to public schools—in forcing Republican politicians to grant black northerners the full fruits of the Reconstruction amendments. He credits Reconstruction-era black activists for inspiring the leadership styles, organizational structures, core principles, and objectives of the twentieth-century civil rights movement.

Still other scholars merge economic, political, and social history during the Reconstruction period. In doing so, they succeed in broadening the traditional meaning of "political." In *Free to Work: Labor Law, Emancipation, and Reconstruction, 1815–1880* (1998), James D. Schmidt charted the evolution of labor law and the development of free labor during much of the nineteenth century. In *Iron Confederacies: Southern Railways, Klan Violence, and Reconstruction* (1999), Scott Reynolds Nelson examines how during Reconstruction southern planters joined northern capitalists in rebuilding southern railroads by reusing remnants of Confederate railways destroyed during the Civil War. Elizabeth Lee Thompson's *The Reconstruction of Southern Debtors: Bankruptcy after the Civil War* (2004) is a pathbreaking study of how congressional bankruptcy law in fact benefited southern planters.

Recent historians have infused an old model—close-in state and regional studies—with the fruits of the new economic, political, and social history. In many cases, these studies add detail and nuance to Foner's interpretations. Significant works in this category include Barbara J. Fields, *Slavery and Freedom on the Middle Ground: Maryland during the Nineteenth Century* (1985); Joseph P. Reidy, *From Slavery to Agrarian Capitalism in the Cotton Plantation South: Central Georgia,*

1800–1880 (1992); Julie Saville, *The Work of Reconstruction: From Slave to Wage Labor in South Carolina, 1860–1870* (1994); Jane E. Dailey, *Before Jim Crow: The Politics of Race in Post-Emancipation Virginia* (2000); John C. Rodrigue, *Reconstruction in the Cane Fields: From Slavery to Free Labor in Louisiana Sugar Parishes, 1862–1880* (2001); Michael W. Fitzgerald, *Urban Emancipation: Popular Politics in Reconstruction Mobile, 1860–1890* (2002); Susan Eva O'Donovan, *Becoming Free in the Cotton South* (2007), which treats southwest Georgia; Leslie A. Schwalm, *Emancipation's Diaspora: Race and Reconstruction in the Upper Midwest* (2009); Aaron Astor, *Rebels on the Border: Civil War, Emancipation, and the Reconstruction of Kentucky and Missouri* (2012); and Stacey L. Smith, *Freedom's Frontier: California and the Struggle over Unfree Labor, Emancipation, and Reconstruction* (2013).[69]

Recent scholars have devoted attention to questions of education, philanthropy, religion, and social uplift during Reconstruction—topics that cry out for additional research. Daniel W. Stowell's *Rebuilding Zion: The Religious Reconstruction of the South, 1863–1877* (1998) provides the best account of the impact of Reconstruction on southern Protestantism, while Edward J. Blum studies how sectional reconciliation diminished northern Protestants' commitment to racial equality in *Reforging the White Republic: Race, Religion, and American Nationalism, 1865–1898* (2005). Paul Cimbala's *Under the Guardianship of the Nation: The Freedmen's Bureau and the Reconstruction of Georgia, 1865–1870* (1997) remains the leading state study of the Freedmen's Bureau. *The Freedmen's Bureau and Reconstruction: Reconsiderations* (1999), edited by Cimbala and Randall M. Miller, includes excellent, up-to-date accounts of the Freedmen's Bureau in eight former Confederate states as well as insightful essays on Ulysses S. Grant, Andrew Johnson, and the Southern Homestead Act. Ronald E. Butchart constructs the world of black students and their teachers in *Schooling for the Freed People: Teaching, Learning, and the Struggle for Black Freedom, 1861–1876* (2010). Mark W. Summers has written several important books on various aspects of Reconstruction, especially on public ethics and political corruption. His fast-paced *The Ordeal of the Reunion: A New History of Reconstruction* (2014) presents a bird's-eye view of Reconstruction as contemporaries witnessed it, which was as a historical moment to reunite the nation, not to remake it.[70]

As a group, recent scholars working on Reconstruction tend to focus on black agency, class, community, group identity, family, gender, local political assertiveness, resistance, and self-help as central themes in their writings. Fortunately, historians no longer pass judgment on Reconstruction or its participants. Rather, they seek to extract meaning from the contingencies, contradictions, and even the margins of the complex postwar story. Today's scholars look beyond interracial or interclass conflict and probe intraracial and intraclass divisions and coalitions. They measure degrees of success or failure rather than thinking in absolutes and seek to understand the broad meaning of disunion, emancipation, Reconstruction, and reconciliation. Constructed memory and the contested meaning of Reconstruction provide yet more avenues for scholars to traverse.

After surveying the historical literature on Reconstruction in 2010, Paul A. Cimbala and Randall M. Miller remarked that "much work on Reconstruction remains locked in limited conceptions of time or space, by focusing on a particular moment or by limiting any comparative perspective." They urge historians to note "that the contours of the unfinished business of the war are more malleable and complicated than any single drawing." Others ponder Reconstruction's chronology. Was there a "long" Reconstruction that began during the Civil War and has yet to be consummated? Cimbala and Miller concluded that "a new generation of scholars has pushed the beginning of Reconstruction ever backward into the antebellum period." They see Reconstruction as "a process on many fronts, working out variously in many places through the war and its aftermath and continuing well into the next century. Then, too, economic, social, and cultural history increasingly informs the approaches of scholars to Reconstruction."[71]

As this chapter has suggested, the historiographical route from Blaine to Rhodes, and then Dunning to Du Bois, Stampp, Foner and beyond, mirrored and continues to mirror American political and intellectual history, as well as contemporary history. Historical writing always has been an unconscious process of engagement between history, the historian, and the world in which she or he resides. Context matters immensely. Taking stock of Reconstruction historiography in 1991, historian Sarah Woolfolk Wiggins observed "that Reconstruction was a time much like our own, one with collisions between state and Federal authority, constant adjustment in race relations, patronage battles, and frantic efforts to stretch shrinking tax revenues to cover expensive public services. These postwar years remind us that today's problems transcend our own time."[72] Not surprisingly, then, by the beginning of the twenty-first century, historians of Reconstruction agreed that Reconstruction signified missed opportunities for true interracial democracy and economic opportunity and social justice for the freedpeople. Today no serious historian paints Reconstruction only as a carnival of alleged horrors committed by Radical Republicans, so-called scalawags, and blacks on a supposedly noble white South, just as no serious historian champions Reconstruction's overthrow by the southern Bourbons as the "redemption" of the South and the beginning of a new day of "freedom" for white southerners.

That said, neo-Confederates, much like the most reactionary among the Dunning authors, continue to underscore what they consider the tragedy of Reconstruction. At the very least, they consider Reconstruction contested ground. In 2003, for example, Frank Conner, author of *The South under Siege* (2002), proclaimed that "any conservative Southerner who has read much about Reconstruction and post-Reconstruction is acutely aware that during those misery-encrusted 32 years, the Yankees did everything in their considerable power to break the spirit of the Southerners. They deliberately held the devastated South on the knife-edge of mass starvation, and continually waved the bloody shirt to fan the nation's hatred of the South." Victorious northerners heaped one draconian punishment upon another on the vanquished Confederates: "The North sought to crush the Southerners' Christian-based independence of spirit and belief in decentralized government and to coerce them into embracing the dominance of the national government and accepting meekly their new status as third-class citizens of the agricultural colonies of the industrialized North."[73] As recently as 2012, the historian general of the United Daughters of the Confederacy defended the proscriptive Black Codes during Presidential Reconstruction as "no worse that the Northern apprentice laws. Northern reformers and radicals, who had been deprived of any contact with field hands, protested that the Code limited the Negroes' civil rights and used this as an excuse to oppose the President's [Andrew Johnson's] reconstruction plans and further hinder the South. These radicals screamed that the South was reviving slavery."[74] Such unreconstructed opinions remain commonplace in popular misunderstandings and myths surrounding Reconstruction.

Of course, today's post-postrevisionist historians see things differently. They hold that despite the determined efforts of the freedpeople and their white friends, North and South, Reconstruction only partially succeeded. As political process, Reconstruction failed because the reconstructionists lacked the local and federal support, and even the will, necessary to effect major societal change. To be sure, Reconstruction at the federal, state, and local levels instituted significant short-term change, but the federal government failed to guarantee the hard-fought gains accomplished in the first flush of the Military Reconstruction Acts of March 1867. The government failed to enforce—in deed as well as in word—the Thirteenth, Fourteenth, and Fifteenth Amendments, as well as the Civil Rights and Enforcement Acts.

As the Freedmen's Bureau withdrew from the South, as white southerners retained control over most southern land and the marketing of agricultural staples, as blacks became farm tenants or sharecroppers, as white paramilitary groups maintained social and racial control by intimidation and violence, the Bourbons systematically overturned Reconstruction, taking control of southern state and local governments. By the mid-1870s, the successes of Reconstruction already had begun to flicker and Jim Crow had begun to flame. To be sure, Reconstruction signified continuity but also degrees of significant change. Today's historians are examining what remained the same and what changed during this transitionary moment in American history. Despite the lengthening shroud of Jim Crow, many black southerners continued to vote in elections and engage politically into the 1890s. In the period 1877-1901, they and their white supporters elected eleven African Americans to the U.S. Congress and achieved political success in the Upper South—in Tennessee, North Carolina, and Virginia.[75]

Nonetheless, as Du Bois wrote with such pathos in 1935, "the slave went free; stood a brief moment in the sun; then moved back again toward slavery."[76] As the great black scholar observed, Reconstruction's bright light had shined only momentarily, snuffed out by what legal historian Alfred L. Brophy recently described as the long "period of deconstruction . . . that followed the short period of Reconstruction."[77] Today, historians continue to study Reconstruction's rise and fall, perhaps inspired by its promise, sobered by its deleterious demise, and dismayed by its long struggle to usher in profound racial change. That contest continues today.

NOTES

Amanda Binder of the J. Murrey Atkins Library, University of North Carolina at Charlotte, provided research assistance for this chapter. Randall M. Miller and Jeffrey J. Crow made valuable suggestions toward improving earlier drafts.

1. Woodrow Wilson, "The Reconstruction of the Southern States," *Atlantic Monthly* 87 (Jan. 1901): 1, 2. In 1907 another historian, William Garrott Brown, also lamented the absence of a first-rate history of Reconstruction. Noting that William A. Dunning's much-anticipated *Reconstruction, Political and Economic, 1865-1877* (1907) had yet to appear, Brown explained that "for trustworthy material" on the topic, "one had to go to the documents and other original sources, to memoirs and biographies, and to monographs which deal, as a rule, only with individual states." See William Garrott Brown, review of *History of the United States from the Compromise of 1850 to the Final Restoration of Home Rule in the South in 1877*, by James Ford Rhodes, *American Historical Review* 12 (Apr. 1907): 681-82.

2. David Y. Thomas, "The South and Her History," *American Monthly Review of Reviews* 26 (Oct. 1902): 464. Burgess wrote in 1893 that "the victorious party should be the more generous and is usually the more fair." See his review of James Ford Rhodes, *History of the United States, from the Compromise of 1850*, vols. I and II, *1850-1860*, *Political Science Quarterly* 9 (June 1893): 342.

3. David Y. Thomas, review of *The Reconstruction Period: The History of North America*, by Peter Joseph Hamilton, *American Political Science Review* 2 (May 1908): 490.

4. David Y. Thomas, *Arkansas in War and Reconstruction, 1861-1874* (Little Rock: Arkansas Division, United Daughters of the Confederacy, 1926), 435.

5. James G. Blaine, *Twenty Years of Congress: From Lincoln to Garfield, with a Review of the Events which led to the Political Revolution of 1860,* 2 vols. (Norwich, Conn.: Henry Hill Publishing, 1884, 1893), 2:93, 94, 107, 203, 304. On Blaine's history, see Charles W. Calhoun, *Conceiving a New Republic: The Republican Party and the Southern Question, 1869-1900* (Lawrence: Univ. Press of Kansas, 2006), 202.

6. Blaine, *Twenty Years of Congress,* 2:241, 420, 421.

7. Ibid., 2:469, 671, 672.

8. John W. Stagg, "Race Problem in the South," *Presbyterian Quarterly* 14 (July 1900): 323.

9. W. P. Trent, "A New South View of Reconstruction," *Sewanee Review* 9 (Jan. 1901): 22, 25, 22-23, 26, 27. Trent noted "the unpardonably cruel lynching of Sam Hose in Georgia" in 1899 to underscore his point. Ibid., 27.

10. Review of *Lincoln's Plan of Reconstruction,* by Charles H. McCarthy, *Southern History Association Publications* 6 (Mar. 1902): 173, 174.

11. William E. Dodd, review of *The Sequel of Appomattox: A Chronicle of the Reunion of the States,* by Walter Lynwood Fleming, *Mississippi Valley Historical Review* 7 (Dec. 1920): 282.

12. Ellis P. Oberholtzer, review of *The Sequel of Appomattox: A Chronicle of the Reunion of the States,* by Walter Lynwood Fleming; *The Cleveland Era: A Chronicle of the New Order in Politics* by Henry Jones Ford; and *The Boss and the Machine: A Chronicle of the Politicians and the Party Organization* by Samuel P. Orth, all in *American Historical Review* 25 (Apr. 1920): 520.

13. Frederic L. Paxon, review of *A History of the United States since the Civil War,* vol. II, *1868-1872,* by Ellis Paxson Oberholtzer, *Mississippi Valley Historical Review* 9 (Dec. 1922): 254.

14. Harvey Wish, *The American Historian: A Social-Intellectual History of the Writing of the American Past* (New York: Oxford Univ. Press, 1960), 145.

15. James Ford Rhodes, *History of the United States from the Compromise of 1850,* 7 vols. (New York: Macmillan, 1892-1906), 5:556; 7:149, 104, 168, 75; 6:309; 7:140; Robert Cruden, *James Ford Rhodes: The Man, The Historian, and His Work* (Cleveland, Ohio: Press of Western Reserve Univ., 1961), 269. Burgess reviewed the first two volumes of Rhodes's *History* in *Political Science Quarterly* 8 (June 1893): 342-46 (quote, 343).

16. William A. Dunning, *Essays on the Civil War and Reconstruction* (1898; repr., New York: Harper Torchbook, 1965), 250, 252, 354, 355.

17. William A. Dunning, *Reconstruction, Political and Economic, 1865-1877* (New York: Harper and Brothers, 1907), 86, 87, 213-14, 219.

18. E. Benjamin Andrews, review of *Reconstruction, Political and Economic, 1865-1877*, by William A. Dunning, *American Historical Review* 13 (Jan. 1908): 371.

19. W. A. D., review of *The Reconstruction Period*, by Peter Joseph Hamilton, and *The Rise of the New South*, by Philip Alexander Bruce, in *Political Science Quarterly* 23 (Mar. 1908): 129.

20. Eric Foner, *Reconstruction: America's Unfinished Revolution, 1863-1877* (New York: Harper and Row, 1988), xx.

21. On the Dunning School, see John David Smith and J. Vincent Lowery, eds., *The Dunning School: Historians, Race, and the Meaning of Reconstruction* (Lexington: Univ. Press of Kentucky, 2013).

22. Vernon L. Wharton, "Reconstruction," in *Writing Southern History: Essays in Historiography in Honor of Fletcher M. Green*, ed. Arthur S. Link and Rembert W. Patrick (Baton Rouge: Louisiana State Univ. Press, 1965), 308.

23. Carl N. Degler, "Suggested Reading," in *Division and the Stress of Reunion, 1845-1876*, by David M. Potter (Glenview, Ill.: Scott, Foreman, 1973), 230.

24. Albert Bushnell Hart, "The Realities of Negro Suffrage," *Proceedings of the American Political Science Association* 2 (1905): 154, 156.

25. Du Bois published this paper as "Reconstruction and Its Benefits" in the *American Historical Review* 15 (July 1910): 795, 799.

26. W. E. B. Du Bois, *Black Reconstruction: An Essay towards a History of the Part Which Black Folk Played in the Attempt to Reconstruct Democracy in America, 1860-1880* (1935; repr., New York: Atheneum, 1973), "To the Reader," n.p., 725.

27. Christopher Phelps, "Introduction," in *Race and Revolution*, by Max Schactman, ed. Christopher Phelps (New York: Verso, 2003), xxv.

28. Du Bois, *Black Reconstruction*, "To the Reader," n.p., 382, 711-16. For a similar contemporary interpretation of Reconstruction as "a profoundly revolutionary epoch," see James S. Allen [Sol Auerbach], *Reconstruction: The Battle for Democracy, 1865-1876* (New York: International Publishers, 1937), 92.

29. A. A. Taylor, review of *Black Reconstruction*, by W. E. Burghardt Du Bois, *New England Quarterly* 8 (Dec. 1935): 610. Also see Taylor's "Historians of the Reconstruction," *Journal of Negro History* 23 (Jan. 1938): 33.

30. Charles H. Wesley, "Racial Propaganda and Historical Writing: The Emancipation of the Historian," *Opportunity: A Journal of Negro Life* 13 (Aug. 1935): 246.

31. On the early revisionists, see Theodore N. Weissbuch, "Literary and Historical Attitudes toward Reconstruction following the Civil War" (PhD diss., State Univ. of Iowa, 1964), 39-69.

32. Francis Butler Simkins, "New Viewpoints of Southern Reconstruction," *Journal of Southern History* 5 (Feb. 1939): 49, 50, 51.

33. W. E. B. Du Bois to Howard K. Beale, January 14, 1935, and enclosed "Suggestions," Howard K. Beale Papers, Wisconsin Historical Society, Madison.

34. Howard K. Beale, "On Rewriting Reconstruction History," *American Historical Review* 45 (July 1940): 808.

35. John Hope Franklin, "Whither Reconstruction Historiography?" *Journal of Negro Education* 17 (Autumn 1948): 448. Other pioneer revisionist scholars who wrote in the 1940s included A. A. Taylor, David Donald, T. Harry Williams, and Vernon L. Wharton.

36. Bernard A. Weisberger, "The Dark and Bloody Ground of Reconstruction Historiography," *Journal of Southern History* 25 (Nov. 1959): 434-36.

37. Eric Anderson and Alfred A. Moss Jr., "Introduction," in *The Facts of Reconstruction: Essays in Honor of John Hope Franklin,* ed. Eric Anderson and Alfred A. Moss Jr. (Baton Rouge: Louisiana State Univ. Press, 1991), x.

38. John Hope Franklin, *Reconstruction: After the Civil War* (Chicago: Univ. of Chicago Press, 1961), 227.

39. Fletcher M. Green, "Introduction," in *The Civil War and Reconstruction in Florida,* by William Watson Davis (1913; repr., Gainesville: Univ. of Florida Press, 1964), xxix, xxxi.

40. Eric Foner, "Foreword," in *Reconstruction: After the Civil War,* by John Hope Franklin, 3rd ed. (Chicago: Univ. of Chicago Press, 2013), xiii.

41. Michael Fitzgerald, "Franklin and His *Reconstruction,*" in ibid., 237, 239.

42. Kenneth M. Stampp, *The Era of Reconstruction, 1865-1877* (New York: Vintage Books, 1965), 184-85.

43. LaWanda Cox, "From Emancipation to Segregation," in *Interpreting Southern History: Historiographical Essays in Honor of Sanford W. Higginbotham,* ed. John B. Boles and Evelyn Thomas Nolen (Baton Rouge: Louisiana State Univ. Press, 1987), 200.

44. Richard N. Current, "Introduction," in *Reconstruction in Retrospect: Views from the Turn of the Century,* ed. Richard N. Current (Baton Rouge: Louisiana State Univ. Press, 1969), x-xi.

45. Kenneth M. Stampp and Leon F. Litwack, "Foreword," in *Reconstruction: An Anthology of Revisionist Writings,* ed. Kenneth M. Stampp and Leon F. Litwack (Baton Rouge: Louisiana State Univ. Press, 1969), viii-ix.

46. Eric Foner, "Reconstruction Revisited," *Reviews in American History* 10 (Dec. 1982): 83.

47. In 1967, LaWanda Cox and John H. Cox, focusing on the motivations of Republican politicians and black enfranchisement, observed a shift away from revisionism, what other scholars would term postrevisionism. They explained that "there is irony in the shifting basis of attack upon the reputation of Republican politicians. Once berated from the right for plots and maneuvers to thwart the popular will and establish Negro suffrage, these whipping boys of history are now in danger of assault from the left for having lacked the boldness, energy, and conviction needed for an earlier and more secure victory." See Cox and Cox, "Negro Suffrage and Republican Politics: The Problem of Motivation in Reconstruction Historiography," *Journal of Southern History* 33 (Aug. 1967): 303-30 (quote, 316).

48. Herman Belz, "The New Orthodoxy in Reconstruction Historiography," *Reviews in American History* 1 (Mar. 1973): 106-7.

49. Michael Fitzgerald, *Splendid Failure: Postwar Reconstruction in the American South* (Chicago: Ivan R. Dee, 2007), 213.

50. Foner, "Reconstruction Revisited," 82-83.

51. See, for example, William S. McFeely, *Yankee Stepfather: General O. O. Howard and the Freedmen* (New Haven, Conn.: Yale Univ. Press, 1968); Michael Les Benedict, *A Compromise of Principle: Congressional Republicans and Reconstruction, 1863-1869* (New York: W. W. Norton, 1974); William Gillette, *Retreat from Reconstruction, 1869-1879* (Baton Rouge: Louisiana State Univ. Press, 1979); Leon F. Litwack, *Been in the Storm So Long: The Aftermath of Slavery* (New York: Alfred A. Knopf, 1979); and Michael Perman, *Reunion without Compromise: The South and Reconstruction, 1865-1868* (Cambridge: Cambridge Univ. Press, 1973).

52. Gillette, *Retreat from Reconstruction*, 450.

53. James McPherson, "Reconstruction Reconsidered," *The Atlantic* 261 (Apr. 1988): 77. On the complexities of land redistribution, for example, see Roger L. Ransom, "Reconstructing Reconstruction: Options and Limitations to Federal Politics on Land Distribution in 1866-67," *Civil War History* 51 (Dec. 2005): 364-77.

54. Richard O. Curry, "The Civil War and Reconstruction, 1861-1877: A Critical Overview of Recent Trends and Interpretations," *Civil War History* 20 (Sept. 1974): 225. For a critical response to Perman's postrevisionism, see LaWanda Cox, "Reconstruction Foredoomed? The Policy of Southern Consent," *Reviews in American History* 1 (Dec. 1973): 541-47.

55. Foner, "Reconstruction Revisited," 83-85, 86, 87.

56. John Hope Franklin, "Mirror for Americans: A Century of Reconstruction History," *American Historical Review* 85 (Feb. 1980): 11, 12.

57. Foner, *Reconstruction*, xxv.

58. Ibid., 402.

59. Noel Ignatiev, "'The American Blindspot': Reconstruction according to Eric Foner and W. E. B. Du Bois," *Labour/Le Travail* 31 (Spring 1993): 246-47.

60. Foner, *Reconstruction*, 603, 604.

61. Kate Masur, review of *Reconstructions: New Perspectives on the Postbellum United States*, ed. Thomas J. Brown, H-CivWar (October 2007), http://www.h-net.org/reviews/showrev.php?id=13650 (accessed July 3, 2013).

62. For useful historiographical essays on scholarship about Reconstruction from the 1970s through the early twenty-first century, see John B. Boles, ed., *A Companion to the American South* (Malden, Mass.: Blackwell Publishing, 2002); Lacy K. Ford, ed., *A Companion to the Civil War and Reconstruction* (Malden, Mass.: Blackwell Publishing, 2005); and Eric Foner and Lisa McGirr, eds., *American History Now* (Philadelphia: Temple Univ. Press, 2011). For an excellent collection of essays on Reconstruction that engages with revisionism and postrevisionism, see Brown, ed., *Reconstructions*.

63. See Robert J. Kaczorowski, *The Politics of Judicial Interpretation: The Federal Courts, Department of Justice, and Civil Rights, 1866-1876* (Dobbs Ferry, N.Y.: Oceana Publications, 1985); Amy Dru Stanley, *From Bondage to Contract: Wage Labor, Marriage, and the Market in the Age of Slave Emancipation* (Cambridge: Cambridge Univ. Press, 1998); Joseph A. Ranney, *In the Wake of Slavery: Civil War, Civil Rights, and the Reconstruction of Southern Law* (New York: Praeger, 2006); Laura F. Edwards, *The People and Their Peace: Legal Culture and the Transformation of Inequality in the Post-Revolutionary South* (Chapel Hill: Univ. of North Carolina Press, 2009); and Pamela Brandwein, *Rethinking the Judicial Settlement of Reconstruction* (Cambridge: Cambridge Univ. Press, 2011).

64. See William Warren Rogers Jr., *Black Belt Scalawag: Charles Hays and the Southern Republicans in the Era of Reconstruction* (Athens: Univ. of Georgia Press,1993); James Alex Baggett, *The Scalawags: Southern Dissenters in the Civil War and Reconstruction* (Baton Rouge: Louisiana State Univ. Press, 2003); Margaret M. Storey, *Loyalty and Loss: Alabama's Unionists in the Civil War and Reconstruction* (Baton Rouge: Louisiana State Univ. Press, 2004); Hyman S. Rubin III, *South Carolina Scalawags* (Columbia: Univ. of South Carolina Press, 2006); Benjamin Ginsburg, *Moses of South Carolina: A Jewish Scalawag during Reconstruction* (Baltimore: Johns Hopkins Univ. Press, 2010); and Frank J. Wetta, *The Louisiana Scalawags: Politics, Race, and Terrorism during the Civil War and Reconstruction* (Baton Rouge: Louisiana State Univ. Press, 2013).

65. The second printing of Gillette's book in 1969 includes a useful epilogue: "The Black Voter and the White Historian: Another Look at Negro Suffrage, Republican Politics, and Reconstruction Historiography," 166-90.

66. Masur, review of Brown, ed., *Reconstructions*.

67. Also see Sharon Ann Holt, *Making Freedom Pay: North Carolina Freedwomen Working for Themselves, 1865-1900* (Chapel Hill: Univ. of North Carolina Press, 2000); Lyde Cullen Sizer, *The Political Work of Northern Women Writers and the Civil War, 1850-1872* (Chapel Hill: Univ. of North Carolina Press, 2000); Nancy Bercaw, *Gendered Freedoms: Race, Rights, and the Politics of the Household in the Delta, 1861-1875* (Gainesville: Univ. Press of Florida, 2003); Jane Turner Censer, *The Reconstruction of White Southern Womanhood, 1865-1895* (Baton Rouge: Louisiana State Univ. Press, 2003); and Carol Faulkner, *Women's Radical Reconstruction: The Freedmen's Aid Movement* (Philadelphia: Univ. of Pennsylvania Press, 2004).

68. Heather Cox Richardson, *West from Appomattox: The Reconstruction of America after the Civil War* (New Haven, Conn.: Yale Univ. Press, 2007), 349, 5.

69. Other important works are Lynda J. Morgan, *Emancipation in Virginia's Tobacco Belt, 1850-1870* (Athens: Univ. of Georgia Press, 1992); Richard Zuczek, *State of Rebellion: Reconstruction in South Carolina* (Columbia: Univ. of South Carolina Press, 1996); Lou Falkner Williams, *The Great South Carolina Ku Klux Klan Trials, 1871-1872* (Athens: Univ. of Georgia Press, 1996); Jeffrey R. Kerr-Ritchie, *Freedpeople in the Tobacco South, Virginia, 1860-1900*

(Chapel Hill: Univ. of North Carolina Press, 1999); Patricia C. Click, *Time Full of Trial: The Roanoke Island Freedmen's Colony, 1862-1867* (Chapel Hill: Univ. of North Carolina Press, 2001); Janette Thomas Greenwood, *First Fruits of Freedom: The Migration of Former Slaves and Their Search for Equality in Worcester, Massachusetts, 1862-1900* (Chapel Hill: Univ. of North Carolina Press, 2009); and Andrew L. Slap, ed., *Reconstructing Appalachia: The Civil War's Aftermath* (Lexington: Univ. Press of Kentucky, 2010).

70. See Summers's earlier works: *Railroads, Reconstruction, and the Gospel of Prosperity: Aid under the Radical Republicans, 1865-1877* (Princeton, NJ: Princeton Univ. Press, 1984); *The Era of Good Stealings* (New York: Oxford Univ. Press,1993); *The Press Gang: Newspapers and Politics, 1865-1878* (Chapel Hill: Univ. of North Carolina Press, 1994); and *A Dangerous Stir: Fear, Paranoia, and the Making of Reconstruction* (Chapel Hill: Univ. of North Carolina Press, 2009). On the Freedmen's Bureau, see also Mary Farmer-Kaiser, *Freedwomen and the Freedmen's Bureau: Race, Gender, and Public Policy in the Age of Emancipation* (New York: Fordham Univ. Press, 2010).

71. Paul A. Cimbala and Randall M. Miller, "Preface," in *The Great Task Remaining before Us: Reconstruction as America's Continuing Civil War*, ed. Paul A. Cimbala and Randall M. Miller (New York: Fordham Univ. Press, 2011), xiv, xiii. On the "long" Reconstruction, see Justin A. Nystrom, *New Orleans after the Civil War: Race, Politics, and a New Birth of Freedom* (Baltimore: Johns Hopkins Univ. Press, 2010), and Gregory P. Downs, *Declarations of Dependence: The Long Reconstruction of Popular Politics in the South, 1861-1908* (Chapel Hill: Univ. of North Carolina Press, 2011).

72. Sarah Woolfolk Wiggins, "Preface," *The Scalawag in Alabama Politics, 1865-1881*, by Sarah Woolfolk Wiggins (1977; repr., Tuscaloosa: Univ. of Alabama Press, 1991), xvii.

73. Frank Conner, "Where We Stand Now: And How We Got Here," in *The Confederate and Neo-Confederate Reader: The "Great Truth" and the "Lost Cause*," ed. James W. Loewen and Edward H. Sebesta (Jackson: Univ. Press of Mississippi, 2010), 385.

74. Retta D. Tindal, "Reconstruction, 1865-1877," *UDC Magazine* 75 (Dec. 2012): 13. Edward H. Sebesta generously provided me with this reference.

75. John David Smith, *When Did Southern Segregation Begin?* (Boston: Bedford/St. Martin's, 2002), 15; Carl N. Degler to the editor, *New York Times Book Review*, July 13, 2008, 6.

76. Du Bois, *Black Reconstruction*, 30.

77. Albert L. Brophy, oral comments at the conference A Radical Notion of Democracy: Law, Race, and Albion Tourgée, 1865-1905, Raleigh, North Carolina, Nov. 4, 2011.

CHAPTER TWO

Presidential Reconstruction

KEVIN ADAMS

Formal studies of Presidential Reconstruction—that is, the period of federal Reconstruction policy that preceded the advent of Congressional or Radical Reconstruction in 1867—have been rare in recent years, a neglect that becomes especially clear when considering the series of impressive studies exploring Reconstruction's final stages that appeared in the first decade of the twenty-first century.[1] Yet even a cursory glance at the recent literature makes it quite clear that historians have not ignored the crucial timespan between the Emancipation Proclamation and the commencement of Congressional Reconstruction with the seating of the Fortieth Congress's Republican supermajority in the spring of 1867. Indeed, works almost too numerous to list constitute this past generation's contribution to historical knowledge concerning the fraught transition from war to peace in the former Confederacy.[2] This outpouring of research has done a marvelous job of exploring the nuances of the time span that constituted Presidential Reconstruction, but remarkably few of these studies have attempted to say very much about Presidential Reconstruction itself.

In large part, this development reflects the evolution of the historical profession since debates over Presidential Reconstruction animated historians of the United States some fifty years ago. As methodological trends favoring studies devoted to sweeping sociocultural constructs (for example, the free labor ideology), specific places, or particular (often marginalized) social groups became more standard, fewer and fewer historians examined Presidential Reconstruction from the perspective of policy formulation or implementation.[3] Not even the resurgence of political history, most evident in the analyses of American state power and institutional development produced by historians, political scientists, and sociologists working in the thriving subfield of American Political Development, has prompted a reconsideration of Reconstruction. Leading works in this field have either dismissed Reconstruction as a "decidedly uncharacteristic period" comprised of "sufficiently peculiar" circumstances to justify passing it by or have portrayed Reconstruction as a moment whose revolutionary potential "was tightly circumscribed" by conservative notions of state power.[4]

Counterintuitively, perhaps the best way to advance the historical discussion about Presidential Reconstruction is to go backward. Two scholarly moves are particularly crucial in this quest. First, one should place Presidential Reconstruction in the realm of policy history, all the while keeping in mind that the set of policies that comprised Presidential Reconstruction intersected with a wide variety of historical experiences on the ground in the American South. Second, one needs to return the president to the forefront of Presidential Reconstruction, without forgetting that other political actors, not to mention the complicated situation found in the postwar South, also influenced Presidential Reconstruction's articulation and implementation.

To illustrate the potential value of these two approaches along with some of the major trends in the study of Presidential Reconstruction, this essay will revolve around President Andrew Johnson, a central character in the ebb and flow of Presidential Reconstruction's historiography. Absolutely central to older interpretations of the period, Johnson's historiographical star burst in the early 1960s, when the fiery president's actions and policies were supplanted by interpretations of Reconstruction that increasingly attributed its successes and failures to sociocultural developments in the North. Even though the best of these interpretations, most notably Eric

Foner's *Reconstruction: America's Unfinished Revolution* (1988), did not dispense with Johnson entirely, the portrait of a Presidential Reconstruction without a president continues to rule the historiographical roost. This development partially results from the powerful insights produced by sociocultural interpretations. At the same time, however, mature consideration of Johnson's political philosophy and style is required in order to understand Presidential Reconstruction on its own terms, and not as a mere precursor to the main event of Congressional Reconstruction. Significantly, once one shifts the scholarly focus back upon Johnson, the absence of a larger synthetic account of the Democratic Party in the nineteenth century as well as the failure to integrate the study of Reconstruction with other major events in nineteenth-century American history become apparent.

The relative lack of attention paid to Johnson today would surprise those historians who wrote in the first few decades of the twentieth century.[5] Chief among these early historians was William A. Dunning of Columbia University, who not only wrote extensively on Reconstruction, but who also trained a generation of historians who worked on the Civil War Era.[6] A quick glance at Dunning's synthetic account for the American Nation series, *Reconstruction: Political and Economic* (1907), exposes the historiographical framework and analytical consensus that undergirded studies of Presidential Reconstruction for much of the next half century. Dunning's treatment of the conflict between Johnson and Republicans in Congress suggests what the field has gained *and* lost in the century since.

Dunning considered Andrew Johnson's personality and character important elements in Presidential Reconstruction, but they did not explain everything that happened between Johnson's ascension to the presidency in the spring of 1865 and the massive Republican electoral victories in the fall of 1866. Johnson, who relied upon "integrity of purpose, force of will, and rude intellectual force" in political life, according to Dunning, was also "as diligent as any man in seeking and weighing the views of all who were competent to aid him." Stolid and reliable, Johnson represented

Dunning's implicit judgment that most Americans were innately conservative. Lacking "the brilliant illusions that beset the chief-justice [Salmon P. Chase] and the other radicals as to the political capacity of the blacks," Johnson also possessed a political worldview that regarded "the audacity of conception" found in the ranks of Republican radicals with extreme suspicion. Sensitive to the weight of historical precedent, and committed to the strict constructionism of the antebellum Democratic Party, Johnson was, in Dunning's estimation, a political realist forced to engage with Radical Republicans inclined to flights of fancy that contravened the laws of nature and the realities of power in the South. Instead, Dunning maintained, Johnson devoted himself to a policy in the nation's best interests: "mercy, conciliation, and an immediate restoration of the old Union and the old constitutional relations."[7]

In analyzing the contest between Johnson and the Republican Party, Dunning identified a series of key historiographical issues that remain important to this day. For example, his account of the demise of Presidential Reconstruction revolved around the notion that Johnson was initially aligned with "the essentially thoughtful and conservative element of the northern voters" in contrast to the Radicals, but that a lack of decorum in public speaking, combined with some ill-timed inflexibility, caused northern voters to lose faith in him.[8] Traces of Dunning's identification of Johnson with northern popular opinion can be seen in the current debate among historians over the extent and influence of moderate political sentiment in the North. Similarly, the precise timing of the breach between the Republican-dominated Thirty-Ninth Congress and the president, which Dunning identified as occurring around the time of Johnson's vetoes of the Freedmen's Bureau Bill and the Civil Rights Act (February and March 1866 respectively), remains an important consideration for scholars interested in the genesis of Radical Reconstruction. And despite Dunning's praise of Johnson's "reverence for the old-time Constitution," as opposed to Republicans' dangerous insistence upon "exact equality between the races in civil status, regardless of any consideration of fact," his somewhat contradictory insistence that Johnson's "narrow and obstinate" stand on principles had produced a resounding electoral victory for Republicans in 1866 strengthened the notion that Johnson's behavior shaped the outcome of Presidential Reconstruction.[9]

Discredited though they may be, Dunning's views shaped the historical debate over Reconstruction for decades. For instance, Dunning's judgment that Johnson was the victim of a hostile and overreaching Congress manipulated by the "aggressive leadership" of Thaddeus Stevens helped reinforce the view that the Radical Republicans were dangerous fanatics.[10] Dunning's related position that self-interested Radicals, "with superfluous ingenuity," exaggerated the extent and seriousness of the vitriol directed against black and white Republicans in the South cast aspersions on the Republican position that were not easily overcome, particularly given Dunning's assertion that Republicans' insistence on suffrage for African Americans would lead "to far worse evils than could ever exist without it." In Dunning's world, racial massacres were not really massacres (and, indeed, could be blamed on the victims), and the notorious Black Codes passed by southern legislatures that embodied Johnson's Reconstruction policy in the South represented a sensible push to craft order out of chaos ("one or two" might have included obnoxious features, he conceded). Dunning's overall conclusion was that "the supporters of the Confederate cause embraced not only the great majority numerically of the population, but also the best it could offer," and it was his conviction that had southern society been left undisturbed, "the better classes" would have allowed African Americans to "settle quietly into that position in southern society to which their usefulness and ability entitled them."[11]

As the social and economic subordination of African Americans deepened in the first half of the twentieth century, Americans absorbed Dunning's perspective as an article of faith, aided by popular accounts like Claude Bowers's *The Tragic Era: The Revolution after Lincoln* (1929).[12] If anything, Bowers extended Dunning's arguments, with Johnson becoming increasingly pure of spirit and the Radicals correspondingly vile.[13] Although African American historians attacked the main components of Dunning's interpretation, their long-standing marginalization within the historical profession lessened the impact of their dissent. Indeed, the editors of the *American Historical Review* failed even to review W. E. B. Du Bois's magisterial *Black Reconstruction in America* (1935).[14]

While some historians (aside from the African American ones just referenced) quibbled with minor particulars of Dunning's interpretation before the 1960s, these studies failed to tarnish Andrew Johnson's stature.[15] Not even the revisionist impulse unleashed by Kenneth M. Stampp's influential account of slavery, *The Peculiar Institution* (1956), an impulse that only gained momentum as Americans paid more attention to the burgeoning civil rights movement, did much to change things.[16] As late as 1959, a judicious survey of developments in the field of Reconstruction historiography noted the urgent need for "a good, new biography of the impeached President."[17] The author apparently was unaware that there was a book project in the works that would change the entire historiographical landscape of Presidential Reconstruction.

Not only did Eric McKitrick's *Andrew Johnson and Reconstruction* (1960) respond to the call for a modern biography of Johnson, but it revealed a sea change in scholarly approaches to Presidential Reconstruction. His task, McKitrick's introduction explained, was to explicate "how Andrew Johnson threw away his own power both as President and as party leader, how he assisted materially, in spite of himself, in blocking the reconciliation of North and South, and what his behavior did toward disrupting the political life of an entire nation."[18] This shot across the bow was only the beginning, for in *Andrew Johnson and Reconstruction* McKitrick took nearly five hundred pages to develop a wide-ranging critique of the scholarly consensus on Reconstruction that Dunning and his students and their followers had helped to shape. By its end, nearly every shibboleth in the first half of the twentieth century's historical consensus came out looking much the worse for wear.

Reinterpreting Andrew Johnson's first two years as president occupied the majority of McKitrick's monograph. In his estimation, Johnson played the leading role in the collapse of Presidential Reconstruction: "If there were to be a real prime mover, a 'causal agent,' such a role would have to be played by the one man—Andrew

Johnson—whose behavior was critical in anything and everything the party did." Painting Johnson as an "outsider," McKitrick pointed out that Johnson's "plebian origins" differed in no significant way from Abraham Lincoln's. While Lincoln made his way in political life as the consummate "insider," quick to employ a winsome bonhomie to ingratiate himself with others, Johnson maintained a perpetually uneasy relationship with his own party and the plantation and other social elites who dominated that political world. Johnson's incessant ambition to escape "grinding destitution" produced in him a temperament that treated life as a "struggle—real, full-bodied, and terrible—against forces specifically organized for thwarting him." In his quest to defeat his many enemies, Johnson relied upon a core of fixed principles that "had served him through all vicissitudes": "equal rights, local self-rule, states' rights as well as Union, and strict constitutionalism." Here McKitrick repeated the personality traits that writers like Bowers had praised but cast these familiar elements in a new light, arguing that Johnson's commitment to principle actually indicated "an easy substitute for concrete thinking." Unsure of his own intellect and unable to handle complex questions, Johnson proved to be the wrong man for a job that required nimble adjustment to a novel situation.[19]

Having painted Johnson in new colors, McKitrick made this image the foundation of an extensive reconsideration of Presidential Reconstruction as a whole. The cast of characters remained the same, but McKitrick subjected their motives, abilities, and actions to fresh scrutiny. For instance, the much maligned Radical Republicans only came to control the Republican caucus, McKitrick maintained, because Johnson's decision to oppose that party's initially moderate Reconstruction policies, like the passage of the 1866 Civil Rights Bill and the drafting of the Fourteenth Amendment, transformed moderates into radicals. McKitrick even argued that Thaddeus Stevens, an unspeakable radical villain in earlier Reconstruction dramas, proved less a mastermind dictating Republican policies, and more a man whose dedication to equality for African Americans placed him on the fringes of his party.[20]

Next, McKitrick insisted that white southerners, previously interpreted as Reconstruction's main victims, bore considerable responsibility for the collapse of Presidential Reconstruction and the onset of Congressional Reconstruction. Southerners refused to adhere to the minimalistic "protocol of defeat" desired by the mass of northerners. They elected former Confederates to public office, repudiated articles of secession and the Confederate debt only with great reluctance in the state constitutional conventions and legislatures created under Presidential Reconstruction, promulgated the odious Black Codes, and mistreated former slaves and Unionists. In short, "the South—perhaps in spite of itself—was contributing, item by item, to a malaise which threatened to undermine the North's initial disposition to support, experimentally, presidential reconstruction." Yet McKitrick did not hold the South entirely responsible for this outcome. Early during the Reconstruction process, Johnson had made clear that he would serve as "their protector against Black Republicans of the North" and, through sins of omission and commission, he encouraged intransigence among southern political elites. As McKitrick succinctly concluded, Johnson, "as advocate for the plaintiff ... had in effect conspired with the defendant."[21]

Not surprisingly, such a profound shift in tone and argument did not sit well with all historians. William B. Hesseltine, for example, struck a strong note of protest against *Andrew Johnson and Reconstruction*, writing "this, indeed, bears only a coincidental relation to the known and observed person and events of the Reconstruction period" and castigating McKitrick for seeing Johnson as "stubborn and irrational" and for not surrendering "abjectly to the moderate program of the Radicals!"[22] Despite McKitrick's significant role in furthering the emergence of a revisionist interpretation of Reconstruction, one that vigorously defended the intent and accomplishments of congressional Republicans' Reconstruction policies against the distortions of the Dunning School, dissent nevertheless appeared. In this case, the most prominent disagreement with McKitrick would come from Michael Perman's *Reunion without Compromise: The South and Reconstruction, 1865-1868* (1973).

Perman introduced a critical new variable in the study of Presidential Reconstruction, insisting that revisionist studies like McKitrick's were "inadequate as well as erroneous" because their focus on Andrew Johnson oversimplified "a complex problem." Because they failed to consider "the attitude of Confederates toward Washington's policies," revisionists only told part of the story. Directly examining those southern politicians who served in state governments formed under Johnson's policy of swift reintegration back into the Union, Perman maintained that white southerners did not passively observe Presidential Reconstruction. No matter their prewar backgrounds (which often revealed less than firm support for secession), southern political leaders immediately after the war made it clear in word and deed that they were "not prepared to ignore their vital interests in pursuit of reunion at any cost."[23]

Most important among these "vital interests" was the continued subordination of the former slaves. If accepting defeat entailed accepting anything that resembled equality between the races, southern political elites insisted that resisting defeat was necessary.[24] Under Johnson's policy of "self-Reconstruction," moreover, southern political leaders believed that "preserving, and even extending, the autonomy which they possessed under the President's policy" was possible. Perman maintained that given the intensity of white southerners' feelings on the status of African Americans and the optimism of southern politicians that they would be able to control the extent of Reconstruction, moderate northern policies based on conciliation and compromise (either between the Republican Party and Johnson or the Johnson administration and the newly formed southern regimes) were "inapplicable and bound to end in disaster sooner rather than later." Instead of being a malicious incompetent, as revisionists like McKitrick charged, Perman insisted that Andrew Johnson was "shackled" during Presidential Reconstruction because he could not renounce the actions of southern politicians (e.g., passing a series of Black Codes on the state level that restricted the freedoms of African Americans) without agreeing with the position of the Republicans. As a result, Presidential Reconstruction actually exposed the "helplessness of the President to influence Southern affairs."[25]

Examining southern leaders on their own terms, not viewing them as symbols filtered through perceptions in Washington, Perman corrected an imbalance long apparent in histories of Reconstruction. In fact, the traditional emphasis on Johnson's battles with Congress reflected this imbalance. Although Perman's study did not take readers into the tactical maneuverings of state legislative sessions and constitutional conventions, his point that the experiences of actual southerners mattered during Reconstruction encouraged historians to explore that period's intricacies through detailed southern state and local studies. Furthermore, the limitations of a top-level and top-down study based mainly on the papers of southern politicians and a few newspapers did not prevent Perman from demonstrating that the southern political elite created during Presidential Reconstruction derived largely from moderates whose policies were rational given their prejudices and their (mis)reading of northern public opinion.

Regardless of its contributions, *Reunion without Compromise* actually held less potential to overthrow the revisionist position than Perman hoped. His reading of the revisionist school was incomplete—rather than engage with the specifics of books like *Andrew Johnson and Reconstruction,* Perman cited only four titles in his introduction without so much as a single reference to a page number—and idiosyncratic. (For example, it is not likely that many revisionists believed that their studies indicated that "radical reconstruction was not inevitable, that the differences between the sections were negotiable, that a formula was available for reconciling the needs and fears of both Congress and the Confederate South.") More significantly, Perman used the southern political elite as foils for a larger argument about the limitations of moderate politics. Writing during the tumult of the late 1960s and early 1970s, he maintained that the postwar situation was "a radical situation that required a radical solution. Anything else was dangerous and delusive and, in the long run, it would fail." According to Perman, sectional peace could only have been achieved at the point of a bayonet: the "whole problem" of Reconstruction "could have been avoided, or at least caused less anxiety, if a mandatory settlement enforced by an occupying army had been imposed on the South." (Here, Perman's assertion that the "South was powerless to resist" appeared to contradict his belief in the agency of southern leaders found elsewhere in the manuscript.) Such a settlement would have been built around the exclusion of Confederate leaders, civil and military, from political life, immediate "suffrage for the freedmen," and "the division of confiscated and abandoned lands for distribution to the freedmen." When the victorious North refused to impose a settlement along these lines—never mind that, as Perman admitted, hardly any northerners conceived of such a harsh peace—it covered "a mailed fist with a velvet glove," and ceded the battle over the South's postwar future from the start.[26] Ultimately, *Reunion without Compromise* was more a story about the North than the South, and more a vehicle to condemn the failings of middle-of-the-road politics in the shadow of the fractious 1960s.[27]

Still, as the 1970s unfolded, it became clear that the terms of the debate over Presidential Reconstruction had changed. By developing such a devastating critique of Johnson, McKitrick had effectively closed off historians' study of Presidential Reconstruction's policy dimensions, even as Perman's challenge faded into the background. The lasting impact of *Reunion without Compromise* lay not in its strident criticism of political moderation, but rather in its discussion of southern political elites, who could easily be assimilated into an interpretation holding that Reconstruction failed because of political incompetence. (Later attempts to resuscitate the reputations of the southern politicians who governed during Presidential Reconstruction, most notably Dan Carter's *When the War Was Over: The Failure of Self-Reconstruction in the South, 1865-1867* [1985], highlighted the very real plight moderate southern leaders faced after the war but also reinforced their utter refusal to discard what Carter called "The Pro-Slavery Argument in a World without Slavery.")[28]

In the place of studies that treated Reconstruction as a sharply contested battle between a Democratic president and a Republican Congress played out in the halls of Washington and in the state houses and conventions of the South, historians of the 1970s increasingly wrote accounts of Reconstruction centered on African

Americans and Radical Republicans, who became the new key actors in studies of Reconstruction. Because the former did not yet possess a political voice during Presidential Reconstruction, analyses of the black experience often moved away from direct engagement with the policies of Presidential Reconstruction and toward local studies concerned with community building and economic change during the transition from slavery to freedom.[29] Moreover, given that the Republican Party only came to control Reconstruction policy after their enormous electoral victories in the fall of 1866, the chronological center of historical studies of Reconstruction moved away from Presidential Reconstruction.

Importantly, the new generation of historical scholarship on Presidential Reconstruction moved beyond the world of politics and increasingly focused on the impact of social factors and cultural values. The 1970s, for instance, witnessed a heated debate between revisionists, who continued the project of critiquing the Dunning School's positions by praising Reconstruction's reform potential, and postrevisionists, who questioned the idealism of the Reconstruction experiment by pointing out Republican policymakers' widely shared racism and ultimate lack of commitment to radical reform. These disagreements over the ideological limitations of Republican politicians who shaped Reconstruction policy, as well as the accomplishments of the short-lived biracial democracies that emerged after southern states were forced to accept universal manhood suffrage to gain readmittance to the Union, expanded historians' understanding of the period immensely. But as historical monographs addressed such topics as southern educational systems, tax regimes, and agricultural policies and tried to explain why northern indifference to the Reconstruction experiment became more prominent in the 1870s, studies of presidential leadership during the early stages of Reconstruction (whether led by Lincoln or Johnson) seemed not only rare, but anachronistic.[30] This trend fit a larger pattern in the historical profession: as historians became increasingly preoccupied with culture and its impact upon historical actors and their societies, older political histories, particularly those devoted to warring political elites, waned in popularity. Hence, when two well-known historians wrote state of the field assessments about Reconstruction historiography in the early 1980s, they could essentially ignore not only Andrew Johnson, but Presidential Reconstruction as a whole.[31]

A glaring error on the first page of Eric Foner's influential 1982 article "Reconstruction Revisited" exemplified the new state of affairs. Glossing over the Dunning interpretation, Foner wrote, "The heroes of the story were President Andrew *Jackson,* whose lenient Reconstruction plans were foiled by the Radicals, and the self-styled 'Redeemers,' who restored honest government" (emphasis added). Counting this reference, Foner's essay only contained three references to Johnson, all of which appeared in the first two pages and were included for the sole purpose of historiographical summary. Andrew Johnson, once the lynchpin of historians' interpretations of Reconstruction, had within a generation been relegated to the historiographical dustbin.[32]

The turn away from the policy and political battles that defined Presidential Reconstruction for earlier generations of historians toward studies interested in how the society and culture of Civil War America shaped developments during Reconstruction continues today. Foner more than any historian played the leading role in this shift in emphasis. In his quest to produce "a coherent, comprehensive, modern account of Reconstruction," Foner's *Reconstruction: America's Unfinished Revolution* depicted Reconstruction as a grand drama about "the centrality of the black experience," the transformation of southern society, particularly in terms of changes in race and class relations, the emergence of a more powerful federal state with "an unprecedented commitment to the ideal of national citizenship" and equal rights, and the ability of economic downturns in the North to transform Reconstruction's direction. While each of these themes had political dimensions, none of them was primarily a story about politics. More to the point, for Foner, none of these themes viewed the political struggle between Johnson and Congress as possessing inherent significance. He explained that "the entire experience of Presidential Reconstruction reveals how profoundly attitudes toward the emancipated slaves and their place in the new social order affected efforts to reshape the Southern polity and economy." Indeed, Foner's belief that "the white South brought Radical Reconstruction upon itself" through its efforts to legally restrain "a volatile black population that regarded economic independence as a corollary of freedom and the old labor discipline as a badge of slavery" tacitly portrayed politicians in Washington as reactive to developments elsewhere. By its final pages, *Reconstruction: America's Unfinished Revolution,* adeptly synthesized decades of research into an analytical framework rooted in social, cultural, and economic history—an approach that also made it easy to downplay the significance of political history.[33]

To be sure, Andrew Johnson and Presidential Reconstruction did not disappear completely from accounts like Foner's, but historians following him now tended to use the story of Reconstruction under Johnson as a colorful warm-up to the main event of Congressional Reconstruction. For example, Foner's acclaimed masterpiece mainly presented a condensed version of McKitrick in his two-chapter overview of Presidential Reconstruction. Although aware of the role southern politicians played in the aftermath of the war, Foner presented with force the notion that Andrew Johnson bore primary responsibility for the failure of Presidential Reconstruction; indeed, "he could not have failed more miserably." Johnson stated clearly to southerners that he would serve as "the white South's champion" and "a protector against the 'ultra fanatics' of the North," particularly through an overly generous amnesty program (initiated in May 1865) that restored civil and political rights to nearly all former Confederates. The quick restoration of political rights to white Confederates in most of the South allowed them to outvote their Republican rivals, giving them "a virtual free hand in regulating the region's internal affairs." Johnson's veto of the Civil Rights Bill, meanwhile, "ended all hope of cooperation with the President," because mainstream Republicans previously inclined to work with him understood that Johnson's veto "repudiated not merely the specific terms of the Civil Rights Act, but the entire principle behind it." Additionally, Johnson's attacks on Congress during the campaign of 1866 caused the president to cross "the line between political debate and uncontrolled harangue" and to surrender "the dignity his office had thrust upon him."³⁴ In all of these examples, Foner followed McKitrick's interpretations closely; Michael Perman's work, meanwhile, was only cited in 9 of the 198 footnotes that appeared in Foner's two chapters on Presidential Reconstruction. Importantly, Foner basically dismissed Perman by ignoring his argument: Foner only cited Perman to provide summary detail concerning the positions taken by southern political elites during Presidential Reconstruction.³⁵

Much more central to Foner's analysis would be an analytical concept that he had helped to popularize and that continues to exert a significant influence on twenty-first-century scholarship. Free labor ideology, the centerpiece of Foner's classic *Free Soil, Free Labor, Free Men: The Ideology of the Republican Party before the Civil War* (1970), posited that American progress rested on the existence of a dynamic society where equality of opportunity guaranteed that the most humble laborer, so long as he remained frugal, avoided vice, and saved his capital, would reap the benefits of social mobility and become an independent business owner.³⁶ Free labor ideology was central to the Republican Party's platform before the Civil War. And during the war—which was, essentially, that party's war against the southern slaveocracy—the Republicans used their newfound power to implement the central tenets of free labor.³⁷ Reconstruction, as Foner made clear in *Reconstruction: America's Unfinished Revolution*, represented an extension of the wartime campaign to make the United States a free labor society. Although "to a large extent irrelevant to the social realities" of the postemancipation South, the free labor ideology guided what Foner called the "amazingly utopian" labors of Freedmen's Bureau agents and the military to remake the conquered South. "United as to the glories of free labor," federal officials in the South undertook the real process of reconstruction, far removed from the halls of Congress.³⁸

Today, historians continue to explain the contours of Reconstruction by pointing to the salience of free labor ideology. Heather Cox Richardson's *The Death of Reconstruction: Race, Labor, and Politics in the Post-Civil War North, 1865-1901* (2001), for example, argued that Republicans during Presidential Reconstruction believed that the former slaves "seemed to be ideal workers of the free labor model"; this mattered because "the happy vision of a prosperous nation could not be realized until the South converted to free labor." Richardson maintained, however, that by the early 1870s, many northerners came to believe that "disaffected" African Americans "who were unwilling to work" sought special privileges from the federal government.[39]

The boundaries of the free labor ideology even expanded to include former Confederates. For instance, William Blair's *Cities of the Dead: Contesting the Memory of the Civil War in the South, 1865-1914* (2004), showed that southern elites immediately after the war urged Confederate veterans to set to work building cemeteries for the Confederate dead so that northern observers would realize that white southerners could thrive as free laborers.[40] Today, even historians whose projects revolve around topics seeming distinct from free labor ideology, like gender, often find it difficult to escape its shadow. Carol Faulkner's *Women's Radical Reconstruction: The Freedmen's Aid Movement* (2004), for example, sought to demonstrate that women working on behalf of the newly freed slaves "articulated an ambitious platform for Reconstruction," rooted in the conviction that "the nation owed former slaves for their years of involuntary labor." But Faulkner's analysis spent just as much time analyzing how free labor fears of dependency held by male politicians and Freedmen's Bureau agents trumped "women's efforts to reconstruct the relationship between the federal government and its citizens." Like Richardson, Faulkner pointed to the debate over the fit between African Americans and a free labor society as central to the early stages of Reconstruction. Unlike Richardson, however, Faulkner's conclusion that male reformers' fears that "charity had corrupted former slaves" by making them dependent on government aid indicated a great deal of unease over African Americans' capacity to thrive in a free labor society.[41]

Analyses rooted in sociocultural constructs like the free labor ideology have clearly pushed historians away from the political and policy battles in Washington that defined the study of Presidential Reconstruction for earlier generations of historians. Given that this state of affairs may not seem problematic to many historians working in the field today, the notion that historians should reconsider President Johnson's place in Reconstruction historiography might seem like a tough sell. Moreover, it is true that a historiographical call to arms for Presidential Reconstruction might also pursue other lines of inquiry—such as the dawning awareness that Reconstruction possibly reflected "war by another means."[42]

At the same time, however, it would seem that integrating federal policy making and policy implementation with the contingencies of power and place that characterize the modern sociocultural emphasis would enrich both approaches, particularly because the historical actors found in the Reconstruction South were well aware of the national political context. Bringing the subject back to Andrew Johnson, for example, one wonders if he might serve as a main player in a sweeping study of the Democratic Party from the antebellum period to the late nineteenth century.[43] Such a study would make the Civil War and Reconstruction the fulcrum of its analysis by pondering the extent to which these eras modified Democratic ideology and political culture, especially with the reintegration of southern Democrats into the national party during Reconstruction.

Furthermore, emphasizing federal policy making would also encourage a sorely needed integration of the Civil War and Reconstruction with contemporary issues like federal Indian and land policy, debates over immigration and naturalization policies, American overseas expansion, and rapid industrial development that American historians have largely walled off from the study of Reconstruction.[44] Particularly in light of the emergence of studies of Reconstruction that encompass new populations and regions (as well as transnational topics) and the inchoate awareness that resonances of Democratic Party ideology—white supremacy, suspicion of federal "centralization," the democratization of economic opportunity for whites at the expense of nonwhites—remained powerful after the Civil War (even if one grants historian Brian Balogh's argument that all nineteenth-century parties supported the situational expansion of federal power), the need for an overarching study that grounds the Democratic Party and its ideology firmly within a nineteenth-century America torn asunder by war only increases.[45]

The intrepid historian who tackles such a study will not only bring insights to the examination of the Civil War and Reconstruction but will better realize Elliot West's intriguing notion of a Greater Reconstruction, lasting from 1845 to 1877, and primarily defined by rapid territorial expansion and the attempt to integrate nonwhites into a white man's republic. And, by utilizing the synthetic device of the Democratic Party to explore fields like federal Indian policy, historians might not only be able to demonstrate to scholars working outside of the Civil War and Reconstruction how the war and the postwar settlement shaped all of American history, but they also might revitalize the study of the war and Reconstruction by drawing concepts and models from fields not usually integrated with Civil War America. For instance, the study of Presidential Reconstruction might particularly benefit from a long tradition of scholarship that connects the grassroots particulars of place and culture with larger federal policies found in the history of the American West.[46] In this way, perhaps, the study of Presidential Reconstruction might return to its historical roots as the study of policy making and policy implementation while simultaneously retaining the impressive insights gleaned from several decades worth of social and cultural history.

NOTES

1. Pamela Brandwein, *Rethinking the Judicial Settlement of Reconstruction* (New York: Cambridge Univ. Press, 2011); Heather Cox Richardson, *West from Appomattox: The Reconstruction of America after the Civil War* (New Haven, Conn.: Yale Univ. Press, 2007); Charles Calhoun, *Conceiving a New Republic: The Republican Party and the Southern Question, 1860-1890* (Lawrence: Univ. Press of Kansas, 2006); Elliot West, "Reconstructing Race," *Western Historical Quarterly* 34 (Mar. 2003): 6-26.

2. An incomplete list of these studies includes Mark Bradley, *Bluecoats and Tarheels: Soldiers and Civilians in Reconstruction North Carolina* (Lexington: Univ. Press of Kentucky, 2009); Judkin Browning, *Shifting Loyalties:*

The Union Occupation of Eastern North Carolina (Chapel Hill: Univ. of North Carolina Press, 2011); Carol Faulkner, *Women's Radical Reconstruction: The Freedmen's Aid Movement* (Philadelphia: Univ. of Pennsylvania Press, 2004); Thavolia Glymph, *Out of the House of Bondage: The Transformation of the Plantation Household* (New York: Cambridge Univ. Press, 2008); Steven Hahn, *A Nation under Our Feet: Black Political Struggles in the Rural South from Slavery to the Great Migration* (Cambridge, Mass.: Harvard Univ. Press, 2003); Kate Masur, *An Example for All the Land: Emancipation and the Struggle over Equality in Washington D.C.* (Chapel Hill: Univ. of North Carolina Press, 2010); Justin Nystrom, *New Orleans after the Civil War: Race, Politics, and a New Birth of Freedom* (Baltimore: Johns Hopkins Univ. Press, 2010); Susan O'Donovan, *Becoming Free in the Cotton South* (Cambridge, Mass.: Harvard Univ. Press, 2009); and Jason Phillips, *Diehard Rebels: The Confederate Culture of Invincibility* (Athens: Univ. of Georgia Press, 2007).

3. In a field as contentious and diverse as American history, exceptions, of course, abound. In fact, one might attribute a large portion of the recent success of James Oakes's *Freedom National* and Hahn's *A Nation under Our Feet* to both works' ability to seamlessly traverse the path between grassroots historical experiences and national policy. See James Oakes, *Freedom National: The Destruction of Slavery in the United States* (New York: W. W. Norton, 2013).

4. Jerry Mashaw, *Creating the Administrative Constitution: The Lost One Hundred Years of American Administrative Law* (New Haven, Conn.: Yale Univ. Press, 2012), 21–22; Brian Balogh, *A Government Out of Sight: The Mystery of Authority in Nineteenth-Century America* (New York: Cambridge Univ. Press, 2009), 293. Mark Wilson, *The Business of Civil War: Military Mobilization and the State, 1861-1865* (Baltimore: Johns Hopkins Univ. Press, 2006), represents a praiseworthy counterweight to the general absence of the Civil War and Reconstruction from American Political Development scholarship on the nineteenth-century state.

5. It should be noted that one can find scholars, such as Paul Bergeron, who maintain that Johnson is unfairly maligned, misunderstood, and unappreciated by "neo-radicals" in the historical profession, although this line of argument tends to founder upon the shoals of Johnson's racism. See Bergeron, *Andrew Johnson's Civil War and Reconstruction* (Knoxville: Univ. of Tennessee Press, 2012). For a perceptive analysis of partisan approaches to Johnson, see Andrew Slap, reviews of *Andrew Johnson's Civil War and Reconstruction,* by Paul H. Bergeron, and *Andrew Johnson,* by Annette Gordon-Reed, in *Civil War History* 59 (June 2013): 254–57.

6. The best recent scholarship on Dunning and his students can be found in John David Smith and J. Vincent Lowery, eds., *The Dunning School: Historians, Race, and the Meaning of Reconstruction* (Lexington: Univ. Press of Kentucky, 2013).

7. William Dunning, *Reconstruction: Political and Economic, 1865-1877* (New York: Harper and Brothers, 1907), 19, 38, 43.

8. Ibid., 82. Dunning contended that had Johnson successfully bolstered the "conservative men" of the Republican Party, a "fair promise" existed that a new "Union Party" could control the country and marginalize extremists on both sides. See Dunning, *Reconstruction*, 43-44. Of course, this begs the questions whether true conservatives remained in a party that had successfully waged a war that had unleashed a social revolution throughout the South.

9. Ibid., 60, 62, 63, 82.

10. Ibid., 51, 63.

11. Ibid., 45, 48, 55, 57-58, 80.

12. Bowers, a committed Democrat who served as an ambassador during the Roosevelt administration, updated Dunning's interpretation by integrating elements of Progressive historiography, notably the notions that a revolutionary conspiracy led by "triumphant industrialists and capitalists" defeated Johnson's "belligerent class consciousness." See Claude Bowers, *The Tragic Era: The Revolution after Lincoln* (Cambridge, Mass.: Literary Guild of America, 1929), 27-28, 141. Other scholarly elaborations of Dunning's thinking include Walter Lynwood Fleming, *The Sequel of Appomattox: A Chronicle of the Reunion of the States* (New Haven, Conn.: Yale Univ. Press, 1919); E. Merton Coulter, *The South during Reconstruction, 1865-1877* (Baton Rouge: Louisiana Univ. Press, 1947). Variants of Dunning that treat the Radicals as the vanguard of a grasping northern capitalism include Howard Beale, *The Critical Year: A Study of Reconstruction* (New York: Harcourt, Brace, 1930), and T. Harry Williams, *Lincoln and the Radicals* (Madison: Univ. of Wisconsin Press, 1941).

13. Bowers, *Tragic Era*, 41, 43, 44, 119. One of the stranger elements of Andrew Johnson's transformation into a martyr at the hands of Bowers involved the latter's rendition of Johnson's disastrous "Swing Around the Circle" speaking campaign as a "veritable triumph" thanks to "uniformly wise, just, patriotic" speeches. See Bowers, *Tragic Era*, 132-33.

14. George Washington Williams, *A History of the African Race in America from 1619 to 1880*, 2 vols. (New York: G. P. Putnam's Sons, 1883), vol. 2; W. E. B. Du Bois, *Black Reconstruction in America: An Essay toward the History of the Part which Black Folks Played in America, 1860-1880* (New York: Harcourt, Brace, 1935); W. E. B. Du Bois, "Of the Dawn of Freedom," in *The Souls of Black Folk: Essays and Sketches*, by W. E. B. Du Bois (Chicago: A. C. McClurg, 1903); Francis Simkins and Robert Woody, *South Carolina during Reconstruction* (Chapel Hill: Univ. of North Carolina Press, 1932) represent some of the better known works in this vein.

15. See, for example, John Cox and LaWanda Cox, "General O. O. Howard and the Misrepresented Bureau," *Journal of Southern History* 19 (Nov. 1953): 427-56; Vernon Lane Wharton, *The Negro in Mississippi* (Chapel Hill: Univ. of North Carolina Press, 1947); C. Vann Woodward, *Reunion and Reaction: The Compromise of 1877 and the End of Reconstruction* (Boston: Little, Brown, 1951).

16. Heather Cox Richardson provides a good gloss of the postwar debate over the economic platform of the Radicals in *The Death of Reconstruction:*

Race, Labor, and Politics in the Post-Civil War North, 1865-1901 (Cambridge, Mass.: Harvard Univ. Press, 2001), 254n16. See also Kenneth Stampp, *The Peculiar Institution: Slavery in the Antebellum South* (New York: Knopf, 1956).

17. Bernard Weisberger, "The Dark and Bloody Ground of Reconstruction Historiography," *Journal of Southern History* 25 (Nov. 1959): 433n23.

18. Eric McKitrick, *Andrew Johnson and Reconstruction*, (1960; repr., New York: Oxford Univ. Press, 1988), 14.

19. Ibid., 66, 85-91.

20. Ibid., 19n6, 20-21, 28-31, 40-41,47, 184-5, 260-67, 276, 279, 298, 329.

21. Ibid., 10, 28-31, 40-41, 172-73, 206, 211, 357.

22. See William B. Hesseltine, review of *Andrew Johnson and Reconstruction*, by Eric McKitrick, *Journal of Southern History* 27 (Feb. 1961): 110-11.

23. Michael Perman, *Reunion without Compromise: The South and Reconstruction, 1865-1868* (New York: Cambridge Univ. Press, 1973), 10, 12

24. The southern refusal to accept—or even recognize—defeat has received its fullest scholarly treatment in Phillips, *Diehard Rebels*.

25. Perman, *Reunion without Compromise*, 93, 347, 154-55.

26. Ibid., 8-10, 12, 14, 347.

27. An interesting comparison might be made here to another influential study that argued, in the aftermath of the 1960s and Watergate, that politics was the problem. See Michael Holt's *The Political Crisis of the 1850s* (New York: Wiley, 1978).

28. Dan T. Carter, *When the War Was Over: The Failure of Self-Reconstruction in the South, 1865-1867* (Baton Rouge: Louisiana State Univ. Press, 1985), 147-75. See also Eric Foner's review of Carter's work in *Georgia Historical Quarterly* 69 (June 1985): 258-61.

29. Two prize-winning accounts in this vein are Leon Litwack, *Been in the Storm So Long: The Aftermath of Slavery* (New York: Knopf, 1979), and Roger Ransom and Richard Sutch, *One Kind of Freedom: The Economic Consequences of Emancipation* (New York: Cambridge Univ. Press, 1977).

30. A sampling of revisionist and postrevisionist interpretations includes Michael Les Benedict, *A Compromise of Principle: Congressional Republicans and Reconstruction, 1863-1869* (New York: W. W. Norton, 1974); William Gillette, *Retreat from Reconstruction, 1869-1879* (Baton Rouge: Louisiana State Univ. Press, 1979); Thomas Holt, *Black over White: Negro Political Leadership in South Carolina during Reconstruction* (Urbana: Univ. of Illinois Press, 1977); Willie Lee Rose, *Rehearsal for Reconstruction: The Port Royal Experiment* (New York: Vintage, 1964); Hans Trefousse, *The Radical Republicans: Lincoln's Vanguard for Racial Justice* (New York: Knopf, 1969); and Joel Williamson, *After Slavery: The Negro in South Carolina during Reconstruction* (Chapel Hill: Univ. of North Carolina Press, 1965).

31. August Meier, "An Epitaph for the Writing of Reconstruction History?" *Reviews in American History* 9 (Mar. 1981): 82-87; Eric Foner, "Reconstruction Revisited," *Reviews in American History* 10 (Dec. 1982): 82-100.

32. Foner, "Reconstruction Revisited," 82-83.

33. Eric Foner, *Reconstruction: America's Unfinished Revolution, 1863-1877* (New York: Harper and Row, 1988), xxiv, 215, 198.

34. Ibid., 251, 190-2, 250, 199, 265.

35. Ibid., 176-280.

36. Eric Foner, *Free Soil, Free Labor, Free Men: The Ideology of the Republican Party before the Civil War* (New York: Oxford Univ. Press, 1970), 11-39.

37. See esp. Heather Cox Richardson, *The Greatest Nation of the Earth: Republican Economic Policies during the Civil War* (Cambridge, Mass.: Harvard Univ. Press, 1997).

38. Foner, *Reconstruction*, 155-57.

39. Richardson, *Death of Reconstruction*, ix, 25, 40, 122-24, 141.

40. William Blair, *Cities of the Dead: Contesting the Memory of the Civil War in the South, 1865-1914* (Chapel Hill: Univ. of North Carolina Press, 2004), 86-87.

41. Carol Faulkner, *Women's Radical Reconstruction: The Freedmen's Aid Movement* (Philadelphia: Univ. of Pennsylvania Press, 2004), 2-3, 14, 148.

42. Richard Zuczek, *State of Rebellion: Reconstruction in South Carolina* (Columbia: Univ. of South Carolina Press, 1996), 1; Gregory P. Downs, *After Appomattox: Military Occupation and the Ends of War* (Cambridge, Mass.: Harvard Univ. Press, 2015). Given the American engagements in Afghanistan and Iraq, it makes sense that the notion that Reconstruction was essentially a low-intensity form of warfare has gained adherents. The current surge of interest in guerilla warfare during the Civil War has encouraged this line of thought as well. See esp. Mark Grimsley, "Wars for the American South: The First and Second Reconstructions Considered as Insurgencies," *Civil War History* 58 (Mar. 2012): 6-36; Edward Ayers, "The First Occupation," *New York Times Magazine*, May 29, 2005; Daniel Sutherland, *A Savage Conflict: The Decisive Role of Guerillas in the Civil War* (Chapel Hill: Univ. of North Carolina Press, 2009); and Zuczek, *State of Rebellion*.

43. While the Whigs and the Republicans have been the foci of broad-gauged studies of party ideology, the Democratic Party, the first national party with origins predating both the Whigs and Republicans, has received less attention. To date, no study explores the continuities in the party's ideologies and constituencies before, during, and after the Civil War, as the utility of Jean Baker's insightful study is limited by its sole focus on the North and its static conception of the Democratic Party's political culture. See Jean Baker, *Affairs of Party: The Political Culture of Northern Democrats in the Mid-Nineteenth Century* (Ithaca, N.Y.: Cornell Univ. Press, 1983). Joel Silbey's *A Respectable Minority: The Democratic Party during the Civil War Era, 1860-1868* (New York: W.W. Norton, 1977) remains an important starting point for those interested in the Democratic Party during the Civil War. For an analogous study of the Republican Party, consult Michael Green, *Freedom, Union, and Power: Lincoln and His Party in the Civil War North* (New York: Fordham Univ. Press, 2004).

44. For a recent study that leans heavily upon the centrality of a Democratic ideology honed by the experiences of war and Reconstruction to western resistance to Indian policy, see Kevin Adams and Khal Schneider, "'Washington Is a Long Way Off': The Round Valley War and the Limits of Federal Power on a California Indian Reservation," *Pacific Historical Review* 80 (Dec. 2011): 557-96.

45. Balogh, *A Government Out of Sight;* Moon-Ho Jung, *Coolies and Cane: Race, Labor, and Sugar in the Age of Emancipation* (Baltimore: Johns Hopkins Univ. Press, 2006); Joshua Paddison, *American Heathens: Religion, Race, and Reconstruction in California* (Berkeley: Huntington/USC Institute on California and the West and the Univ. of California Press, 2012); D. Michael Bottoms, *An Aristocracy of Color: Race and Reconstruction in California and the West, 1850-1890* (Norman: Univ. of Oklahoma Press, 2013); Stacey L. Smith, *Freedom's Frontier: California and the Struggle over Unfree Labor, Emancipation, and Reconstruction* (Chapel Hill: Univ. of North Carolina Press, 2013); Nicholas Guyat, "America's Conservatory: Race, Reconstruction, and the Santo Domingo Debate," *Journal of American History* 97 (Mar. 2011): 974-1000; Nicholas Clayton, "Managing the Transition to a Free Labor Society: American Interpretations of the British West Indies during the Civil War and Reconstruction," *American Nineteenth Century History* 7 (Feb. 2006): 89-108.

46. See esp. Jeffrey Ostler, *The Plains Sioux and U.S. Colonialism from Lewis and Clark to Wounded Knee* (New York: Cambridge Univ. Press, 2004); David Chang, *The Color of the Land: Race, Nation, and the Politics of Landownership in Oklahoma, 1832-1929* (Chapel Hill: Univ. of North Carolina Press, 2010); Elliott West, *The Last Indian War: The Nez Perce Story* (New York: Oxford Univ. Press, 2009). On the Greater Reconstruction, see esp. xx-xxiii.

CHAPTER THREE

Radical Reconstruction

SHEPHERD W. MCKINLEY

The historiography of Congressional, or as it is more popularly known, Radical, Reconstruction, has been a "dark and bloody ground" paralleling the arcs of race relations and politics in the United States.[1] After Reconstruction's end, the so-called Dunning School of historians, the students of Columbia University's William A. Dunning, adopted the white South's victimized voice, hanging (this time in effigy rather than by ropes) the Radical Republicans, providing the dominant historical interpretation of the period 1867–1877 for most of the twentieth century.

Revisionist historians began attacking the Dunning interpretation in the 1930s and within three decades had rehabilitated Radical Reconstruction generally and the Radicals in particular. Federal intervention in racial questions and the civil rights laws of the 1960s seemed, to these historians, to justify Congressional Reconstruction. In fact, historians often label the modern civil rights movement as the Second Reconstruction. As the optimism of the civil rights movement faded in the 1970s and all but disappeared during Reagan's America, a breed of so-called postrevisionist scholars discovered that the Radicals had not been so radical after all, that Radical Reconstruction had been a rather conservative affair. In 1988, historian Eric Foner reconciled the revisionist and postrevisionist viewpoints and ended the century-long debate over whether the era was a lost revolutionary moment (as described by liberals and progressives) or a chamber of horrors (as defined by conservatives and reactionaries). Although no post-postrevisionist historiographic school has yet emerged, recent historians have generally followed Foner's lead, exploring previously neglected aspects of Radical Reconstruction. They underscore the Reconstruction Era's essential complexity, again suggesting how historiography tends to mirror political and social thought at any given time. Today's scholars argue that although Reconstruction defies facile conclusions, even an overall synthesis, close study of the topic nevertheless improves our understanding of this most wrenching period in American history.

The Dunning School represented the first scholarly generation to interpret Radical Reconstruction. Dunning's Columbia mentor John W. Burgess, Dunning himself, and later their students utilized primary sources and sought to create histories using the so-called scientific historical method. To a large extent, these historians succeeded in moving the writing on Reconstruction away from rank partisanship, and their scholarship helped reunify northern and southern whites. However, not surprisingly, the works of the Dunning School authors also reflected the era's racist attitudes and justified the emerging Jim Crow laws. The school's interpretation of Radical Reconstruction remained ingrained in the popular imagination decades after the revisionist onslaught of the 1950s and 1960s undermined its once glowing reputation.[2]

In general, most Dunningites portrayed Reconstruction-era white southerners as willing to admit defeat, to be fair to the newly freed blacks, to genuinely seek readmission to the Union, and to accept Abraham Lincoln's and Andrew Johnson's Reconstruction plans. Labeling most Republicans as Radicals, the Dunning scholars accused the party of Thaddeus Stevens and Charles Sumner of plotting to overthrow Presidential Reconstruction in order to secure political domination of the South and to punish former Confederates and their allies. (Later, Progressive historians such as Charles and Mary Beard substituted an economic motive for the political one; they viewed Radicals as mere "agents of Northern capitalism.") The Dunningites believed that the Radicals empowered the allegedly dishonest carpetbaggers and scalawags and ignorant freedmen in order to dominate and plunder white southerners. They almost uniformly considered black suffrage as Reconstruction's original sin. Radical Reconstruction represented, so the Dunningites' narrative went, an unparalleled period of corruption, and therefore, native white southerners were justified in violently and fraudulently resisting and then overturning it. Beneath this interpretation lay the belief of innate black inferiority. White Republican manipulation of blacks, the Dunningites charged, proved the latter's inability to shoulder the responsibilities of full citizenship and thereby proved the wisdom of limiting, by any and all means, the blacks' civil and political rights.[3]

Although Civil Rights Era historians tended to besmirch the Dunning School historians as a homogenous group of racists and apologists for white supremacy, recent scholarship on the Dunning scholars has identified variations as to their motivations and interpretations. For example, Burgess's belief in the Teutonic germ theory constituted part of a worldview that justified colonialism and elite rule. Dunning himself praised some Radical Reconstruction policies and maintained that in fact the South would have benefited from a longer military occupation. His tone on racial matters evolved over time. While in *Essays on the Civil War and Reconstruction and Related Topics* (1897) he disapproved of black suffrage, Dunning's overt racism became less restrained in the more popular work, *Reconstruction: Political and Economic, 1865-1877* (1907). By espousing the "black rapist beast" myth in the latter book, Dunning solidified his school's racist reputation in the twentieth century. That said, three of his students—James W. Garner, Paul L. Haworth, and C. Mildred Thompson—embraced liberal views on race for their day.[4] Overlooked by revisionists and postrevisionists, these variations within the Dunning School expose a generation deeply imbued with racism yet searching for a scholarly understanding of the still-deeply controversial era. For them, Reconstruction constituted "recent" history.

Just as most Dunningites supported Jim Crow, the racial modus operandi of their day, revisionists of the 1950s and 1960s largely embraced the civil rights movement of *their* day and emphasized the noble motives behind and significant achievements of Radical Reconstruction.[5] But significant challenges to the Dunning School actually began much earlier, with the efforts of black authors including the lawyer and politician John R. Lynch and the Harvard University-trained historian W. E. B. Du Bois. They and others laid the groundwork for future revisionists, including mainstream scholars Howard K. Beale and Francis Butler Simpkins before World War II and the more widely accepted Civil Rights Era syntheses of John Hope Franklin and Kenneth M. Stampp. By the late 1960s, the revisionists had virtually destroyed the credibility of the Dunning interpretation, at least among most mainstream scholars.[6]

Several decades after he served in Congress, Lynch sought to correct what had become the generally accepted version of Radical Reconstruction by publishing what he considered the "facts" of the period.[7] In 1935, Du Bois exposed what he considered to be the Dunning scholars' essential racism and highlighted the hitherto ignored agency of the black working class. He declared that "one fact and one alone explains the attitude of most recent writers toward Reconstruction; they cannot conceive of Negroes as men; in their minds the word 'Negro' connotes 'inferiority' and 'stupidity.'" Far from being the horrific era that Burgess and Dunning had described, Radical Reconstruction, according to Du Bois, was a period of "mystic years" when "a majority of thinking Americans in the North believed in the equal manhood of black folk." Du Bois considered Stevens and Sumner heroes. He chided white southern leaders for lacking common sense and described President Johnson as "pitiful." Northern Republicans' abandonment of black civil rights and suffrage was for Du Bois a national tragedy, not the return to rational governance portrayed by Dunning and his students. Seeking to refute the Dunningites' celebration of Redemption as a victory by southern whites, Du Bois, a Marxist, attributed the decline of Reconstruction to "Northern industry" gaining control over "abolition-democracy" within the Republican Party.[8]

Neither Lynch nor Du Bois completely overturned the Dunning interpretation of Reconstruction, but revisionist criticism by white historians grew more common and pointed in the 1930s and 1940s. Calling in 1939 for "more moderate, saner, perhaps newer views" of the period, especially regarding black suffrage, Simkins complained that too many historians described Radical Reconstruction "as a melodrama involving wild-eyed conspirators whose acts are best described in red flashes upon a canvas."[9] The following year, Beale praised members of the Dunning School for their "meticulous and thorough research" but sensed that a new generation of historians (including Simkins, C. Vann Woodward, and Vernon L. Wharton) was starting to dismantle the previous orthodoxy. And Beale insisted that "every future historian must reckon with" Du Bois's insistence on the centrality of black agency in understanding the Reconstruction saga.[10] In 1959, Bernard A. Weisberger criticized white historians generally for not understanding "the nettle of the race conflict," and specifically he argued that their assumptions of black inferiority, Redeemers' virtue, and Radical corruption had led to faulty analysis. He praised contemporary revisionists T. Harry Williams, David Donald, John and LaWanda Cox, and others but bemoaned the fact that no new Reconstruction synthesis had yet emerged.[11]

The revisionist wave crested in the 1960s. With their recasting of heroes and villains, the revisionists espoused a thorough overhaul of the old Dunning interpretation. The new consensus judged Johnson to be an incompetent racist and the Republicans to be legitimate reformers. Radical Reconstruction was, according to the revisionists, one of the most admirable moments in American history.[12] Black historian John Hope Franklin's 1961 synthesis, *Reconstruction: After the Civil War,* was notable for its restraint and balance. He employed remarkable tact when referring to the Dunningites or when describing Johnson's responses to the Radicals' overrides of his presidential vetoes. Emphasizing black agency and praising black politicians during southern Republican rule, Franklin nevertheless admitted that some African American politicians had been corrupt—a favorite criticism leveled by the Dunningites. Although Franklin's book received mixed reviews, *Reconstruction: After the Civil War* marked an important milestone in the overturning of the Dunning School interpretation of Reconstruction.[13]

Kenneth M. Stampp's *The Era of Reconstruction, 1865-1877*, appearing in 1965, expanded the revisionists' critique, more explicitly attacking the Dunning School and underscoring the linkages between the first Reconstruction of the 1860s and the Second Reconstruction a century later. Stampp explained that "Dunningites overlooked a great deal," including the fact that "nobility and idealism" did not die in 1865. Reflecting the general influence of the civil rights movement on revisionists, Stampp declared that white southerners "refused to forgive or forget those years of humiliation when Negroes came close to winning equality" and added that the three Reconstruction amendments, the Thirteenth, Fourteenth, and Fifteenth, were of "crucial importance," both in the 1860s and the 1960s. And in noting the shortcomings of Radical Reconstruction in protecting blacks' economic, political, and civil rights, Stampp anticipated later postrevisionists' arguments. Together, Franklin and Stampp launched the influential revisionist critique of Reconstruction that dominated 1960s historiography. Writing at a time of massive civil rights reform, revisionists put blacks at the center of the Reconstruction story and emphasized such accomplishments of the southern Radical and so-called black and tan governments as advances in southern education and the redefinition of a national citizenship. The biggest tragedy of Radical Reconstruction, Franklin, Stampp, and other revisionists maintained, was not black suffrage but rather that Radical Reconstruction was not radical enough.[14]

As civil rights reform waned in the 1970s, so too did historians' optimism about past racial progress. The new, postrevisionist school of historians of Reconstruction that supplanted the revisionist interpretation questioned whether radicalism was any part of Reconstruction at all. The postrevisionists' emphasis on continuity and moderation as essential characteristics of Reconstruction marked a major reinterpretation of both the Dunning and revisionist schools. According to the postrevisionists, Congressional Reconstruction never was the revolutionary moment that earlier historians had claimed it to be. In fact, historians Eric McKitrick, John and LaWanda Cox, Michael Les Benedict, and Michael Perman found that moderate Republicans were the guiding forces behind the era's legislation. Other scholars argued that northerners' commitment to the freedpeople was weak, that the war's long-term impact on the nation's race problem (supposedly building a foundation for securing black civil rights) was not as great as historians previously had believed, and that the expansion of federal power on the national level was not long lasting. State studies of Louisiana, Florida, and Mississippi revealed that Republican governments failed to help former slaves substantially. Documenting indifference by federal and state officials toward the freedpeople, Leon Litwack proclaimed that white planters retained control of southern agriculture and that land reform never materialized. No part of the revisionist cannon went unscathed. Historians accused northern educators of exporting social control or cultural imperialism to the South. But as Foner concluded, "Denial of change does not in itself provide a compelling interpretation." No postrevisionist study of Reconstruction emerged to supplant Franklin and Stampp's syntheses.[15]

Foner's scholarship in the 1980s marked a significant crossroads in the historiographical landscape. In a 1982 article, he lamented that historians had "failed to produce a coherent modern portrait of Reconstruction either as a specific time period or as the effort of American society to come to terms with the results of the Civil War and the consequences of emancipation." Foner found it ironic that the postrevisionists' emphasis on continuity relegated blacks to be "passive victims of white manipulation." Understanding the strength and complexity of black agency during Radical Reconstruction was crucial. Foner believed that "rather than simply emphasizing conservatism and continuity, a coherent portrait of Reconstruction must take into account the subtle dialectic of continuity and change in economic, social, and political relations as the nation adjusted to emancipation."[16]

Foner's *Reconstruction: America's Unfinished Revolution, 1863-1877* (1988) was a masterpiece and remains one of the most important works on Reconstruction ever published. It is the reigning synthesis, assessing and uniting the best revisionist and postrevisionist scholarship on Reconstruction. In his book, Foner borrowed from revisionists an interest in investigating to what extent "southern society was remodeled," how race relations evolved, the rise of the national state, and the transformation of the North. He described Reconstruction as "the beginning of an extended historical process: the adjustment of American society to the end of slavery." Reconstruction signified a noble effort that "left behind an altered landscape," especially in the form of religious, social, and educational gains for blacks. Foner also gave the postrevisionists their due, noting that "Reconstruction can only be judged a failure" and that "the inequalities" preserved during Redemption "still afflict our society today." Most significantly, he refocused historians' attention on southern blacks. While Foner recognized that Reconstruction contained revolutionary elements, he nevertheless insisted that the revolution started in 1865 went "unfinished" in 1877, just as the civil rights reform of the 1950s and 1960s remained a work in progress in 1988. Sympathizing in his epilogue with the postrevisionists' emphasis on the "failure" of Radical Reconstruction, Foner the revisionist declared, "Perhaps the remarkable thing about Reconstruction was not that it failed, but that it was attempted at all and survived as long as it did." Yes, Reconstruction was an overall "failure" and a "tragedy," he noted, but its successes "provided the base" and "legal strategy" for the modern civil rights movement.[17]

Foner's book began with an excellent summary of Reconstruction historiography and then, in covering the era's main events and themes, he struck a balance between revisionism and postrevisionism, identifying patterns both of change and continuity in the dozen postwar years. President Johnson, Foner argued, greatly broadened support for the Radicals' appeal for black suffrage by ignoring the minimal demands of moderate and conservative Republicans. Radicals, for their part, were neither angels nor devils. According to Foner, Stevens's contemporaries identified in him "egoism, self-righteousness, and [a] stubborn refusal to compromise," but they also credited him with an unwavering belief in "the principle of equality before the law." The Radicals possessed a civil, not economic, ideology and believed that an expanded federal government was a means to the end.[18]

For example, they avoided taking extreme positions on such volatile questions as land confiscation and redistribution. In order to gain moderates' backing, Radicals compromised on economic support for the freedpeople. Foner observed that each "Radical element" within the Reconstruction Acts of 1867 "appeared balanced by a moderate one." Military rule on paper did not translate into a thoroughly radicalized South. For all the Republicans' success, Johnson remained influential in the Reconstruction process, southern state and local governments generally retained their previous leaders, and federal troops rarely intervened to help blacks. Foner concluded that "Congressional Reconstruction was indeed a radical departure" that "inspired blacks with a millennial sense of living at the dawn of a new era." But he acknowledged that the lack of essential economic support undermined the former slaves' efforts to shape independent lives. Foner's nuanced analysis defied easy generalizations of just how "radical" Radical Reconstruction in fact was. His book pointed out that Reconstruction's reality was much more complicated than simplistic assessments of radicalism or conservatism or success or failure.[19]

Historian Michael Perman ended his enthusiastic book review of Foner's work with a rhetorical question, asking "What is left to be done?"[20] Until the publication of Douglas Egerton's *The Wars of Reconstruction: The Brief, Violent History of America's Most Progressive Era* (2014), recent historians have shied away from writing a synthesis on Reconstruction, deferring to Foner's monumental work. As a result, no discernable school has yet emerged to replace it. Historians following Foner have generally investigated specific topics he mentioned or touched upon. Monographs and edited collections explore legal, political, religious, social, and psychological aspects of the era, as well as recent trends in Reconstruction historiography. Many of these studies venture into various parts of the country and among multiple constituencies to understand Radical Reconstruction's impact on local battles over policy and practice. Increasingly, historians are illuminating the full contributions of blacks, working-class whites, women, and religious leaders to the successes and failures of Reconstruction. Seemingly less influenced than their predecessors by contemporary race relations, the most recent generation of students of Radical Reconstruction shows signs of accepting the Fonerian balance of revisionism's optimism and postrevisionism's disappointments. As a result, they emphasize the era's complexity, diversity, and contingency.

Legal historians, for instance, have begun reexamining traditional narratives about Radical Reconstruction. In her investigation of the U.S. Supreme Court, Pamela Brandwein argues against the "common wisdom" that the "state action" doctrine of the Waite Court (1874-1888) protected southern white perpetrators of racial and political intimidation and violence from the authority of the Fourteenth and Fifteenth Amendments and therefore undermined federal efforts to ensure the safety and rights of blacks. The doctrine, she states, did not enable the "definitive abandonment" (which began instead of ended with the *Plessy v. Ferguson* decision of 1896) but rather opened "broad possibilities" for enforcement and protection.[21] James D. Schmidt examines "the role of law in the creation of free labor" as a way to understand further postwar labor struggles. He positions freedpeople's daily experiences during Radical Reconstruction into southern and northern contexts and finds that the tensions between northern "conservatives" (who "looked backward to the right to security and direct state enforcement of work") and northern "liberals" (who "looked forward to the right to quit with or without state policing of the perimeters of the labor market") migrated to the South. In the end, vagrancy laws became another form of the abandonment of the freedpeople.[22]

Recent historians also have taken an increasing interest in the origins and motivations of scalawags during Radical Reconstruction. In the first regionwide study of southern white Republicans, James Alex Baggett seeks to bring scalawags out of "the shadows" and "to see their origins in the light of circumstances surrounding them." His "collective biography" of elite scalawags finds, for example, that many of the men were teachers and lawyers, better educated than most white southerners but less wealthy, educated, and politically experienced than southern Democratic leaders. These elite scalawags were a diverse lot before the war, and Baggett investigates their many reasons for joining the party and the tensions within the Republicans' southern coalition.[23] Hyman Rubin III's study of South Carolina's scalawag leadership finds that they were unusual in that most of the men had been former Confederates, not Unionists or antebellum Whigs, and that they had a larger influence on the party than their numbers might suggest. The most distinguishing characteristic of the South Carolina scalawags was racial moderation. While hardly racial progressives, they nonetheless were not wedded to white supremacy. According to Rubin, they grew to accept black political activity and to "embrace racial equality as a core political principle."[24]

Historians investigating individual southern Republican leaders, including carpetbaggers and blacks, have also illuminated their origins and motives. In his book on the former U.S. Colored Troops officer and Freedmen's Bureau agent Marshall H. Twitchell, Ted Tunnell does not engage in "carpetbagger rehabilitation" but rather demonstrates that northerners who came south like Twitchell were "neither saints nor heroes." Tunnell concludes that Twitchell's experience in Louisiana was "a metaphor for the real tragedy of Reconstruction, the crushing of the closest thing to liberal democracy the South had ever known."[25] Richard L. Hume and Jerry B. Gough provide the first comprehensive examination of state constitutional convention delegates during Radical Reconstruction. The authors find "diversity and complexity," and their data confirms Foner's general conclusion that radicals, moderates, blacks, and whites all made sizeable contributions to shaping the Republican agenda in the South.[26]

Gender analysis represents an important new direction in recent studies. Peter W. Bardaglio argues that Reconstruction was a period of change and continuity on questions of race and gender. Postbellum fears of miscegenation and black male sexuality led southern white Democrats to reevaluate the basis of antebellum laws banning interracial sex and push for new restrictive laws that utilized the state-regulated institution of marriage to limit federal meddling. The intensified efforts against intermarriage also had strong political implications; during Republican rule, some state legislatures had suspended miscegenation laws, a fact not lost on Democratic politicians during and after Radical Reconstruction. Even some blacks supported the measures as a way to keep white men away from black women.[27] Laura F. Edwards studies the politics of race, class, and gender in postwar Granville County, North Carolina, and finds that the Civil War and emancipation "shook the antebellum household to its foundation," initiating struggles over legal identity within households—especially that of head of household—that became "highly contested" in the public sphere. Freedpeople and common whites successfully, if briefly during Radical Reconstruction, seized the power of household head, previously the realm of only white men with property, for all men regardless of race or class. Democrats retook political control from Republicans during the 1870s not just by fraud and violence but also through manipulating traditional gender norms.[28] Carol Faulkner reveals the struggles of and between black and white women working within the freedmen's aid movement, the various organizations devoted to rally an activist federal government to help former slaves. "Like the most radical of Radical Republicans," the women demanded political equality and economic independence for blacks and women and that the nation take full "responsibility" for slavery. These women reformers labored against the more moderate policies of the men in the Republican Party and Freedmen's Bureau, but they also struggled among themselves to understand each other's worlds. Freedwomen resisted white middle-class women's efforts to make their daughters servants, while the middle-class white women considered such resistance as evidence of laziness. Faulkner declares that although "stymied in its time," the movement's "philosophy of federal responsibility and action remained a strong current in women's reform for the next century."[29]

Post-Foner historians also have delved deeper into the intersections of religion and politics. Victor B. Howard identifies northern radical Christians who backed Radicals during and after the Civil War and lists the ways they "played a significant role in molding and supporting" Radical Reconstruction. Howard argues that the church was "the conscience" of the party and "the mainstay" of the Radicals' agenda. He documents, for example, radical Christians who urged impeachment of President Johnson and contributed ideas to the Reconstruction Acts and the Fifteenth Amendment.[30] Daniel W. Stowell finds that white southerners, evangelical northerners (and some scalawags), and the freedpeople had completely different interpretations of God's allegiances to and design for the South. Each group searched for divine meaning in battlefield losses, emancipation, and political setbacks. They disagreed on whether Radical Reconstruction was a punishment for the sins of slavery and secession or merely a severe test for white southerners. Stowell argues that racial and sectional factors were more important than class, gender, and denominational differences in dividing American Christians. Although northerners and freedpeople separately sought to assert their "vision" for "religious reconstruction" after the Civil War, the white southerners' one was the most enduring.[31] Gaines M. Foster states that emancipation began the shift in white southern attitudes toward supporting the creation and enforcement of national moral laws. The so-called Bible Belt originated with southern "Christian lobbyists" calling for federal power. He emphasizes that "political Reconstruction" was a watershed period that influenced the course of national religious reform into the next century; a federal government that brought an end to slavery could, the Christian lobbyists believed, eliminate other immoral practices. Foster also sees parallels between northerners' efforts to use the state to reform the South's political and labor relations during Radical Reconstruction and southerners' desires to use the state as a vehicle to enact moral reform.[32] In *Vale of Tears: New Essays on Religion and Reconstruction* (2005), editors Edward J. Blum and W. Scott Poole continue the scholarly revival in placing religion and the religious at the center of Radical Reconstruction. Several authors in Blum and Poole's anthology argue that Republicans and former Confederates utilized religious language, such as the word redemption, to advance their respective political agendas. Many contributors to their work indicate that southern white religious leaders substantially added to the rise in racial violence throughout Reconstruction.[33]

Historian James K. Hogue seeks to understand other origins for the violence that helped destroy Radical Reconstruction. In examining the links between politics and force in five New Orleans street battles, he argues that "Reconstruction politics became the continuation of civil war by other means." Radical Reconstruction in Louisiana constituted what Hogue terms a failure of "nation building." It featured Union and Confederate veterans using skills learned in the war to influence political outcomes during peacetime. By applying military analysis to this often most "uncivil" era, Hogue reveals previously ignored elements in the decline of the southern Republican coalition.[34] Heather Cox Richardson similarly challenges traditional notions of chronology. While Hogue sees the war ending in 1877, Richardson—agreeing with Dunning—finds that Reconstruction ended around 1900 with black disfranchisement. Based on evidence in the northern popular press, she argues that the radical impulse among Republicans began to fade after 1872 as they perceived increasing class conflict.[35]

Recently, historians also have begun to delve into the broad psychological aspects of Reconstruction. Bruce Baker begins to explore "the history of the meaning of Reconstruction" in South Carolina by examining who first created various commonly held memories of Reconstruction and why they crafted them. He also carefully delineates between the memory constructed by whites to maintain white supremacy and the blacks' "countermemory" of the era designed to push back against white propaganda and preserve the history of black achievement. While the former memory helped justify Jim Crow, the latter formed the foundation for the modern civil rights movement.[36] Mark Wahlgren Summers also looks northward to understand the demise of Radical Reconstruction, focusing on policy driven by "fears, often unreasonable, phantasms of conspiracy, dreads and hopes of renewed civil war" and concerns "that the republic itself lay in peril." Once this general anxiety had subsided, support for the extraordinary measures subsided as well. Reconstruction failed, Summers argues, because northerners came to view it as a success; no longer sensing that the nation was on the verge of destruction, they willingly abandoned the radical schemes that had seemingly saved it.[37]

Inspired no doubt by Foner's *Reconstruction,* numerous collections of essays have appeared that emphasize the degree to which complexity, diversity, and contingency are hallmarks of Radical Reconstruction, North and South. In *The Facts of Reconstruction: Essays in Honor of John Hope Franklin* (1991), editor Eric Anderson summarizes the book's contributors' major findings involving ideology, race, class, and chronology. He notes that the "political ideas behind Reconstruction," not just the competing interests, were important and that historians analyzing the Republicans must not judge their beliefs and ideologies based on today's standards. Anderson declares that blacks' "expectations and demands" were the keys to understanding how and why Reconstruction evolved and that whites' racial beliefs were diverse and changing rather than monolithic. He argues that Republicans generally avoided class appeals and denies that there was any "lower-class insurgency" in the South during Radical Reconstruction. Finally, Anderson describes Reconstruction as a "long-term process," not confined to the traditional 1865-1877 chronology.[38] Two collections focus on prominent historians of the Dunning and revisionist schools and offer readers the opportunity through multiple biographies to understand the evolution of Reconstruction historiography in the twentieth century. Editor Glenn Feldman's *Reading Southern History: Essays on Interpreters and Interpretations* (2001) provides a thematic complement to the biographically oriented, edited works by Arthur S. Link and Rembert W. Patrick (1965) and John B. Boles and Evelyn Thomas Nolen (1987) and engages in classic debates about race, class, and continuity. In their *The Dunning School: Historians, Race, and the Meaning of Reconstruction* (2013), editors John David Smith and J. Vincent Lowery present a reassessment of ten Dunningites and the Dunning School's negative reputation among later generations of scholars. Perhaps surprisingly, the contributors maintain that the Dunning-inspired historians, though not without intellectual blinders and flaws of omission and commission, contributed impressive scholarship. Indeed, their work was more diverse, and their attitudes toward blacks and Radical Reconstruction more nuanced and complicated, than historians generally acknowledge. The essays recognize the Dunningites' Jim Crow-era racism but argue that dismissing the scholars and their influential assessments of Reconstruction is a mistake.[39]

Two recent collections that combine Reconstruction historiography with new scholarship on the volatile era are especially noteworthy. Lacy K. Ford's anthology, *A Companion to the Civil War and Reconstruction* (2005), includes eight strong chapters on politics, economics, labor, women, and legacies of the war during Reconstruction. He finds in general that the authors identify "mixed and disappointing results" during the era. More specifically, Ford notes that the economically radical implications of Reconstruction policies did not die in 1877 but rather after 1945, when the South began a period of true national economic integration (which seemed to close off more radical alternatives).[40] Thomas J. Brown's edited *Reconstructions: New Perspectives on the Postbellum United States* (2006) provides yet another excellent update on the state of Reconstruction historiography, a genre that Brown argues "now thrives less as a form of combat than as a collective building on a solid foundation." Brown and the other contributors examine economics, race, politics, foreign policy, constitutional questions, intellectual and cultural life, and memory. While readers of either of these collections will not find direct challenges to Foner's balance between revisionism and postrevisionism, the authors nonetheless wrestle with such important categories of analysis as religion, labor, and gender. These topics continue to cry out for further historical analysis.[41]

More recently, in a 2012 article, Adam Fairclough signals a potentially significant turn in the apparent consensus among historians on Radical Reconstruction. Writing in the *Journal of the Historical Society,* Fairclough argues that presentist condemnations of Dunning School racism obscured the fact that "despite their bias, the 'Dunningites' got many things right," especially their criticism of black voting. Radical Reconstruction was too radical, he believes, because Republican imposition of universal suffrage provoked defiance by southern whites and because the policy did not have enough political support in the North. The experiment was doomed without the use of more federal power and institutions. Directly challenging Foner's assessment, Fairclough maintains that Dunning and company were "closer to the mark" than the revisionists in evaluating the appropriateness of black suffrage, "a political error," he argues, "whose failure was foreordained." In fact, "the damaging consequences of that error far outweighed any lasting benefits." Fairclough asserts that Foner, in his "over-optimistic reading of Reconstruction's legacy," misses the ugly truth: Radical Reconstruction was a complete failure, and blacks suffered greatly after gaining the vote.[42]

It remains to be seen if Fairclough's interpretation will gain traction. Predictably, those historians responding to the article attacked it. In his response, Michael Fitzgerald agrees that a reappraisal of the Dunning school was in order, but he defends Foner, arguing that black suffrage was a major factor in the creation of public schools, sharecropping (as opposed to postwar plantation labor organized in the slave-like manner of closely supervised gangs or squads), and constitutional reform. Fitzgerald's strongest point is his reference to the three Reconstruction-era amendments to the U.S. Constitution. Indeed, it is hard to imagine the emergence of the twentieth-century civil rights movement without the Thirteenth, Fourteenth, and Fifteenth Amendments. Michael A. Ross and Leslie S. Rowland, two other respondents to Fairclough's article, disagree with Fairclough's assertion that modern scholars view the Dunning works as "worthless" and argue convincingly that "emancipation, not suffrage, initiated the white onslaught against former slaves." In his response to Fairclough, J. Mills Thornton insists that far from empowering blacks and inciting unified white resistance, black suffrage (and its support from northern Radicals) mobilized white planters to manipulate black votes against white yeomen farmers; the harmful effects of Radical Reconstruction on democracy were wider, he argues, than even Fairclough acknowledges.[43]

The scholarship since Foner's classic work suggests a vibrancy in examining Radical Reconstruction that is unlikely to diminish anytime soon.⁴⁴ Foner's synthesis still reigns as the state of the historiographic art, and most scholars view their new work as extending the path he blazed. Whether or not Fairclough's recent challenge to Foner's interpretation signals a seismic shift in the historiography of Radical Reconstruction, it nevertheless raises an interesting point about the ongoing reassessment of the Dunning, revisionist, and postrevisionist schools.

While revisionists targeted the spirit of Jim Crow that lay at the core of the Dunning School interpretation, and postrevisionists reacted to what they considered Civil Rights Era revisionists' naïveté and optimism regarding racial change, recent scholars seem willing to reassess all previous historiographic schools and to adopt what is of value in the old interpretations and discard what is not. Scholars continue to follow Foner's leads, integrating the many groups and influences into the narrative while noting the successes and failures of Radical Reconstruction. They accept Foner's argument that the era was complicated and the start of a long-term and national adjustment to emancipation. Indeed, the newer interpretations continue to underscore Reconstruction as an era of extreme complexity. Historians in the twenty-first century portray Radical Reconstruction as a mixture of continuity and change, and they detect varying degrees of conservatism and progressivism within political parties and religious and ethnic groups in the South and the North. They emphasize not just the importance of black agency but also the interaction of political, economic, legal, and social forces in shaping the period. Finally, recent scholars appreciate the importance of the legacies and memories of Radical Reconstruction and in doing so, they argue convincingly that the post–Civil War years were among the most fundamental in American history.

NOTES

1. Bernard A. Weisberger, "The Dark and Bloody Ground of Reconstruction Historiography," *Journal of Southern History* 25 (Nov. 1959): 427.

2. John David Smith, "Introduction," in *The Dunning School: Historians, Race, and the Meaning of Reconstruction*, ed. John David Smith and J. Vincent

Lowery (Lexington: Univ. Press of Kentucky, 2013), 1-7, 9, 11, 16, 18, 21-22, 37-38; James S. Humphreys, "William Archibald Dunning: Flawed Colossus of American Letters," in ibid., 77.

3. Eric Foner, *Reconstruction: America's Unfinished Revolution, 1863-1877* (New York: Harper and Row, 1988), xix-xx; Smith, "Introduction," 2-3, 7, 9-10, 19-20, 23-25; Humphreys, "William Archibald Dunning," 77-78, 86-87.

4. Smith, "Introduction," 4-6, 8, 21-22, 36; Humphreys, "William Archibald Dunning," 81-87; Shepherd W. McKinley, "John W. Burgess, Godfather of the Dunning School," in Smith and Lowery, eds., *The Dunning School*, 56; W. Bland Whitley, "James Wilford Garner and the Dream of a Two-Party South," in ibid., 114, 122-23; J. Vincent Lowery, "Paul Leland Haworth: The 'Black Republican' in the Old Chief's Court," in ibid., 203-4, 206-9; William Harris Bragg, "C. Mildred Thompson: A Liberal among the Dunningites," in ibid., 287-91, 293-94.

5. Smith, "Introduction," 3-4; Vernon Burton, review of *Reconstruction: America's Unfinished Revolution, 1863-1877*, by Eric Foner, *South Carolina Historical Magazine* 91 (July 1990): 217-20.

6. Foner, *Reconstruction*, xxi-xxii.

7. John R. Lynch, *The Facts of Reconstruction* (New York: Neale Publishing, 1913), 10; Foner, *Reconstruction*, 610.

8. W. E. B. Du Bois, *Black Reconstruction in America 1860-1880* (1935; repr., New York: Atheneum, 1992), "To the Reader," 182-87, 265, 275-77, 280, 322, 368, 381, 431, 726, 731; David Levering Lewis, "Introduction," in *Black Reconstruction in America 1860-1880*, by W. E. B. Du Bois (1935; repr., New York: Atheneum, 1992), xi.

9. Francis B. Simkins, "New Viewpoints of Southern Reconstruction," *Journal of Southern History* 5 (Feb. 1939): 50-51; Foner, *Reconstruction*, 610.

10. Foner, *Reconstruction*, xxi; Howard K. Beale, "On Rewriting Reconstruction History," *American Historical Review* 45 (July 1940): 807-9.

11. Weisberger, "Dark and Bloody Ground," 428-34, 436-37, 439.

12. Foner, *Reconstruction*, xxi-xxii.

13. John Hope Franklin, *Reconstruction: After the Civil War* (1961; repr., Chicago: Univ. of Chicago Press, 1994), 48-49, 71, 144-46; Avery Craven, review of *Reconstruction: After the Civil War*, by John Hope Franklin, *Journal of Southern History* 28 (May 1962): 255-56; Hans L. Trefousse, review of *Reconstruction: After the Civil War*, by John Hope Franklin, *American Historical Review* 67 (April 1962): 745-46; Eric L. McKitrick, review of *Reconstruction: After the Civil War*, by John Hope Franklin, *Mississippi Valley Historical Review* 49 (June 1962): 153-54.

14. Kenneth M. Stampp, *The Era of Reconstruction, 1865-1877* (1965; repr., New York: Vintage Books, 1967), 6-9, 12-13, 15, 20-22; John Hope Franklin, review of *The Era of Reconstruction, 1865-1877*, by Kenneth M. Stampp, *Journal of Negro History* 50 (Oct. 1965): 286-88; Eric Foner, "Reconstruction Revisited," *Reviews in American History* 10 (Dec. 1982): 83.

15. Burton, review of *Reconstruction*, 218; Foner, "Reconstruction Revisited," 83-87; Foner, *Reconstruction*, xxii-xxiv.
16. Foner, "Reconstruction Revisited," 87-91, 94-95.
17. Foner, *Reconstruction*, xxi-xxvii, 602-4, 612.
18. Ibid., 230.
19. Ibid., 277, 278, 281.
20. Michael Perman, review of *Reconstruction: America's Unfinished Revolution, 1863-1877*, by Eric Foner, *Reviews in American History* 17 (Mar. 1989): 78; John M. Giggie, "Rethinking Reconstruction," *Reviews in American History* 35 (Dec. 2007): 546.
21. Pamela Brandwein, *Rethinking the Judicial Settlement of Reconstruction* (Cambridge: Cambridge Univ. Press, 2011), 1-3, 18; Michael Kent Curtis, review of *Rethinking the Judicial Settlement of Reconstruction*, by Pamela Brandwein, *American Political Thought* 1 (Spring 2012): 161; Pamela Brandwein, "A Judicial Abandonment of Blacks? Rethinking the 'State Action' Cases of the Waite Court," *Law & Society Review* 41 (June 2007): 343-44. Brandwein also explores related issues in *Reconstructing Reconstruction: The Supreme Court and the Production of Historical Truth* (Durham, N.C.: Duke Univ. Press, 1999).
22. James D. Schmidt, *Free to Work: Labor Law, Emancipation, and Reconstruction, 1815-1880* (Athens: Univ. of Georgia Press, 1998), 1, 6; Christopher Waldrep, review of *Free to Work: Labor Law, Emancipation, and Reconstruction, 1815-1880*, by James D. Schmidt, *Journal of Southern History* 66 (Aug. 2000): 616-17.
23. James Alex Baggett, *The Scalawags: Southern Dissenters in the Civil War and Reconstruction* (Baton Rouge: Louisiana State Univ. Press, 2003), xxii, 2-3, 7-8, 13; Joe P. Dunn, review of *The Scalawags: Southern Dissenters in the Civil War and Reconstruction*, by James Alex Baggett, *South Carolina Historical Magazine* 104 (Oct. 2003): 281-83.
24. Hyman Rubin III, *South Carolina Scalawags* (Columbia: Univ. of South Carolina Press, 2006), xii, 1-2, 18-19; Stephen A. West, review of *South Carolina Scalawags*, by Hyman Rubin III, *Journal of Southern History* 73 (Aug. 2007): 717.
25. Ted Tunnell, *Edge of the Sword: The Ordeal of Carpetbagger Marshall H. Twitchell in the Civil War and Reconstruction* (Baton Rouge: Louisiana State Univ. Press, 2001), 2-5, 307; John C. Rodrigue, review of *The Edge of the Sword: The Ordeal of Carpetbagger Marshall H. Twitchell in the Civil War and Reconstruction*, by Ted Tunnell, *Georgia Historical Quarterly* 85 (Winter 2001): 651-53.
26. Richard L. Hume and Jerry B. Gough, *Blacks, Carpetbaggers, and Scalawags: The Constitutional Conventions of Reconstruction* (Baton Rouge: Louisiana State Univ. Press, 2008), 1-2, 7-8; Michael Les Benedict, review of *Blacks, Carpetbaggers, and Scalawags: The Constitutional Conventions of Reconstruction*, by Richard L. Hume and Jerry B. Gough, *Arkansas Historical Quarterly* 68 (Summer 2009): 230-31.
27. Peter W. Bardaglio, *Reconstructing the Household: Families, Sex, and the Law in the Nineteenth-Century South* (Chapel Hill: Univ. of North Carolina

Press, 1995), 177-83; Steven M. Stowe, review of *Reconstructing the Household: Families, Sex, and the Law in the Nineteenth-Century South,* by Peter W. Bardaglio, *Journal of American History* 83 (June 1996): 187-88.

28. Laura F. Edwards, *Gendered Strife and Confusion: The Political Culture of Reconstruction* (Urbana: Univ. of Illinois Press, 1997), 3-9; Elizabeth R. Varon, review of *Gendered Strife and Confusion: The Political Culture of Reconstruction,* by Laura F. Edwards, *Journal of American History* 84 (Mar. 1998): 1517-18; Diane Miller Sommerville, review of *Gendered Strife and Confusion: The Political Culture of Reconstruction,* by Laura F. Edwards, *Journal of Southern History* 64 (Aug. 1998): 566-68.

29. Carol Faulkner, *Women's Radical Reconstruction: The Freedmen's Aid Movement* (Philadelphia: Univ. of Pennsylvania Press, 2004), 1-8, 152; Louise Newman, review of *Women's Radical Reconstruction: The Freedmen's Aid Movement,* by Carol Faulkner, *Journal of Southern History* 71 (Feb. 2005): 177-78.

30. Victor B. Howard, *Religion and the Radical Republican Movement, 1860-1870* (Lexington: Univ. Press of Kentucky, 1990), ix, 1, 149.

31. Daniel W. Stowell, *Rebuilding Zion: The Religious Reconstruction of the South, 1863-1877* (Oxford: Oxford Univ. Press, 1998), 5-8; Paul Harvey, review of *Rebuilding Zion: The Religious Reconstruction of the South, 1863-1877,* by Daniel W. Stowell, *Journal of Southern History* 65 (Nov. 1999): 887-88.

32. Gaines M. Foster, *Moral Reconstruction: Christian Lobbyists and the Federal Legislation of Morality, 1865-1920* (Chapel Hill: Univ. of North Carolina Press, 2002), 3, 6-7, 225; Elizabeth Clement, review of *Moral Reconstruction: Christian Lobbyists and the Federal Legislation of Morality, 1865-1920,* by Gaines M. Foster, *New York History* 85 (Winter 2004): 71-73.

33. Edward J. Blum and W. Scott Poole, "Introduction," in *Vale of Tears: New Essays on Religion and Reconstruction,* ed. Edward J. Blum and W. Scott Poole (Macon, Ga.: Mercer Univ. Press, 2005), 2-3, 9; Kimberly R. Kellison, "Parameters of Promiscuity: Sexuality, Violence, and Religion in Upcountry South Carolina," in ibid., 35; John Patrick Daly, review of *Vale of Tears: New Essays on Religion and Reconstruction,* ed. Edward J. Blum and W. Scott Poole, *South Carolina Historical Magazine* 109 (Oct. 2008): 322-23.

34. James K. Hogue, *Uncivil War: Five New Orleans Street Battles and the Rise and Fall of Radical Reconstruction* (Baton Rouge: Louisiana State Univ. Press, 2006), 2-3, 9, 13; Mark Elliott, "Nation-Building Begins at Home," *Reviews in American History* 35 (June 2007): 239-42, 245-46; Dennis C. Rousey, review of *Uncivil War: Five New Orleans Street Battles and the Rise and Fall of Radical Reconstruction,* by James K. Hogue, *Journal of Southern History* 73 (Nov. 2007): 928-29.

35. Heather Cox Richardson, *The Death of Reconstruction: Race, Labor, and Politics in the Post-Civil War North, 1865-1901* (Cambridge, Mass.: Harvard Univ. Press, 2001), xii-xv; Michael Perman, "An Autopsy for Reconstruction," *Reviews in American History* 30 (June 2002): 252-54.

36. Bruce E. Baker, *What Reconstruction Meant: Historical Memory in the American South* (Charlottesville: Univ. of Virginia Press, 2007), 2, 9, 11, 13, 15;

Charles J. Holden, review of *What Reconstruction Meant: Historical Memory in the American South*, by Bruce E. Baker, *South Carolina Historical Magazine* 111 (July-Oct. 2010): 181-82.

37. Mark Wahlgren Summers, *A Dangerous Stir: Fear, Paranoia, and the Making of Reconstruction* (Chapel Hill: Univ. of North Carolina Press, 2009), 2, 6; Joel M. Sipress, review of *A Dangerous Stir: Fear, Paranoia, and the Making of Reconstruction*, by Mark Wahlgren Summers, *History Teacher* 43 (May 2010): 471-72.

38. Eric Anderson, "Afterword: Whither Reconstruction Historiography?" in *The Facts of Reconstruction: Essays in Honor of John Hope Franklin*, ed. Eric Anderson and Alfred A. Moss Jr. (Baton Rouge: Louisiana State Univ. Press, 1991), 220-28.

39. Glenn Feldman, "Introduction: The Pursuit of Southern History," in *Reading Southern History: Essays on Interpreters and Interpretations*, ed. Glenn Feldman (Tuscaloosa: Univ. of Alabama Press, 2001), 1-6; Smith, "Introduction," 3-5, 9-11.

40. Lacy K. Ford, "Introduction: A Civil War in the Age of Capital," in *A Companion to the Civil War and Reconstruction*, ed. Lacy K. Ford (Malden, Mass.: Blackwell Publishing, 2005), 2, 13-19.

41. Thomas J. Brown, "Introduction," in *Reconstructions: New Perspectives on the Postbellum United States*, ed. Thomas J. Brown (Oxford: Oxford Univ. Press, 2006), 3-6; Giggie, "Rethinking Reconstruction," 547.

42. Adam Fairclough, "Was the Grant of Black Suffrage a Political Error? Reconsidering the Views of John W. Burgess, William A. Dunning, and Eric Foner on Congressional Reconstruction," *Journal of the Historical Society* 12 (June 2012): 157, 159-60, 165-66, 169-73, 176-77, 182-83, 186-88.

43. Michael W. Fitzgerald, "Reconstruction Reengineered: Or, Is Doubting Black Suffrage a Mistake?," *Journal of the Historical Society* 12 (Sept. 2012): 242-47; Michael A. Ross and Leslie S. Rowland, "Adam Fairclough, John Burgess, and the Nettlesome Legacy of the 'Dunning School,'" ibid., 250-51, 255, 264; J. Mills Thornton, "Class Conflict and Black Enfranchisement in Alabama," ibid., 238-40. Fairclough defends his earlier article against these critics in "Congressional Reconstruction: A Catastrophic Failure," ibid., 271-82.

44. Other recent scholarly additions to the historiography of Radical Reconstruction include Eric Foner, "The Supreme Court and the History of Reconstruction—And Vice-Versa," *Columbia Law Review* 112 (Nov. 2012): 1585-1606; Peter Kolchin, "Comparative Perspectives on Emancipation in the U.S. South: Reconstruction, Radicalism, and Russia," *Journal of the Civil War Era* 2 (June 2012): 203-32; Mark Wahlgren Summers, "What Fresh Hell is This? Revisiting Reconstruction," *Register of the Kentucky Historical Society* 110 (Summer-Autumn 2012): 559-74.

CHAPTER FOUR

Reconstruction

Emancipation and Race

R. BLAKESLEE GILPIN

In March 1913, W. E. B. Du Bois wrote a public letter to the soon-to-be-inaugurated twenty-eighth president of the United States, Woodrow Wilson. The election of 1912 represented the capstone of Southern Redemption and a symbolic deliverance from Reconstruction for Democrats in the former Confederacy. Du Bois witheringly explained to a man well aware that "for the first time since the emancipation of slaves the government of this nation . . . [passes] into the hands of the party which a half century ago fought desperately to keep black men as real estate in the eyes of the law."[1]

As he cataloged postbellum outrages, Du Bois coupled the nation's failed promises with the inextinguishable hopes of African Americans. "We want to be treated as men," he explained, "We want to vote. We want our children educated. We want lynching stopped. We want no longer to be herded as cattle on street cars and railroads. We want the right to earn a living, to own our own property and to spend our income unhindered and uncursed."[2] "It will take more than general good will on your part," Du Bois explained, "to foil the wide conspiracy to make Negroes known to their fellow Americans not as flesh and blood but as beasts of fiction."[3] Unfortunately, Wilson was as deluded by those fictions as any American. Just two years after his inauguration, Wilson's friend Thomas Dixon, the immensely popular North Carolinian novelist, convinced the president to screen the first film ever shown in the White House, D. W. Griffith's *The Birth of a Nation* (1915). The film was an adaptation of Dixon's virulently racist and pathologically inaccurate trilogy about Reconstruction and the Ku Klux Klan. Dixon's novels and Griffith's film depicted barbaric blacks let loose on the South after the Civil War and focused on the insatiable and depraved political and sexual appetites of emancipated slaves. These fictional black antagonists were obsessed with taking over southern politics and forcing "themselves upon white women."[4] The heroes who rescued the nation from this interracial nightmare and mockery of democratic politics were the hooded nightriders of the Klan. Wilson physically embraced both Dixon and Griffith when the screening ended. "It is like writing history with lightning," the president reportedly remarked, "my only regret is that it is all so terribly true."[5]

Wilson's reaction underscores one of the most harrowing aspects of Reconstruction historiography: its radical partisanship. By 1935, after Du Bois had survived what historian Vernon Burton has called "the nadir of race relations in America," Du Bois published his flawed jewel, *Black Reconstruction*.[6] With a heavy hand on the Marxist tiller, Du Bois called attention to Americans' refusal to recognize blacks as human beings. As during his struggles to steer the National Association for the Advancement of Colored People (NAACP) in more radical directions, Du Bois made impassioned pleas about the nation's persistent (and often conscious) misunderstanding of its history (in this case the years 1865-1877) and the explicitly racist consequences that came as a result.

Apart from a few well-intentioned accounts in the 1890s, southerners and southern sympathizers quickly dominated Reconstruction historiography with racist condemnations of these chaotic years. From the fringe of the Left came little-read or unappreciated (inside or outside the academy) attempts to catalog the terrorist violence and black political advancements that followed emancipation.[7] Mainstream interpretations migrated from narratives of Reconstruction as a wrongheaded misadventure to a tragic debacle imposed by an overreaching and corrupt federal government. Du Bois's *Black Reconstruction* certainly fit the marginalized leftist mold, but the book did more than celebrate the brief and unprecedented experiment in progressive government or reveal the ways the federal government failed to deliver on the human and democratic advances of the Civil War. More presciently, Du Bois exposed how American historians had, in the words of his biographer, David Levering Lewis, "congealed racist interpretations of Reconstruction in the popular mind as solidly as had D. W. Griffith's film."[8]

Du Bois trenchantly described the field of Reconstruction history as "devastated by passion and belief." "Sheer necessity," he explained, required his work to serve as "an arraignment of American historians and an indictment of their ideals." Why had the historical profession systematically ignored the many black triumphs and countless white outrages while totally misinterpreting the broader themes of the postbellum years? "With a determination unparalleled in science," Du Bois explained, "the mass of American writers have started out so to distort the facts of the greatest critical period of American history as to prove right wrong and wrong right.... It simply shows that with sufficient general agreement and determination among the dominant classes, the truth of history may be utterly distorted and contradicted and changed to any convenient fairy tale that the masters of men wish."[9]

Beyond Griffith and Wilson, who reflected and channeled popular prejudice, Du Bois considered most outrageous the school of historians associated with Columbia University's William A. Dunning, who collectively and persistently legitimized this erroneous claptrap. Dunning did more than write what became standard texts on the Reconstruction Era; he trained a phalanx of historians (many but not all of them southerners) who would produce an exhaustive array of histories on the antebellum South, the Civil War, and Reconstruction. The far-reaching effects of their scholarship on America, infecting textbooks, monographs, and popular histories, is hard to exaggerate.[10] Films like *Birth of a Nation* and *Gone with the Wind* (1939) and best-selling books like Claude Bowers's *The Tragic Era* (1929) revealed the devastating influence of Dunning and his acolytes on the country's popular consciousness. Unfortunately, the insidious effect of these historians on the country's understanding of Reconstruction (as well as the Civil War and slavery itself) would resonate for generations.[11]

In the past few decades, historians have invoked Dunning and his students but rarely seem to have actually read them.[12] Du Bois's label for the group—"Anti-Negro"—was simply a variation on his formulation in *Black Reconstruction* of a field guided by "passion and belief." That basic fault line guides Reconstruction historiography even today.[13] For a century, from 1865 to 1965, the most reliable predictor of whether historians could appreciate the complexities of Reconstruction was their opinion of the relative humanity, intelligence, and fitness for democratic citizenship of black Americans. In other words, the greater the degree of racial prejudice on the part of the historian, the more severely Reconstruction would be condemned. From the 1960s, the explicitly pro- and anti-Negro binary became more subtly expressed but no less passionately practiced.[14]

It would be dramatic understatement to describe the field of Reconstruction history, particularly as it related to emancipation, as rather bleak until the later 1950s and the 1960s.[15] Du Bois's voice was not singular in the long intellectual winter of Dunning's dominance, but his was notably shrill amidst the near silence for his sharp-tongued characterizations of the prejudice and ignorance dominating the profession. It was at midcentury that a group of similarly minded scholars emerged to challenge the Dunning school. Dubbed by critics and enthusiasts as "the revisionists" because they were revising Dunning (who, incidentally, was revising the work of James Ford Rhodes), Fawn Brodie, Eric L. McKitrick, and John and LaWanda Cox all used biography and high politics to challenge the Dunning School's dogged hold on Americans' understandings of Reconstruction.[16] Nonetheless, it was not until the publication of landmark syntheses by John Hope Franklin and Kenneth Stampp that the historiography seemed to turn away from Dunning at last.[17] Franklin and Stampp "turned the prevailing orthodoxy upside-down," as Michael Perman (a notable contributor to the scholarship that followed them) explained.[18]

Their immensely popular and influential books shifted the historiographical dynamic. Part of this change was simply the emerging intellectual climate of the 1960s—the civil rights movement started to wear away long-standing racial prejudices and historical blindspots.[19] Instead of having to argue *for* or *against* Reconstruction—arguing implicitly or explicitly that blacks were unfit for citizenship and that the changes wrought by emancipation were bad—Franklin and Stampp symbolized the emergence of a new scholarly paradigm.

The editorial note in Franklin's *Reconstruction: After the Civil War* explained (in another dramatic understatement) that "the Reconstruction era has properly been called the bloody battleground of American historians." Franklin demonstrated remarkable equanimity throughout his study, but when he wrote of the "wild, nightmarish fear" of blacks that formed a through line from the antebellum to the Reconstruction South, one recognizes the driving emotional impulse of Dunning and his pupils.[20] With the rest of his voluminous output, Franklin, both in his scholarship and wide-ranging accomplishments in the profession, exerted tremendous influence on scholars like Vernon Burton, John Boles, Michael Les Benedict, and innumerable others.[21] Franklin understood his position and used it deliberately, in his own rendering, to help produce better history. Franklin's 1979 presidential address to the American Historical Association, "Mirror for Americans: A Century of Reconstruction History," revealed his long-held hopes for the field. "We would do well," he wrote, "to cease using Reconstruction as a mirror of ourselves."[22]

Across historical fields, the 1960s and 1970s also witnessed a widespread democratization of scholarly inquiry.[23] Reflected across time periods and areas of specialty, the 1970s experienced an unprecedented broadening of historical inquiry. In this sense, depending on which godfather or spiritual mentor one cares to invoke, the fruits of this scholarship could be seen as the postrevisionist school but, in fairness to his prescience, the Du Bois school might be more accurate. To invoke Du Bois's call to Woodrow Wilson, post-1960s historians used dogged archival efforts but also new interpretive tools "to make Negroes known to their fellow Americans."

Since the 1960s, several generations of scholars have explored incredibly diverse subject matter to assess the achievements, setbacks, and symbolism that arrived with emancipation in the Reconstruction Era. For this reason, the work of the last fifty years lacks even the intellectual similarities of the original revisionists. What that scholarship shares is a desire to give voice (and perhaps more controversially) agency to those ignored by Dunning and those who revised him.

Within that broader shift, a slew of state studies in the 1970s seemed to point the field toward a revision of the revisionists—particularly with critiques of the Republican program and greater emphasis on the conservatism of Reconstruction's progressive experiment.[24] Still, by decade's end, new research in the Du Bois-Franklin-Stampp mold again dominated the field. In *Masters without Slaves* (1977), James L. Roark explored white resistance to emancipation and black citizenship but argued that planters lost something irretrievable in the war (slaves and complete legal control) even while they remained politically, socially, and economically dominant. This loss, Roark wrote, partly explained their desperate fears and even more desperate commitment to segregation.

That said, if the decade belonged to one book, it was Leon Litwack's *Been in the Storm So Long: The Aftermath of Slavery* (1979), which marked a new interest in the lives and struggles of emancipated slaves. In the spirit of Du Bois's work, Litwack's first lines are dedicated to "the Negro's humanity," in this case via Ralph Ellison. Litwack represents the final strand of DNA that made possible the thriving renaissance of Reconstruction studies in the late twentieth and early twenty-first centuries. While that historiography may be a heated one, historians over the past half century have established the era as both impossible to ignore and inconceivable to look at without wincing. As one recent assessment of the field explained, the "very identity of modern America first emerged during Reconstruction."[25] We have come a long way since Dunning, and even if Americans may want to forget Reconstruction, out of shame if nothing else, historians have made it increasingly difficult to do so.

In the family tree of Reconstruction, Du Bois carried the literature to Franklin and Stampp, which brought the field to Litwack. These historians all begot Eric Foner. Despite occupying a similar august perch at Columbia University, Eric Foner does not quite approach William Dunning's scholarly influence or cultural clout. However, Foner looms over the field of Reconstruction historiography because of the popular reception of his work and the influence of his interpretations on a wide range of scholars. Although emerging from graduate school in 1969, a historiographical moment dominated by John Hope Franklin, Foner's upbringing thrust him in a different direction. From his blacklisted father, Jack D. Foner, Eric Foner "came to appreciate how present concerns can be illuminated by the study of the past . . . how a commitment to social justice could infuse one's attitudes towards the past."[26] Indeed, Foner's work has quite explicitly been motivated by Du Boisian passion and belief.

Inspired in great part by Ira Berlin's landmark editing project, *Freedom: A Documentary History of Emancipation*, Foner set out to show how revolution, however half-baked and aborted, defined Reconstruction.[27] Accordingly, Foner boldly marked the ground he hoped to reclaim in 1983 with *Nothing But Freedom: Emancipation and Its Legacy*. Steven Hahn (whose work on similar themes has also been important) argued that Foner's short study directed scholars' attention back to the questions of freedom and Reconstruction rather than leaving American historians endlessly and grimly obsessing over slavery.

Foner's hugely popular landmark study, *Reconstruction: America's Unfinished Revolution, 1863-1877* (1988), and the abridged *A Short History of Reconstruction, 1863-1877* (1990), won nearly every book prize awarded by the historical profession. His work also captured, condensed, and established an emerging interpretation of the Civil War and Reconstruction Era that could be called emancipationist, documenting the unfulfilled promises and connections between the American Revolution, Reconstruction, and beyond. Foner, like Du Bois before him, targeted his work at Dunning, whose interpretation he described as the "everlasting shame" of the historical profession. According to Foner, Dunning and his students depicted blacks as ignorant, barbaric children and posited that the eventual "restoration of lands to the planters provided for a future better for the negroes." Foner lamented how far-reaching these ideas became, a process he described as freezing the mind of the white South (and much of the rest of the country as well) in a set of antebellum stereotypes and white supremacist redeemers' propoganda.[28]

Following the publication of Foner's *Reconstruction*, historian Michael Perman asked, "What is left to be done?"[29] Foner responded by publishing even more extensively on worldwide movements of emancipation, Abraham Lincoln, and the entirety of American history. Most recently, Foner is probably best-known as the author of the number one-selling high school and college textbook in the United States: *Give Me Liberty! An American History* (2005), whose title underscores the basic slant of the emancipationist school. Describing the series of constitutional amendments that formed the legal backbone of emancipation, Foner writes that the U.S. Constitution changed from an expression of "federal-state relations and the rights of property into a vehicle" of "freedom and . . . protection against misconduct by all levels of government."[30] The broader story of Reconstruction, Foner insists, is one of glorious triumphs and harrowing setbacks, a narrative where emancipation began to realize promises of the founding era just as it set in motion transformations that crested in the civil rights movement of the twentieth century and continues in various ways to the present. In all of his work, Foner celebrates the centuries-long struggle of black Americans to gain equal rights alongside other groups not initially included by the founding fathers. Foner's *Forever Free: The Story of Emancipation and Reconstruction* (2005), takes up these issues even more explicitly. Reconstruction was "an era of noble dreams," Foner explains, and learning its history "can serve as an inspiration for the unfinished task of forging from the ashes of slavery a society of interracial democracy and social justice."[31]

Foner's work thus marks another shift in the historiography. If Franklin and Stampp symbolized scholars' exodus from the Dunning school, anything written after 1989 was somehow communicating with Foner's widely read and celebrated work. In an era where it is no longer acceptable in scholarly discourse or polite conversation to openly or even subtly espouse racial prejudice, the debate over Reconstruction had clearly evolved (some might say even shifted tectonically). In this sense, Du Bois was again a prescient observer. The questions scholars of Reconstruction have asked in the past twenty-five years revolve around the complex dynamics of black citizenship and the moment when southern redemption began (and what forms it took). So while it can be dismaying to learn that undergraduates never encountered Reconstruction in any form in their high school American history courses, it is nonetheless reassuring that historians have moved past the binary of condemnation versus celebration of black fitness for citizenship (and the related celebration of antebellum life and the justification of secession).

In the post-Foner historiography, scholars have approached Reconstruction invariably and necessarily as a richer canvas of tragedy and promise. Thus, in the past two decades especially, historians have sought to measure in what ways the South changed for whites and blacks, the degree to which blacks exercised agency, how many blacks were killed by white supremacists, and how various groups experienced Reconstruction.

The historical literature on redemptive violence includes studies of political violence both broadly construed—studies of the origins of the Ku Klux Klan—and close examinations of specific incidents such as the Colfax Massacre.[32] Historian Allen Trelease was one of the first to explore the South's darkest response to emancipation, the Ku Klux Klan. In *White Terror* (1971), Trelease described the origins and practices of this highly organized and deeply political group to show how disturbingly widespread and organic this "terrorist organization aim[ed] at the preservation of white supremacy" really was.[33] Trelease systematically explored the group's history, particularly its origins in antebellum slave patrols, and its three distinct periods, stretching eventually from Reconstruction to the interwar period to the civil rights struggle and through to today. George Rable's work extended past the Klan and included various forms of informal violence designed to challenge black suffrage and Republican rule. His work remains the most comprehensive account of the many forms of violence aimed at restoring the hierarchy and control of slavery.[34] Among many recent monographs on lynching and the violence of social control, the most compelling is Philip Dray's immensely powerful *At the Hands of Persons Unknown: The Lynching of Black America* (2002).[35] Dray terms the ritual murder of more than ten thousand black Americans in the postbellum years simply "a holocaust!" Further, he considers this period, which he defines as encompassing the end of the Civil War into the 1970s, "a systematized reign of terror that was used to maintain the power whites had over blacks, a way to keep blacks fearful and to forestall black progress and miscegenation." Startling in his evidence and conclusions, Dray confronts us with the shame of Reconstruction and connects this violent and racist terrorism with its myriad legacies in contemporary America.

Not surprisingly, beginning in the 1950s, historians explored the high politics of Reconstruction. Depending on their interpretive bent, their work continued either to celebrate the virtues or condemn the foibles and failures of Republican congressmen, senators, and presidents from 1865 to 1877.[36] By the 1970s, scholars like Michael Les Benedict began to explore the motives, passage, and effects of the Thirteenth, Fourteenth, and Fifteenth Amendments to the Constitution. More recently, Benedict has made important reconsiderations of Andrew Johnson and the legislative and constitutional actions of the postwar period.[37] Harold Hyman's *A More Perfect Union* (1973) was another important study of the constitutional revolution of 1865-1877, painting congressional leaders as more bumbling than heroic in their landmark changes.[38] Michael Vorenberg has explored similar material, examining the landmark Reconstruction amendments but using them to link politics, race, and waning radicalism in the postbellum years.[39] In the context of emancipation and Reconstruction, Annette Gordon-Reed's recent critical biography *Andrew Johnson* (2011), is especially noteworthy, capturing a presidency whose legacy, she explains, has "haunted the nation ever since."[40]

Historians have increasingly focused on these haunting echoes, whether in the White House or in more modest political circumstances in the South. Dan Carter's *When the War Was Over* (1984) addressed the immediate postwar situation in the South, running against the scholarly grain in trying to rehabilitate or at least humanize those "racists" who remained "fanatically opposed" to change, particularly when it came to "black political participation."[41] Richard Zuczek's more recent work on South Carolina has helped broaden our understanding of the political response to Johnson and Radical Republicans, shedding light on the space between the Klan and formal Democratic politics. In works like *State of Rebellion* (1996), Zuczek drew a considerably bleaker picture than Foner, detailing how doggedly white southerners resisted any changes after the Civil War as they retained racial control through political violence and organization.[42] Zuczek's scholarship stands out from a number of other excellent state studies that charter similar changes in the former Confederate states. These works, by J. William Harris, Carl Moneyhon, and Julie Saville, underscore the dynamic local studies of freedpeople's political involvement.[43] Much like the highly politicized and contentious scholarship on slavery, Reconstruction historiographical battles have been fought over how black citizenship expressed itself and how resistance to it took shape.

Only a scholar as dogged and brilliant as Steven Hahn could document so thoroughly the trials and triumphs of black engagement with politics.[44] Hahn's *Roots of Southern Populism* (1983) focused mainly on poor whites in Georgia during the antebellum, Civil War, and Reconstruction eras.[45] In *A Nation under Our Feet* (2003), Hahn argued for the continuity of black political involvement, explaining that "slaves did express and act according to their individual wills, fashion collective norms and aspirations, contest the authority of their owners on many fronts, build institutions to mobilize their resources and sensibilities, produce leaders who wielded significant influence, and in ways we still have yet to appreciate fully, press on the official arenas of politics at the local, state, and national levels."[46]

Hahn's work reveals how under Foner's umbrella, scholars have utterly abandoned the Dunning notion of "black rule." Despite rejecting Dunning's labels and conclusions, Hahn's research reveals a far more pervasive degree of participation and organization by blacks than previous historians had uncovered or may still be willing to acknowledge. In this context, Hahn ends up carving out an important space between emancipation itself and what he calls "the removal of African Americans . . . from the southern body politic."[47] Hahn does not document the "lengthy offensive by which white employers and property owners attempted to construct a postemancipation regime of domination and subordination," mainly because he so persistently argues terrorist violence did not extinguish black political hopes.[48] Indeed Hahn seems to argue, particularly in *The Political Worlds of Slavery and Freedom* (2009), that Reconstruction itself needs to be more purposefully tied to the Civil War and antebellum periods as well as to the Jim Crow era and beyond.[49] In other words, the struggle for freedom was long and black actors had been asserting their roles for centuries and would continue to do so, regardless of the opposition.

Hahn's focus on the political lives of freedpeople and his call for a longer timeline structured by the themes of Reconstruction fits neatly with Heather Andrea Williams's *Help Me to Find My People* (2012). Williams's book, ostensibly a study of family, follows the struggles of African Americans during and after slavery to trace the "love and loneliness and grief . . . anger . . . fear, joy, hope, and despair" slaves and emancipated African Americans experienced as they tried to preserve or reunite families.[50] Williams's work helps us to reconsider the binary of Dunning and Du Bois and see in Reconstruction a more ambiguous mixture of hope and outrage, persistence and despair. In this capacity, Williams's attention to emotion, that quintessentially human response to history as it unfolds, is one way of making sense of the chaos and complexities of Reconstruction.

Under the broad rubric of bringing the lens of gender to a field dominated by men and male historical protagonists and antagonists, historians Glenda Gilmore, Laura Edwards, Jane Dailey, and Hannah Rosen have provided thought-provoking studies of the gendered dimension of political organization, terrorist violence, and the chaotic contestation of black suffrage in the Reconstruction period.[51] Tera Hunter's *To Joy My Freedom* (2003) is especially notable as a study that takes Reconstruction and joins it not to the Civil War but to the outrages of the Jim Crow South. Throughout her wide-ranging exploration of the "everyday networks" of working black women's lives, Hunter artfully blends primary and secondary sources. At one point, Hunter quotes a fairly reflective white Atlantan: "What could be more pitiful," the woman observed, "than to live in such nightmarish terror of another race that you have to lynch them, push them off sidewalks, and never be able to relax your venomous hatred for one moment?" Hunter answered that rhetorical meditation with a statement that informs each page of her book: "African-Americans bore the burden of this bad dream every day."[52]

Despite a similarly keen appreciation for new sources and sharply drawn arguments, Heather Cox Richardson's work seems to sail in the opposite direction, but she is equally concerned with expanding the scholarly vision of Reconstruction. While some may dispute Richardson's conclusions, her research has stretched conceptions of Reconstruction northward in *The Death of Reconstruction* (2001) and westward in *West from Appomattox: The Reconstruction of America after the Civil War* (2007). Throughout her work, Richardson tends to minimize race in favor of labor and migration. In so doing, she shows northern Republicans afraid of the creeping potential of freedmen's labor activism and its implications in their own backyards as well as along the expanding frontier.[53] Richardson explains that the relentless "focus on the South and its morass of racial problems" has distracted historians from labor, industrialization, urbanization, and westward expansion.[54]

Two other recent books turn the state studies of yesteryear somewhat on their heads. Both John Rodrigue and Moon-Ho Jung look at Louisiana—a famously defiant hot spot in the process of emancipation, Reconstruction, and redemption.[55] While Rodrigue follows a somewhat more conventional path by filling out the story of neglected parts of Louisiana, Jung's story concerns the little-known importation of Chinese laborers to sugar plantations during Reconstruction. Jung's fascinating work takes on an even more intriguing historiographical dimension in the author's invocation of Du Bois's prescience and "revolutionary . . . global framework" of "superexploitation of the dark proletariat." As Jung writes of Du Bois, "More than any other work, Du Bois's landmark study has guided my interpretation of the age of emancipation."[56]

Jung's work underscores another trend in recent Reconstruction historiography, where the need for big bold claims may simply refashion ideas that have circulated for some time. In many ways, the journalist Douglas A. Blackmon repackages the work of the late 1970s by James L. Roark and others in *Slavery by Another Name* (2008). Blackmon's provocative subtitle, *The Re-Enslavement of Black Americans from the Civil War to World War II*, reveals what is inside: an easily readable distillation packaged as a polemic. Blackmon argues that Jim Crow should be renamed for the process that began in earnest at Appomattox. "Only by acknowledging the full extent of slavery's grip on U.S. society," he writes, "its intimate connections to present-day wealth and power, the depth of its injury to millions of black Americans, the shocking nearness in time of its true end—can we reconcile the paradoxes of current American life."[57]

Blackmon's eagerness to show readers the contemporary legacies of Reconstruction implies that knowledge about the past smooths the way toward reconciling its traumas and legacy. In much the same vein, Douglas Egerton's *The Wars of Reconstruction* (2014) offers a concise synthesis on this disputed period. Twenty-six years following Foner's monumental 1988 effort, carving new intellectual space requires Egerton, known for his controversial work on slave rebels Denmark Vesey and Gabriel Prosser, to try out different approaches and analysis of mostly familiar material. In fairness, Egerton had his work set out for him in a way Foner could only have dreamed about during the 1980s. With so many rich contributions to the historiography, there is no easy way to synthesize such diverse strands of scholarship. As such, Egerton works in the activist framework set forth by Du Bois, attempting to blend equally together elements of the work of Hahn, Foner, and Dray.

But Egerton, much in the spirit of his subjects, also experiments with different methods. He utilizes a far more intimate anecdotal approach than his predecessors, employing individual characters like Robert Vesey, Denmark's son, to capture the long history of Reconstruction. In this capacity, Egerton heeds the call of scholars like Hahn and Burton to expand Reconstruction's periodization. In so doing, his book underscores the roots and legacy of slavery in the origins, path, and aftermath of what he emphasizes was a moment of glorious progressive experimentation. Thus, unlike Foner, Egerton chooses to emphasize the experimental nature and boldness of the radical vision rather than the promise of Reconstruction. As Egerton concludes, "Reconstruction was that better future, the nation's first truly progressive era." Lamenting the lack of memorials in present-day Charleston, he explains that "no forest of statues can make up for that lost potential or can erase the guilt" of Reconstruction. Egerton writes that when America builds "as many monuments" to men like Robert Smalls and Octavius Catto as there are to "proslavery politicians and Confederate generals, we will know that Americans have finally come to understand the meaning of those decades."[58]

That said, in the throes of passion and belief, where historians and the public have never seemed to agree on when or what Reconstruction was or if it was good or bad, it is difficult to know whether monuments will ever signify public understanding. Moreover, as any examination of the historiography of Reconstruction (or nearly any field of history) reveals, it is inevitable that future historians will revise the conclusions of the present. One can only hope that scholarship will heed the lessons that each of these works has taught the broader field of American history. As Eric Foner recently lamented, touching on the real endgame of scholarship driven by social justice, "I wish I could say that the general public has absorbed the changes in interpretations of Reconstruction that I and many others have promoted."[59]

Historians no doubt will continue to find new connections and analytical tools, trying both passionately and objectively to convince people to accept Reconstruction as one of the most vital and revealing periods in the history of the United States. But perhaps that wiser approach to engaging the public is accepting the unlikelihood of that day ever coming to pass and remaining keenly aware that historians of Reconstruction will always be contesting hostile territory, both in the past and the present.

Notes

1. The letter appeared in *The Crisis,* the magazine Du Bois edited for the National Association for the Advancement of Colored People. W. E. B. Du Bois, "Open Letter to Woodrow Wilson," *The Crisis* 5 (Mar. 1913): 236, http://teachingamericanhistory.org/library/document/open-letter-to-woodrow-wilson (accessed Mar. 10, 2014).
2. Ibid.
3. Ibid.
4. Richard Wormser, *The Rise and Fall of Jim Crow* (New York: St. Martin's Press, 2003), 121.
5. Jennifer D. Keene, "Wilson and Race Relations," in *A Companion to Woodrow Wilson,* ed. Ross A. Kennedy (London: John Wiley, 2013), 144.
6. O. Vernon Burton, David Herr, and Matthew Cheney, "Defining Reconstruction," in *A Companion to the Civil War and Reconstruction,* ed. Lacy K. Ford (Malden, Mass: Blackwell Publishing, 2005), 301. Burton, Herr, and Cheney may be invoking Rayford W. Logan's *The Negro in American Life and Thought: The Nadir* (New York: Dial Press, 1954), although Logan was referring to the years 1877-1901.
7. Alrutheus A. Taylor's works in the 1920s and 1940s provided important counterparts to Du Bois but received even less attention. See *The Negro in South Carolina during the Reconstruction* (Washington, D.C.: Association for the Study of Negro Life and History, 1924), *The Negro in the Reconstruction of Virginia* (Washington, D.C.: Association for the Study of Negro Life and History, 1926), and *The Negro in Tennessee, 1865-1880* (Washington, D.C.: Association for the Study of Negro Life and History, 1941). See also Francis B. Simkins and Robert H. Woody, *South Carolina during Reconstruction* (Chapel Hill: Univ. of North Carolina Press, 1932); Vernon Lane Wharton, *The Negro in Mississippi, 1865-1900* (Chapel Hill: Univ. of North Carolina Press, 1947); and George Brown Tindall, *South Carolina Negroes, 1877-1900* (Columbia: Univ. of South Carolina Press, 1952).
8. David Levering Lewis, "Introduction," in *Black Reconstruction in America, 1860-1880,* by W. E. B. Du Bois (1935; repr., New York: The Free Press, 1992), vii.
9. Ibid., xvi.
10. Dunning's achievements are assessed with far more equanimity in John David Smith and J. Vincent Lowery, eds., *The Dunning School: Historians, Race, and the Meaning of Reconstruction* (Lexington: Univ. Press of Kentucky, 2013). Even C. Vann Woodward, with three immensely important

books and dozens of students, enjoyed but a fraction of Dunning's influence on the field of American history.

11. In his pathbreaking work of 1907, *Reconstruction: Political and Economic*, Dunning effectively hijacked Americans' narrative of how blacks and the South fit into the nation's history. "On the arrival of Union troops after January 1, 1863 (the effective date of the Emancipation Proclamation), Dunning infamously wrote, "The policy of emancipation was systematically carried out, with the result that great masses of blacks, withdrawn from their wonted routine, wasted away in idleness, want, and disease." Accordingly, Dunning condemned the Civil War as an illegal debacle that unleashed forces upon blacks which they were utterly unprepared for and which the South neither wanted nor needed. Notable as Dunning was for his carefully documented research, the historian became best known for the state-by-state studies his students undertook of the Reconstruction period—fleshing out Dunning's approach across the states of the former Confederacy. His students also branched out. Dunning's most influential student, Ulrich Bonnell Phillips, expanded the Dunning thesis deeply and broadly in his landmark work, *American Negro Slavery* (1918). Phillips taught still more of his countrymen that Africa was a horrific and barbaric place and that slaves were better off in bondage. Slavery was "a positive benefit to the people who constituted its merchandise." If slavery were such a good thing, then freedom and citizenship for blacks, that ground which would be so brutally contested during Reconstruction, was, in the words of John W. Burgess, "the most soul-sickening spectacle that Americans have ever been called upon to behold." See William A. Dunning, *Reconstruction: Political and Social, 1865-1877* (New York: Harper and Brothers, 1907), 11; Ulrich B. Phillips, *American Negro Slavery* (New York: D. Appleton, 1918), 95; and John W. Burgess, *Reconstruction and the Constitution 1866-1876* (New York: Charles Scribner's Sons, 1902), 34.

12. The essays in Smith and Lowery's *The Dunning School* credit Dunning and his acolytes for the many things, good and bad, that they contributed to the profession and the field. Smith explains that the essays complicate our dismissal of the school as merely one-dimensionally racist. What was worthwhile about their approach, the essays collectively ask, and what should we know about, as Eric Foner explains that the Dunningites' "intellectual formation, social backgrounds, personal experiences, and research methods, and the overall trajectories of their careers," are important to understand. Eric Foner, "Foreword," in Smith and Lowery, eds., *The Dunning School*, ix.

13. Du Bois, *Black Reconstruction*, 726.

14. For more on the deep influence of objectivity on U.S. historiography, see Peter Novick, *That Noble Dream: The "Objectivity Question" and the American Historical Profession* (Cambridge: Cambridge Univ. Press, 1988).

15. The main exceptions were scholarly articles, especially Howard K. Beale's "On Rewriting Reconstruction History," *American Historical Review*

45 (July 1940): 807-27. But given the dominance of the Dunning School, expecting scholarly articles to dislodge these interpretations was akin to using a .22 to incapacitate a grizzly bear.

16. Fawn Brodie, *Thaddeus Stevens: Scourge of the South* (New York: Norton, 1959); Eric L. McKitrick, *Andrew Johnson and Reconstruction* (Chicago: Univ. of Chicago Press, 1960); John Cox and LaWanda Cox, *Politics, Principle, and Prejudice, 1865-6: Dilemma of Reconstruction America* (New York: Free Press of Glencoe, 1963).

17. John Hope Franklin, *Reconstruction: After the Civil War* (Chicago: Univ. of Chicago Press, 1961), and Kenneth M. Stampp, *The Era of Reconstruction, 1865-1877* (New York: Alfred A. Knopf, 1965). Franklin's landmark textbook about the African American experience, *From Slavery to Freedom*, also deserves mention in this context. First published by Alfred A. Knopf in 1947, it has gone through nine editions and sold more than three million copies.

18. Michael Perman, *Emancipation and Reconstruction* (Wheeling, Ill.: Harlan Davidson, 2003), 147.

19. The historian William Bragg argues in "C. Mildred Thompson: A Liberal among the Dunningites," in Smith and Lowery, eds., *The Dunning School*, that it was pesky 1960s radicals and the blight of political correctness that allowed historians to finally shelve Dunning. Whatever the accuracy of Bragg's claims, the upshot was that by 1970, things had begun to change.

20. Daniel Boorstin, "Introduction," in Franklin, *Reconstruction: After the Civil War*, vii, 3.

21. See Burton, Herr, and Cheney, "Defining Reconstruction," 302.

22. John Hope Franklin, "Mirror for Americans: A Century of Reconstruction History," *American Historical Review* 85 (Feb. 1980): 1-14.

23. Roy Rosenzweig and David Thelen, *The Presence of the Past: Popular Uses of History in American Life* (New York: Columbia Univ. Press, 1998), 4.

24. Joe Gray Taylor, *Louisiana Reconstructed, 1863-1877* (Baton Rouge: Louisiana State Univ. Press, 1974); Jerrell H. Shofner, *Nor Is It Over Yet: Florida in the Era of Reconstruction, 1863-1877* (Gainesville: Univ. Presses of Florida, 1974); Carl Moneyhon, *Republicanism in Reconstruction Texas* (Austin: Univ. of Texas Press, 1980).

25. Burton, Herr, and Cheney, "Defining Reconstruction," 299.

26. Jon Wiener, "In Memoriam: Jack D. Foner," *AHA Perspectives* (Apr. 2000), http://www.historians.org/publications-and-directories/perspectives-on-history/april-2000/in-memoriam-jack-d-foner (accessed Mar. 10, 2014).

27. Ira Berlin et al., eds., *Freedom: A Documentary History of Emancipation, 1861-1867*, 6 vols. (New York: Cambridge Univ. Press, 1982-2013).

28. Eric Foner, *Reconstruction: America's Unfinished Revolution, 1863-1877* (New York: Harper, 1988), 609, 610. See also Eric Foner, *A Short History of Reconstruction* (New York: Harper, 1988). Other works by Eric Foner that deal directly with Reconstruction include *The Fiery Trial: Abraham Lincoln and American Slavery* (New York: Norton, 2010); *Our Lincoln: New Perspectives on*

Lincoln and His World (New York: Norton, 2008); *Who Owns History? Rethinking the Past in a Changing World* (New York: Hill and Wang, 2002); (and Olivia Mahoney), *America's Reconstruction: People and Politics after the Civil War* (New York: Harper Perennial, 1995); *Slavery and Freedom in Nineteenth-Century America* (New York: Oxford Univ. Press, 1994); *Freedom's Lawmakers: A Directory of Black Officeholders during Reconstruction* (New York: Oxford Univ. Press, 1993); (ed.), *A House Divided: America in the Age of Lincoln* (New York: Norton, 1990); *Nothing But Freedom: Emancipation and Its Legacy* (Baton Rouge: Louisiana State Univ. Press, 1983); *Politics and Ideology in the Age of the Civil War* (New York: Oxford Univ. Press, 1980); and *Free Soil, Free Labor, Free Men: The Ideology of the Republican Party* (New York: Oxford Univ. Press, 1970). See also Richard Follett, Eric Foner, and Walter Johnson, *Slavery's Ghost: The Problem of Freedom in the Age of Emancipation* (Baltimore: Johns Hopkins Univ. Press, 2011).

29. Michael Perman, "Eric Foner's Reconstruction: A Finished Revolution," *Reviews in American History* 17 (Mar. 1989): 73-78.

30. Eric Foner, *Give Me Liberty! An American History*, 3rd ed., vol. 1 (New York: Norton, 2011), 607.

31. Eric Foner, *Forever Free: The Story of Emancipation and Reconstruction* (New York: Alfred A. Knopf, 2005), 238.

32. Nicholas Lemann, *Redemption: The Last Battle of the Civil War* (New York: Farrar, Straus and Giroux, 2006). See also Stephen Budiansky, *The Bloody Shirt: Terror after Appomattox* (New York: Viking, 2008).

33. Allen W. Trelease, *White Terror: The Ku Klux Klan Conspiracy and Southern Reconstruction* (1971; repr., Baton Rouge: Louisiana State Univ. Press, 1995), 11.

34. George C. Rable, *But There Was No Peace: The Role of Violence in the Politics of Reconstruction* (Athens: Univ. of Georgia Press, 1984).

35. Philip Dray, *At the Hands of Persons Unknown: The Lynching of Black America* (New York: Modern Library, 2002). See also Ashraf Rushdy, *American Lynching* (New Haven, Conn.: Yale Univ. Press, 2012); Crystal Feimster, *Southern Horrors: Women and the Politics of Rape and Lynching* (Cambridge, Mass.: Harvard Univ. Press, 2009); Michael Fellman, *In the Name of God and Country: Reconsidering Terrorism in American History* (New Haven, Conn.: Yale Univ. Press, 2010); Amy Louise Wood, *Lynching and Spectacle: Witnessing Racial Violence in America, 1890-1940* (Chapel Hill: Univ. of North Carolina Press, 2009).

36. Michael W. Fitzgerald, *Splendid Failure: Postwar Reconstruction in the American South* (Chicago: Ivan R. Dee, 2007).

37. See these works by Michael Les Benedict: *The Impeachment and Trial of Andrew Johnson* (New York: Norton, 1973); *A Compromise of Principle: Congressional Republicans and Reconstruction* (New York: Norton, 1974); *The Fruits of Victory: Alternatives in Restoring the Union, 1865-1877* (Lanham, Md.: Univ. Press of America, 1986); and *Preserving the Constitution: Essays on Politics and the Constitution in the Reconstruction Era* (New York: Fordham Univ. Press, 2006).

38. Harold M. Hyman, *A More Perfect Union: The Impact of the Civil War and Reconstruction on the Constitution* (New York: Alfred A. Knopf, 1973).

39. Michael Vorenberg, *Final Freedom: The Civil War, the Abolition of Slavery, and the Thirteenth Amendment* (Cambridge: Cambridge Univ. Press, 2001). See also Michael Vorenberg, "Reconstruction as Constitutional Crisis," in *Reconstructions: New Perspectives on the Postbellum United States*, ed. Thomas J. Brown (New York: Oxford Univ. Press, 2006), 141-71.

40. Annette Gordon-Reed, *Andrew Johnson* (New York: Times Books/Henry Holt, 2011), back cover.

41. Dan T. Carter, *When the War Was Over: The Failure of Self-Reconstruction in the South, 1865-1867* (Baton Rouge: Louisiana State Univ. Press, 1984), 3.

42. See Richard Zuczek, *State of Rebellion: Reconstruction in South Carolina* (Columbia: Univ. of South Carolina Press, 1996). Also, see his essays: "The Government's Attack on the Ku Klux Klan: A Reassessment," *South Carolina Historical Magazine* 97 (Jan. 1996): 47-64; "The Last Campaign of the Civil War: South Carolina and the Revolution of 1876," *Civil War History* 42 (Mar. 1996): 18-31; and "I Stand Here the Equal of Any Man: The Life of Robert Smalls," in *The Human Tradition in the Civil War and Reconstruction Era*, ed. Steven E. Woodworth (New York: Scholarly Resources, 1999), 199-212.

43. J. William Harris, *Deep Souths: Delta, Piedmont, and Sea Island Society in the Age of Segregation* (Baltimore: Johns Hopkins Univ. Press, 2001); Carl H. Moneyhon, *The Impact of the Civil War and Reconstruction in Arkansas: Persistence in the Midst of Ruin* (Baton Rouge: Louisiana State Univ. Press, 1994); Julie Saville, *The Work of Reconstruction: From Slave to Wage Laborer in South Carolina, 1860-1870* (New York: Cambridge Univ. Press, 1994). These works also serve as an important precursor to Steven Hahn's later work.

44. Lerone Bennett Jr., the radical black intellectual and editor of *Ebony* magazine, wrote *Black Power U.S.A.: The Human Side of Reconstruction, 1867-1877* (New York: Johnson Publishing, 1967), a work very much in the spirit of Du Bois and 1960s black radicalism. It was not widely read and remains underappreciated. The historian Michael W. Fitzgerald anticipated some of Hahn's work in *The Union League and Social Change in the Deep South during Reconstruction* (Baton Rouge: Louisiana State Univ. Press, 1989) and *Urban Emancipation: Popular Politics in Reconstruction Mobile* (Baton Rouge: Louisiana State Univ. Press, 2002).

45. Steven Hahn, *The Roots of Southern Populism: Yeoman Farmers and the Transformation of the Georgia Upcountry, 1850-1890* (New York: Oxford Univ. Press, 1983).

46. Steven Hahn, *A Nation under Our Feet: Black Political Struggles in the Rural South from Slavery to the Great Migration* (Cambridge, Mass.: Belknap Press of Harvard Univ. Press, 2003), 15.

47. Ibid., 441.

48. Ibid.

49. Vernon Burton, David Herr, and Matthew Cheney make much the same argument in "Defining Reconstruction," using the historiography of Reconstruction to argue for broadening the chronology.

50. The historian Mark Smith has examined similar dynamics of emotion and the senses in antebellum and Civil War history. In "The Past as a Foreign Country: Reconstruction, Inside and Out," in Brown's *Reconstructions*, Smith pointed historians to the work of Jay Sexton as significant in urging more international studies of Reconstruction. See also Jay Sexton, *The Monroe Doctrine: Empire and Nation in Nineteenth-Century America* (New York: Hill and Wang, 2011).

51. Glenda Gilmore, *Gender and Jim Crow: Women and the Politics of White Supremacy in North Carolina, 1896-1920* (Chapel Hill: Univ. of North Carolina Press, 1996); Laura Edwards, *Gendered Strife and Confusion: The Political Culture of Reconstruction* (Urbana: Univ. of Illinois Press, 1997); Jane Dailey, *Before Jim Crow: The Politics of Race in Postemancipation Virginia* (Chapel Hill: Univ. of North Carolina Press, 2000); Hannah Rosen, *Terror in the Heart of Freedom: Citizenship, Sexual Violence, and the Meaning of Race in the Postemancipation South* (Chapel Hill: Univ. of North Carolina Press, 2000).

52. Tera Hunter, *To Joy My Freedom: Southern Black Women's Lives and Labors after the Civil War* (Cambridge, Mass.: Harvard Univ. Press, 2003), 97, 129.

53. Heather Cox Richardson, *The Greatest Nation of the Earth: Republican Economic Policies during the Civil War* (Cambridge, Mass.: Harvard Univ. Press, 1997). See particularly Heather Cox Richardson, *The Death of Reconstruction: Race, Labor and Politics in the Post-Civil War North, 1865-1901* (Cambridge, Mass.: Harvard Univ. Press, 2001), which revises and revisits many of the arguments David Montgomery made in *Beyond Equality: Labor and the Radical Republicans, 1862-1872* (New York: Alfred A. Knopf, 1967); Heather Cox Richardson, "North and West of Reconstruction: Studies in Political Economy," in Brown, *Reconstructions*, 66-90; Heather Cox Richardson, *West from Appomattox: The Reconstruction of America after the Civil War* (New Haven, Conn.: Yale Univ. Press, 2007); Heather Cox Richardson, *Wounded Knee: Party Politics and the Road to an American Massacre* (New York: Basic, 2010).

54. Richardson, *West from Appomattox*, 4.

55. John C. Rodrigue, *Reconstruction in the Cane Fields: From Slavery to Free Labor in Louisiana's Sugar Parishes, 1862-1880* (Baton Rouge: Louisiana State Univ. Press, 2001); Moon-Ho Jung, *Coolies and Cane: Race, Labor, and Sugar in the Age of Emancipation* (Baltimore: Johns Hopkins Univ. Press, 2006).

56. Jung, *Coolies and Cane*, 222.

57. Douglas A. Blackmon, *Slavery by Another Name: The Re-Enslavement of Black Americans from the Civil War to World War II* (New York: Random House, 2008), 402.

58. Douglas Egerton, *The Wars of Reconstruction: The Brief, Violent History of America's Most Progressive Era* (New York: Bloomsbury, 2014), 357.

59. Eric Foner, email to author, April 27, 2014.

CHAPTER FIVE

Reconstruction
National Politics, 1865-1877

EDWARD O. FRANTZ

It was once easy to disparage national politics during the Reconstruction Era. Whether one was a southerner or a northerner, a liberal or a conservative, many a historian looked at the political era spanning from 1865 to 1877 with disdain. Corruption, scandal, terror, and pettiness supposedly characterized the era, and the politicians of the day reportedly were unable to solve the major problems of the time. The occupants of the executive mansion were so maladroit that a mere forty years after Rutherford B. Hayes's death, the novelist Thomas Wolfe wondered, "Garfield, Arthur, Harrison and Hayes. . . . Which had the whiskers, which the burnsides: which was which?"[1] As historians in general and biographers in particular focused on national politics of the Civil War and Progressive Eras, the politics of Reconstruction seemed like a distant, awkward cousin who was, at best, tolerated but frequently better to ignore. Despite this overarching trend, careful, quality scholarship on national politics during this period always was available to those who sought it out. For those adventuresome enough to dig, the national politics of the Reconstruction Era provided not only sensational headlines, but also key debates about the evolution of the modern American state.

This essay focuses largely on works written since 1982, with special attention to the most influential interpretations that helped to usher in subsequent research. Although historians of national politics during the Reconstruction years have produced high quality scholarship, much of that work nevertheless has remained more obscure than it should be. As late-twentieth-century historiographical trends toward social and cultural history have enriched our approach to the past, and as new generations of historians coming of age after the idealism of the 1960s entered the profession, fewer scholars found studying traditional political history generally, and of the nineteenth century in particular, attractive. That said, scholars have entered into an era of renewed, vibrant interest in politics during the age of Reconstruction.

Eric Foner's monumental *Reconstruction: America's Unfinished Revolution* (1988) is the most authoritative interpretation of Reconstruction. Many may find Foner's historical synthesis daunting, but the scope of his original research proved even more impressive. Aware of Reconstruction's complexity, Foner raised questions as to whether one could even consider Reconstruction as a single entity. In some states, he explained, politics proved to be so divided that one might struggle even to talk definitively about a common experience. Generalizing on a national level, therefore, seemed even riskier. Nevertheless, Foner's approach, intent, and argument influenced generations of students and remain dominant today. By placing the black experience at the center of Reconstruction, Foner touched on so many different fields (including race, class, labor, economics, ideology, and politics) that his book became the definitive Reconstruction text of the era. Looking to W. E. B. Du Bois's analysis in *Black Reconstruction* (1935) for inspiration, Foner created the kind of magnum opus to which many historians aspire but few will ever reach.

How is Foner most useful for understanding national politics during the age of Reconstruction? First, even though Foner placed African Americans at the center of his Reconstruction story, he never lost sight of the national political scene. Even if, as former Democratic Speaker of the House of Representatives Thomas "Tip" O'Neill asserted, all politics are local, national politics were vitally important to African Americans. It was the federal government that provided a framework for the expanded African Americans rights advanced in the form of the Thirteenth, Fourteenth, and Fifteenth Amendments. It was the federal government that experimented with the Freedmen's Bureau, and it was the federal court system, intimately tied to the political system, that helped to minimize the most far-reaching goals of liberal reformers over the course of Reconstruction.

As with many studies written after the civil rights movement, race occupies a central place in Foner's argument. It is here that Foner's ability to analyze state and national levels pays particular dividends. White southern Democrats were not alone in using racial appeals to rally their constituents. Indeed, northern Democrats were equally adept at playing the race card. In Foner's telling, the 1868 election—the first presidential election held since the end of the Civil War—"centered on white supremacy."[2] The Democratic nominee for president, New York governor Horatio Seymour, was not a racial demagogue. His running mate, Frank Blair, however, was. With Blair on the attack, the Democrats had a candidate who played on white racial fears. He insinuated that the expansion of the federal government would benefit African Americans at the expense of whites. This argument, one should note, proved to be highly malleable and effective for more than one hundred years of American politics, as racial demagogues would argue that big government was a special favor to African Americans that came at the expense of the white working class.

Foner's book contains numerous laments of missed opportunities. None of these matters more to Foner than the idea of a centralized government that could protect its citizens. Accordingly, Foner considered the contested election of 1876 and subsequent Compromise of 1877 significant because "1877 marked a decisive retreat from the idea, born during the Civil War, of a powerful nation state protecting the fundamental rights of American citizens."[3]

Although from the late 1980s onward Foner's work redirected historians' interpretation of national politics during Reconstruction, scholars nonetheless continued to rely on earlier studies. Among the most lasting interpretations of politics during Reconstruction are William Gillette's *Retreat from Reconstruction* (1982) and Michael Perman's *The Road to Redemption* (1984). Both scholars pay close attention to variation in time and place as well as to the regional variations of Reconstruction politics. Their interest lies at the macro level, but their work also provides close case studies of state and local politics. Perman's book constructs an interpretative chronology that helps explain the big picture. First, Perman investigates what he terms "The Politics of Convergence," covering 1869-1873. During the period between 1869 and 1873, he explains, both political parties sought competitive advantage by appealing to moderate, mainstream voters. Both Republicans and Democrats targeted former southern Whigs as part of that strategy. Next, Perman examines what he calls "The Politics of Divergence," lasting from 1874-1879. Here he elucidates how conservative southerners, whom historians typically call Bourbons, regained the political power that they had lost during the Civil War and Congressional Reconstruction. The cost for obtaining this power, he argues, was "a politics of balance, inertia and drift" that plagued the South for generations.[4] Throughout his work, Perman successfully steers clear of adopting a reductionist explanation of whom to "blame" for the end of Reconstruction.

Gillette's *Retreat from Reconstruction, 1869-1879* succeeds admirably in examining how the leadership of Ulysses S. Grant's administration contributed to the uncertainty of Reconstruction politics. Gillette is unsparing in his criticism of Grant's Reconstruction policies, noting that they rarely seemed to react to southern politics in any coherent manner. Gillette's was the most powerful argument of the post-1960s era encouraging historians to look beyond the Compromise of 1877 for explanations of Reconstruction's collapse. Gillette argues that "if reconstruction ever had a chance, it was during Grant's administration, when the Republicans controlled . . . both the presidency and Congress for the first time during the postwar period."[5] Gillette concedes that an inadequate bureaucracy, insufficient funds, racism, and other factors undermined the Grant administration's ability to enact robust Reconstruction policies. But, he forcefully argues, the problem was internal, not external. The

Republicans, and Grant in particular, were most responsible for the failures of Reconstruction. Gillette concludes his book on a pessimistic note, arguing that the South "had never been truly reconstructed or reformed, and in many respects it had not been fundamentally changed."[6] Though Foner and others challenged Gillette's point, scholars nonetheless will still find much to value in his work because of its scope and engagement with primary sources.

Like Gillette, George C. Rable wrote prior to Foner's influential synthesis and focused on the national political system. Rable's *But There Was No Peace: The Role of Violence in the Politics of Reconstruction* (1984) points out the central role of violence in understanding the limits of political action in the Reconstruction South. Rable wrote his book well before "terror" and "terrorism" took on new meanings to Americans in the twenty-first century. He therefore seemed not only to appreciate the role that racial terror could play in the United States through the 1960s, but also anticipated the ways in which the foreign foes of the United States could resist American dominance. Extreme violence often worked, according to Rable: "Although Americans have often been loath to concede that violence may bring about needed change, terrorism in the Reconstruction Era was instrumental in achieving the ends desired by its perpetrators." Rable unearths chilling evidence that violence served as a reactionary force in southern politics. He concludes that "the Reconstruction legacy legitimized the use of force in southern society."[7]

More interested in American culture broadly defined, historian David Blight explores competing ideologies following the Civil War. Blight points out that the quest for racial justice, or what he describes as the "emancipationist memory" of the Civil War, comprised part of a competing set of ideologies during the postwar decades. Blight also identifies a "reconciliationist memory" as well as a "white supremacist memory" of the war. Following the end of the conflict, Blight argues, the forces of reconciliation and white supremacy triumphed over the celebration of emancipation. Blight's pathbreaking *Race and Reunion* (2001) draws heavily upon literature and American culture to provide a paradigm for understanding the political processes at play following Appomattox.

In *The Door of Hope: Republican Presidents and the First Southern Strategy, 1877-1933* (2011), Edward Frantz explores the political terrain hinted at in Blight's book. By examining the travel of Republican presidents from Rutherford B. Hayes to Herbert Hoover, Frantz demonstrates that what he calls the "legacy of liberation" had longer meaning and rhetorical staying power among Republican presidents than many previous historians realize. That said, when making concrete political decisions, most Republicans in the late nineteenth and early twentieth centuries closed what Theodore Roosevelt frequently called "the Door of Hope" on African Americans. Although Frantz's work covers a chronological period generally associated with the Gilded Age and Progressive Era, it demonstrates that many of the political legacies stemming from the Civil War and Reconstruction were far more complicated than many historians of the 1960s had realized.

If Foner, Blight, and Frantz positioned race at the center of their discussions, other historians pointed out that political discussions centered on other themes as well. Heather Cox Richardson's *The Death of Reconstruction* (2001) posited that northerners' commitment to African American rights never was as fervent as historians trained during the Civil Rights Era had assumed. Instead, she argues that "free labor ideology," also the focus of Foner's influential *Free Soil, Free Labor, Free Men* (1970), helps to explain a narrower conception of the meanings of freedom among northern Republicans following the end of the war. Richardson maintains that as the United States embraced a more industrialized economy during the Reconstruction years, the popular press prioritized societal harmony over free labor. She concludes that white northerners stopped supporting questions of African American rights not because of racism alone, but also "because African-Americans came to represent a concept of society and government that would destroy the free labor world."[8] In other words, to northern Republicans, emancipated slaves were less dangerous to the free labor system than they had been under slavery, but they still were a threat to the emerging industrial economy because of their desire for a more expansive federal government.

Charles C. Calhoun's *Conceiving a New Republic: The Republican Party and the Southern Question, 1869-1900* (2006) provides an even more powerful examination of ideology following the Civil War. Whereas previous historians assessed how and why Republicans "abandoned" southern blacks and their white Republican allies, Calhoun believes that the idea of republicanism was a central force of post–Civil War political thought and rhetoric. Calhoun underscores the often complex and contradictory understandings of republicanism. Republicans defined republicanism "most fundamentally . . . as the rule by the people through the instrument of representative government."[9] Of course, key debates about who "the people" were and what the proper relationship was between people and the federal government lay at the heart of this concept. Calhoun's work built upon earlier books by Vincent J. De Santis, Stanley P. Hirshson, and Rayford W. Logan, scholarship that vilified Republican politicians for lacking sufficient moral fiber to lead. Moreover, by focusing on a time period that includes both Reconstruction and its aftermath, Calhoun's study breaks down the simplistic chronology historians too often employ when studying the postwar era.

In another important work, Calhoun's *From Bloody Shirt to Full Dinner Pail: The Transformation of Politics and Governance in the Gilded Age* (2010), the author provides a more streamlined approach not only to republicanism in general but to the broader political system. "In the Gilded Age," Calhoun writes, "if politics was blood sport, it was so because politics was in most people's blood."[10] This approach contains two vital observations that any student of the post–Civil War period should remember, because they illustrate the vitality of the two-party system. First, Calhoun argues that the election of 1868 demonstrated that the Democratic Party was more powerful than observers would have expected, because "even with a relatively weak candidate [Horatio Seymour], the Democrats had managed a more than respectable showing against the savior of the Union."[11]

Second, Calhoun redirected scholars' attention to the salience of the 1874 congressional election. The Democrats did well enough in that election to win control of the House of Representatives. According to Calhoun, the Forty-Third Congress, which closed on

March 4, 1875, signaled the end of the era of Republican dominance. This insight matters because nearly every American history textbook cites the contested presidential election of 1876 as the turning point for Reconstruction, with the implicit argument that the 1876 campaign led to the abandonment of the freedpeople and their southern Republican allies to Democratic "redeemers." Calhoun, however, insists that the results of the 1874 election were clear: Republicans could not expect to dominate national politics if they focused solely on Reconstruction. Moreover, once Republicans had to share one of the branches of government with their Democratic counterparts, enacting policy would prove to be far more difficult than it previously had been. Once divided government (where one party does not monopolize the legislative and executive branches) characterized Washington, D.C., any progress on Reconstruction issues would be nearly impossible to achieve. This key observation helps demonstrate the limits and possibilities that one could reasonably expect from American political leaders during the mid-1870s. If strong Reconstruction policies could be achieved only along partisan lines, then Reconstruction clearly was a more fragile political experiment than many historians have realized.[12]

In a compelling recent article, historian Nicholas Barreyre calls attention to the important effects of the Panic of 1873 on the nation's political system. Arguing persuasively that too few historians have focused on the political consequences of the devastating economic downturn, Barreyre encourages scholars to examine the "politics of the 1873 crisis." By this the author contends that although the panic was financial in nature, the most important ramifications manifested themselves in politics. Barreyre points to the implications of the panic in shaping the political realities that made it difficult for Democrats as well as Republicans to come to grips with a compelling response to the panic. Governing effectively for the remainder of the 1870s proved to be an even greater challenge. Among other things, Barreyre argues, the political response broke down along regional rather than party lines. Southerners and westerners were more willing to pursue an expansive currency than their eastern counterparts, who stressed "sound money."[13] Sound money, in the context of the nineteenth century, meant a currency based on gold. These debates may seem trivial to some modern readers, but they were of central importance to politics for more than twenty years. The issue famously culminated in the so-called Battle of the Standards during the election of 1896, when Republican William McKinley, who backed the gold standard, defeated Democrat William Jennings Bryan, who advocated the free and unlimited coinage of silver. Barreyre helps historians by demonstrating the deep roots of that debate.

Historian Andrew Slap shares Calhoun's and Barreyre's insights about the complexity and fluidity of political ideas during the 1870s. Slap is among a growing coterie of scholars taking a fresh look at the Liberal Republican movement that culminated in the 1872 presidential election. In that year, reformers coalesced around the candidacy of longtime *New York Tribune* editor Horace Greeley as president and Missouri's Benjamin Gratz Brown as vice president. Concentrating on corruption, civil service reform, and good government, this group was particularly strong in the Northeast. Reform ideas were compelling enough (and the perception of the Grant administration's corruption was prevalent enough) that the Democratic Party, desperate to regain control of the presidency, joined with the Liberal Republicans in their campaign against Grant. Although Grant won by a margin of over 200 in the Electoral College, Slap nonetheless insists that historians should not overlook the ideas espoused by the losing party. Revising earlier historians, most notably John G. Sproat (who had characterized the reformers as ineffective and effete elitists in his derisively titled *"The Best Men": Liberal Reformers in the Gilded Age* [1968]), Slap argues that one needs to understand liberal republicanism as a movement and the political party itself as distinct political forces. To Slap, the movement and the party were not one and the same. To make his case, Slap employs an extremely narrow definition of the "true" liberal republican leadership, identifying twenty-three individuals who, their contemporaries all agreed, were central leaders of the reform movement. They were not, however, particularly skilled politicians. The political party that would emerge in 1872, which Slap distinguishes with capital letters, bore little resemblance to the ideals advanced by the original leaders. Though the small size of Slap's sample limits the value of his argument, he makes a valuable contribution because he insists on taking political actors and political ideas during the 1870s seriously. Slap also forges a clear link with Calhoun when he argues that "classic republicanism best explains" the Liberal Republicans' "thoughts and actions."[14]

Historian Mitchell Snay also looks at national politics with an appreciation for the complexity of political expression. His *Fenians, Freedmen, and Southern Whites* (2010) examines three groups that historians rarely have considered in the same analysis. Snay does so in order to focus on the seemingly divergent groups' sense of civic nationalism. He defines this concept by stating "civic nationalism can be said to exist where primary loyalty is given to common citizenship in a nation state governing a specific territory."[15] Voting, Snay argues, became the key way for each group to express its civic nationalism. His study demonstrates the limits of this nationalism while also showing the divergent ways in which the interests of each group played out. Perhaps Snay's most important contribution is the approach he takes in explaining the Civil War's political magnitude. The war, Snay argues, "was a modernizing and liberalizing experience that unintentionally raised the aspirations of groups who had recently been marginalized from the mainstream of American political power."[16]

Snay does not explore conceptions of proper manhood and masculinity in detail. But his study points to the obvious ways in which the civic nationalism of freedmen, Irish Americans, and southern whites was informed by gender. Fortunately, historians can link Rebecca Edwards's *Angels in the Machinery* (1997) to Snay's argument with great success. Because her subjects did so, Edwards employs a narrow definition of politics in the nineteenth century. "To them," Edwards writes, "politics was the system by which factions and parties won control of government through elections."[17] Like Snay, Edwards argues that the Civil War served to widen the political horizons for a number of political actors. Like Calhoun's work, much of Edwards's book covers a time period well beyond the scope of the 1870s. This wider scope assists her argument that both Republicans and Democrats pointed to new definitions of political participation involving women. Northern Republicans, Edwards explains, "displayed growing commitment to a maternal family ideal" while Democrats believed Republicans "threatened the authority of the independent white men, upon which rested both civic and household order."[18] Yet even as male politicians from both sections talked about women, women themselves slowly began testing the boundaries of political propriety. Not until the Progressive Era, Edwards maintains, would Americans realize the promises of greater female political participation. Her study, however, argues that the transformation was rooted in the era of Reconstruction.

Whereas Rebecca Edwards demonstrates changes in political process involving women and gender roles, historian Steven Hahn examines African American political struggles in rural areas both before and after the Civil War. In doing so, Hahn's *A Nation under Our Feet: Black Political Struggles in the Rural South from Slavery to the Great Migration* (2003) modifies traditional interpretations of Reconstruction-era politics. Ambitiously linking African American political practice and attitudes from slavery through the era of World War I, Hahn insists "that African Americans in the rural South contributed to the making of a new political nation while they made themselves into a new people—a veritable new nation as many of them came to understand it."[19] Hahn's impressive undertaking has profound implications for a number of different subfields within the historical profession. Indeed, in Hahn's telling, African American identity and the post-Civil War American nation became inextricably linked. Even though the majority of the chapters in *A Nation under Our Feet* focus on a local and micro level, one needs to understand how the processes described in Hahn's book affected national politics.

Hahn provocatively argues that the political strategies which African Americans developed in the Reconstruction South continued on into "the organizing tradition" of the twentieth century. Identifying Marcus Garvey and civil rights activist Ella Baker as part of this tradition, Hahn provides a link for historians interested in the grassroots activism advocated by groups like the Student Nonviolent Coordinating Committee of the 1960s.[20] Although Hahn's book makes few connections to the national political scene and to traditional electoral politics, any serious scholar hoping to probe the meaning of political life during the era of Reconstruction should consult his work.

Students should also include biographies in their assessment of the political components of the Reconstruction period. Although such a statement would have been absurdly self-evident a generation ago, many scholars have eschewed the genre for its perceived lack of intellectual and methodological sophistication. Fortunately, shrewd historians of the Reconstruction period have ignored the attempt to marginalize the role of biography. Presidential biographies are particularly instructive for the light they shed on national politics of the era. The best biography of Johnson remains Hans L. Trefousse's *Andrew Johnson: A Biography* (1989), in which the author goes to considerable lengths to understand the seventeenth president. To his credit, Trefousse refuses to demonize Johnson for his well-known personality and behavioral characteristics—his temper, lack of moderation, and racial attitudes—traits considered severe even by 1860s standards. Unlike Abraham Lincoln, whom scores of historians have praised for his ability to grow intellectually, Trefousse concludes that "Johnson was a child of his time, but he failed to grow with it."[21]

Rutherford B. Hayes has probably received the least biographical coverage of the presidents who occupied the White House during Reconstruction. Hayes was fortunate, however, to have found a very able biographer in Ari Hoogenboom. His *Rutherford B. Hayes: Warrior and President* (1995) deserves far wider readership than it has received. Hoogenboom judges Hayes a far more capable politician than many of his critics have acknowledged. And far from being indifferent to the fate of freedpeople, Hayes in fact showed a lasting commitment to African American civil rights. Hoogenboom interprets Hayes, especially his moderation and statesmanship, in a manner similar to Jean Edward Smith's more recent interpretations of Dwight D. Eisenhower.[22] Hoogenboom considers Hayes a "pragmatic reformer" who "took steps toward establishing the modern presidency."[23] Hoogenboom's exemplary biography captures Hayes's goals, as well as the real limits that economic depression, divided government, and political unrest imposed upon his presidency.

In recent years, Ulysses S. Grant has enjoyed a relative surge in interest from historians. In his award-winning *Grant: A Biography* (1982), William S. McFeely excoriated Grant for poor leadership, racism, and general incompetence. More recent works have been more sympathetic to the hero of the Union. Joan Waugh's *U. S. Grant: American Hero, American Myth* (2009) aptly traces the different ways in which Americans have remembered Grant. She thereby pinpoints the ebb and flow of his popularity. Waugh makes an especially valuable contribution in showing how adherents to the mythology of the Lost Cause contributed to the diminution of Grant's reputation.

If Waugh's book marked a turning point in the interpretation of Grant, historian Brooks Simpson has dedicated even more time and energy to rehabilitating the eighteenth president's reputation. Both Simpson's *Ulysses S. Grant: Triumph over Adversity, 1822-1865* (2000) and his earlier work, *Let Us Have Peace: Ulysses S. Grant and the Politics of War and Reconstruction, 1861-1868* (1991), cast Grant as a more sympathetic, complex, and human figure than had many earlier scholars. Simpson has not yet completed a book-length assessment of Grant's presidency, and therefore his interpretation of Grant remains incomplete. That said, in 1998 Simpson offered an appetizing hors d'oeuvre in his comparative volume, *The Reconstruction Presidents,* which treats Lincoln, Johnson, Grant, and Hayes and serves up an assessment of presidential leadership. Simpson's work underscores complexity, context, and contingency and is especially favorable toward Grant. In *The Reconstruction Presidents,* Simpson implored scholars to avoid evaluating presidential leadership through the prism of twentieth-century racial attitudes. "A scholarship grounded in seeking out moral shortcomings may assuage a scholar's conscience," he concluded, "but in the end it marks no improvement upon a search for flawless heroes."[24]

Two other writers—Jean Edward Smith and H. W. Brands—deserve special mention for their astute one-volume studies of Grant's military and political careers. Given Grant's centrality to the military history of the Civil War and then Reconstruction, and his reflections on his military career in his two-volume *Personal Memoirs of Ulysses S. Grant* (1885), many other authors have been unable to create a framework that could encompass the vastness of his life. Although neither Smith nor Brands provides pathbreaking conceptual or interpretive insights, both authors nonetheless successfully demonstrate the vital nexus between Grant's political life and his earlier military career.[25]

If biography is useful for comprehending the political scene, so too is a book that on first glance might seem to have little connection to electoral politics. Although Richard White's *Railroaded: The Transcontinentals and the Making of Modern America* (2012) has more wide-ranging interests, it also provides an original and fresh view of the political world of the 1870s. White focuses closely on politics within the context of American railroad expansion in this period. He notes how the extensive lobbying by such railroad magnates as Tom Scott and Collis P. Huntington helped to shape the very fabric of political life in deeply corrupting ways. He cautions that procedural votes as well as investigative journalism of the era might in fact be misleading. He also implies that a giant campaign of obfuscation makes interpreting the politics of this era particularly tricky. "Much of this duplicity," White says, "was embedded in the loyalty of friends."[26]

For example, railroad magnates gained favors by liberally awarding passes to potential political allies. Railroad managers used the rhetoric of friendship to inform their lobbying efforts. But affection, according to White, was not central to such friendship, because it "was a code: a network of social bonds that could organize political activity."[27] White's *Railroaded* also demonstrates that the growing concern which Americans would have with monopolies derived largely from the power of railroad companies and their leaders. "By the 1870s," he explains, "special privilege and monopoly had become synonymous with corporations."[28]

Two more studies have both widened and deepened our understanding of the national political scene during Reconstruction. Jackson Lears is among the recent historians who consider a broader chronology for understanding Reconstruction's legacy. Lears's *Rebirth of a Nation: The Making of Modern America, 1877-1920* (2010) identifies what he calls the force of regeneration in motivating American reform movements from the end of the Civil War onward. This quest for rebirth was both deep and far-reaching, Lears claims. He argues that in order to "understand the public transformations of this period, we need to return to their origins in private feeling."[29] In so doing, Lears simultaneously pushes Reconstruction's legacy forward and the roots of Progressive Era reform backward in a masterpiece of synthetic interpretation. Lears argues that the quest for regeneration did not die when Reconstruction finally ended. Instead, what he calls the "Unionist narrative" contributed to the emergent American nationalism of the late nineteenth century in which northerners "forged a powerful link between war and regeneration."[30]

In his *Declarations of Dependence: The Long Reconstruction of Popular Politics in the South, 1861-1908* (2011), historian Gregory P. Downs provides another exciting and important conceptual reinterpretation of Reconstruction. Focusing largely on North Carolina politics, Downs uses a concept he calls "patronalism" to explain the importance of relationships in fostering new forms of political identity. Patronalism, according to Downs, was an intentional strategy designed to create a politics of dependence in which government worked "through favors not programs."[31] This concept allows Downs to connect average citizens to a variety of would-be political patrons and to demonstrate that the political system was more pragmatic and flexible than its critics realized. Downs argues that the concept of patronalism further allows one to extend the political legacies of the 1860s well into the 1890s, thereby also agreeing with a number of scholars who have argued for a more capacious definition of Reconstruction. Although Downs readily acknowledges strategic differences among groups of Americans, he nevertheless believes that patronalism is useful for understanding politics as practiced in large urban political machines in the North, too.

Recent histories covering the national political scene during the period from 1865 to 1877 have been incredibly vibrant. Serious academic work has helped to demonstrate the strength and richness of political expression during this period. Few times in American history have brimmed with more political possibility than the immediate post–Civil War years. For that reason, much remains to be understood about the ways that local and state politics interacted with (and helped to transform) the national political system. Particularly because historians of American foreign relations tend to privilege twentieth-century topics, there is an even greater opportunity to connect the outward thrust of the American national state with domestic politics during the "long" Reconstruction Era.

American schoolchildren may always struggle to remember, as did Thomas Wolfe, which of our Reconstruction presidents had facial hair and how those who did differed from each other. But a number of scholars long ago jettisoned the simplistic formulas that rendered political activity following Abraham Lincoln's presidency and preceding that of Theodore Roosevelt a tragic wasteland of incompetence. Whether future generations contemplate a "long Reconstruction" or a "long Progressive era," they surely will realize that the period between 1865 and 1877 remains central to understanding what the nineteenth century was, and what the twentieth century could become.

Notes

1. Thomas Wolfe, *From Death to Morning* (1932; repr., New York: Scribner, 1935), 121.
2. Eric Foner, *Reconstruction: America's Unfinished Revolution* (New York: Harper and Row, 1988), 341.
3. Ibid., 582.
4. Michael Perman, *The Road to Redemption: Southern Politics, 1869–1879* (Chapel Hill: Univ. of North Carolina Press, 1984), 277.
5. William Gillette, *Retreat from Reconstruction, 1869–1879* (1979; repr., Baton Rouge: Louisiana State Univ. Press, 1982), xii.
6. Ibid., 379.

7. George C. Rable, *But There Was No Peace: The Role of Violence in the Politics of Reconstruction* (1984; repr., Athens: Univ. of Georgia Press, 2007), 191.

8. Heather Cox Richardson, *The Death of Reconstruction: Race, Labor, and Politics in the Post-Civil War North, 1865-1901* (Cambridge, Mass.: Harvard Univ. Press, 2001), 245. See also Heather Cox Richardson, *West of Appomattox: The Reconstruction of America after the Civil War* (New Haven, Conn.: Yale Univ. Press, 2008).

9. Charles C. Calhoun, *Conceiving a New Republic: The Republican Party and the Southern Question, 1869-1900* (Lawrence: Univ. Press of Kansas, 2006), 3.

10. Charles C. Calhoun, *From Bloody Shirt to Full Dinner Pail: The Transformation of Politics and Governance in the Gilded Age* (New York: Hill and Wang, 2010), 9.

11. Ibid., 16.

12. Ibid., 39.

13. Nicolas Barreyre, "The Politics of Economic Crises: The Panic of 1873, the End of Reconstruction, and the Realignment of American Politics," *Journal of the Gilded Age and Progressive Era* 10 (Oct. 2011): 403-23.

14. Andrew L. Slap, *The Doom of Reconstruction: The Liberal Republicans in the Civil War Era* (New York: Fordham Univ. Press, 2006), xxi.

15. Mitchell Snay, *Fenians, Freedmen, and Southern Whites: Race and Nationality in the Era of Reconstruction* (Baton Rouge: Louisiana State Univ. Press, 2010), 8.

16. Ibid., 175-76.

17. Rebecca Edwards, *Angels in the Machinery: Gender in American Party Politics from the Civil War to the Progressive Era* (New York: Oxford Univ. Press, 1997), 9.

18. Ibid., 12-13.

19. Steven Hahn, *A Nation under Our Feet: Black Political Struggles in the Rural South, from Slavery to the Great Migration* (Cambridge, Mass.: Belknap Press of Harvard Univ. Press, 2003), 9.

20. Hahn cites the pioneering work of Charles Payne in discussing the organizing tradition. This work quickly became central to some of the more sophisticated analyses of the civil rights movement. See Charles M. Payne, *I've Got the Light of Freedom: The Organizing Tradition and the Mississippi Freedom Struggle* (Berkeley: Univ. of California Press, 2005).

21. Hans L. Trefousse, *Andrew Johnson: A Biography* (New York: W. W. Norton, 1989), 379.

22. For a favorable interpretation of Eisenhower, see Jean Edward Smith, *Eisenhower: In War and Peace* (New York: Random House, 2013).

23. Ari A. Hoogenboom, *Rutherford B. Hayes: Warrior and President* (Lawrence: Univ. Press of Kansas, 1995), 2-3.

24. Brooks D. Simpson, *The Reconstruction Presidents* (Lawrence: Univ. Press of Kansas, 1998), 6.

25. Jean Edward Smith, *Grant* (New York: Simon and Schuster, 2001); H. W. Brands, *The Man Who Saved the Union: Ulysses Grant in War and Peace* (New York: Doubleday, 2012).

26. Richard White, *Railroaded: The Transcontinentals and the Making of Modern America* (New York: W. W. Norton, 2011), 132-33.

27. Ibid., 100.

28. Ibid., 111.

29. Jackson Lears, *Rebirth of a Nation: The Making of Modern America, 1877-1920* (New York: Harper Perennial, 2010), 5.

30. Ibid., 18.

31. Gregory P. Downs, *Declarations of Dependence: The Long Reconstruction of Popular Politics in the South, 1861-1908* (Chapel Hill: Univ. of North Carolina Press, 2011), 3.

CHAPTER SIX

Reconstruction

Gender and Labor

J. VINCENT LOWERY

Historians have always described the transition from slavery to free labor in the South as a difficult process. Historiographical debates have turned on assessments of freedpeople's struggle for autonomy, planters' determination to preserve some semblance of the old order, and the intent of northern Republicans and government agents. Recent scholarship incorporating the theme of gender to the study of this transition illustrates the distinctive experiences of freedwomen and refines the meaning of freedom to account for their experiences and the complexities of this process.[1]

At the turn of the twentieth century, Columbia University professors John W. Burgess and William A. Dunning trained the first generation of professional historians, many of them southern born, who studied Reconstruction. African American historian W. E. B. Du Bois summarized the primary qualities of their works: "First, endless sympathy with the white South; second, ridicule, contempt, or silence for the Negro; third, a judicial attitude towards the North." Whereas the Dunningites argued that Congress committed a grievous error by empowering African Americans, Du Bois, influenced by Marxism, proposed that the failure of black and white workers to unite in common cause represented the greatest fault of Reconstruction. Race, not class interests, determined poor whites' actions. According to Du Bois, "The old anti-

Negro labor rivalry between white and black workers kept the labor elements after the war from ever really uniting in a demand to increase labor power by Negro suffrage and Negro economic stability." African Americans consequently found themselves forced back into a condition resembling slavery, while white workers were "directed in the South by the same methods that were dominating [them] in the North." Although most scholars did not embrace Du Bois's Marxist interpretation of Reconstruction, a new generation of historians who shared his sympathetic view of African Americans and his negative assessment of southern whites had emerged by the mid-twentieth century.[2]

Speaking to the Southern Historical Association at its annual meeting in New Orleans in 1938, historian Francis B. Simkins called for the objective study of Reconstruction, a challenge echoed by Howard K. Beale at a subsequent meeting. Simkins, coauthor of the revisionist *South Carolina during Reconstruction* (1932) with Robert H. Woody, proposed that such research would reveal that "freedpeople bargained themselves into an agricultural situation unlike that of slavery and from their viewpoint advantageous." Simkins argued that sharecropping represented "a revolutionary reform more important in the actual life of the freedmen than the sensational but largely unsuccessful political changes attempted at the time." Beale criticized the Marxist interpretation of Reconstruction but nonetheless credited Du Bois with providing historians with a clearer perspective on the African American experience "that every future historian must reckon with." Beale anticipated that previous scathing critiques of freedpeople and their northern allies would give way to more balanced perspectives. By the mid-twentieth century, the sway of the Dunning School interpretation began to ease as revisionist scholars questioned their predecessors' conclusions, particularly the belief that Reconstruction was in fact a "tragic era."[3]

In *The Era of Reconstruction, 1865-1877* (1965), Kenneth M. Stampp synthesized the emerging revisionist consensus on the era. Whereas the Dunningites credited President Andrew Johnson and the newly reconstructed southern state governments with reasonably resolving the nation's postwar dilemmas, Stampp and his fellow revisionists blamed the president and the governments established under his Reconstruction plan for the plight of freedpeople. The revisionists observed southern whites' refusal to accept the former slave's new status: "The future for him was that of an illiterate, unskilled, propertyless, agricultural worker" who must be compelled to labor. The Dunning School accepted this condition as the natural one for African Americans, but revisionists rejected this labor system as merely a "return to a modified form of involuntary servitude," which Stampp, writing during the time of the civil rights movement, proclaimed "introduced the whole pattern of disenfranchisement, discrimination, and segregation into the postwar South."[4]

Republicans, particularly the Radical Republicans, once deemed the source of disorder during Reconstruction, were heralded by revisionists like Stampp for their efforts on behalf of freedpeople, mired in a "condition of economic helplessness." Land reforms desired by Radicals failed to materialize, one of the great shortcomings of the Republican plan of Reconstruction. Sounding a critical note, historian John Hope Franklin argued "there was no significant breakup of the plantation system during and after [R]econstruction. . . . [W]hile it was not slavery, [it] was nevertheless one of due subordination in every conceivable way." Stampp excused Republicans for this shortcoming, suggesting the problems of the postwar era resulted from their lack of understanding of the economic plight of freedpeople and the resistance of landowners and employers. Moreover, he argued that Republicans deserved credit for their work through the Freedmen's Bureau, which "played a constructive role in the transformation of the Negro from slave to citizen." That its work ended in 1869 signaled the challenges of reorganizing southern society and economy through federal intervention and doomed the Reconstruction experiment, eliminating the one agency through which Republicans could truly protect the interests of African Americans. Franklin was less forgiving of the Republicans' abandonment of Reconstruction, noting that few African Americans criticized their northern allies, "but all had good reason to be unhappy about their condition at the end of Reconstruction."[5]

While revisionists charted the political and social dimensions of Reconstruction, other scholars examined the economic history of the era. In the early 1970s, scholars began employing econometric analysis to the study of the past. In *One Kind of Freedom: The Economic Consequences of Emancipation* (1977), economists Roger L. Ransom and Richard Sutch applied this method to the study of Reconstruction. Ransom and Sutch argued that "the lack of progress in the postemancipation era was the consequence of flawed economic institutions erected in the wake of the Confederate defeat." In this environment, freedpeople were particularly susceptible to economic exploitation because of their lack of education and skills emerging out of slavery. Yet Ransom and Sutch argued that freedpeople "asserted their independence and insisted upon institutional arrangements more to their liking than those envisioned for them by whites." The economists proposed that freed slaves withdrew their labor in a manner that "duplicated (perhaps emulated) the work-leisure patterns of other free Americans." This withdrawal "was [also] a voluntary response to new patterns of incentives in the postemancipation economy." Ransom and Sutch detected the highest rates of withdrawal among women, children, and the elderly, with a decline in "man-hours per capita" of 28 percent to 37 percent. Scholars have long debated freedpeople's withdrawal of their labor, just as observers at the time questioned this pattern. Planters doubted that former slaves could thrive without coercion, yet blacks' intransigence reflected their desire to assert their newly acquired freedom. Ransom and Sutch attributed the eventual adoption of sharecropping to planters' realization "that small-scale operations produced rents at least equivalent to those anticipated under the plantation system." This arrangement, however, further exacerbated freedpeople's prostrate condition, preserving the economic inequalities of the postemancipation South.[6]

In 1986, Gerald David Jaynes built upon the work of Ransom and Sutch in *Branches without Roots: Genesis of the Black Working Class in the American South, 1862-1882*. Jaynes argued that Radicals seized upon the Freedmen's Bureau to transform the South, introducing the free labor system to replace slavery. They encountered opposition by former slaveholders, who doubted the ability of freedpeople to labor effectively without compulsion and wished to continue to exert absolute authority. Freedpeople appealed to the Freedmen's Bureau for protection from landholders. In the cash-starved South, blacks worked for a share of the crop. Under the direction of General O. O. Howard, bureau agents protected laborers' pay beginning in 1866. Jaynes explained that a share of the crop provided an advantage over wages because of these protections. Yet he noted that the "long pay" system rewarding freedpeople with a share of the crop was fraught with problems. Planters relentlessly worked to maintain the upper hand in relations with laborers, seeking to preserve some semblance of antebellum labor control. Landlords seized control of crops and demanded labor from their tenants while relying on vigilante groups to impose their will upon the freedpeople. Jaynes repeated the assertion made by Ransom and Sutch that freedwomen withdrew their labor, although he noted that this withdrawal only reached significant levels in 1867. He concluded "that the desire to keep women from having to perform fieldwork existed generally among both sexes seems beyond dispute." He later proclaimed, "To state that the labor force participation of female agricultural workers fell after emancipation is to do little more than state the obvious." Citing an 1869 political convention in Georgia, Jaynes argued that African American men expressed their desire "to consume this luxury."[7]

With the Dunning School vanquished, Eric Foner's *Reconstruction: America's Unfinished Revolution, 1863-1877* (1988) synthesized a generation of scholarship, completing the historiographical revolution started by Du Bois while signaling the advance of the postrevisionist school. Revisionists celebrated Reconstruction's potential for change and the groundwork it laid for the Second Reconstruction during the civil rights movement, but postrevisionists questioned the revolutionary character of Reconstruction, identifying continuity as its defining characteristic, "question[ing] whether much of importance had happened at all." Yet Foner also criticized this school, noting that these scholars "ended up returning blacks to their traditional status as passive victims of white manipulation."

He instead argued that "a coherent portrait of Reconstruction must take into account the subtle dialectic of continuity and change." Situating African Americans at the center of the story of Reconstruction, Foner explored the era's great democratic potential and its heartbreaking shortcomings. In contrast to Stampp's claims, Foner argued that the Freedmen's Bureau, charged with assisting freedpeople in their transition from slavery to freedom and protecting them from exploitation, "seemed to consider black reluctance to labor the greater threat to its economic mission." Despite the efforts of General Howard to support former slaves' pursuit of land and independence, Johnson's restoration of former Confederates' land placed African Americans in a vulnerable position. They eventually embraced sharecropping "because it seemed so far removed from 'our former management.'" Even in the rice country, where the semiautonomous task system persisted, freedpeople struggled to counter employers' authority. The presumed advantages of sharecropping soon withered, as the credit system upon which croppers depended took its toll. The labor struggles of freedpeople thus represented one aspect of Foner's "unfinished revolution."[8]

Former slaves relied upon their mobility for any advantage in these struggles. While historian Jonathan Wiener asserted that "planters regained control of the South and crushed both black and white workers under their heels as they traveled along a Prussian road to modernization," other scholars, such as Harold Woodman and Gavin Wright, detected a high degree of mobility among freedpeople. Confronting this historiographical disagreement, William Cohen argued that the contradictory evidence of labor control and mobility actually revealed divergent interests among planters and employers. In *At Freedom's Edge: Black Mobility and the Southern White Quest for Racial Control, 1861-1915* (1991), Cohen contended that those planters who commanded black labor attempted to restrict the movement of freedpeople, while those in need of workers encouraged mobility to satisfy their own labor shortages. Cohen recognized the role that the Freedmen's Bureau played in fulfilling the needs of the latter. In contrast to Foner's more critical assessment of agents' work, Cohen commended officials for their achievements in protecting the rights of freedpeople across the South despite the agency's sparse resources. Former slaves enjoyed a degree of success combatting employers' efforts to impose control upon them, sustaining a degree of mobility locally and, with the assistance of bureau officials and labor agents, long-distance movement throughout the South.[9]

Although freedpeople turned to government agencies for support during Reconstruction, they also waged their own battles. In *The Work of Reconstruction: From Slave to Wage Labor in South Carolina, 1860-1870* (1994), Julie Saville argued that the freedmen and freedwomen "gradually mounted public and collective repudiations of the personal sovereignty on which their masters' and mistresses' right to command human property had rested. At the same time, they challenged the emergent claims that subjection to landowners' management and to the discipline of an abstract market constituted freedom." Recognizing the freedpeople's uneven struggle to acquire land and therefore achieve independence in a region carved up by General William Tecumseh Sherman's Special Field Order No. 15, Saville observed the organizational strategies of freed slaves who relied on kinship networks to claim land and supplies. They also formed "neighborhood leagues" to bargain from a position of strength, recognizing their own vulnerability as freedpeople. These organizations sought to improve the terms of labor, combatted terminations and evictions, and even appealed for land from Republican officeholders. As Saville noted, former slaves found themselves at odds not only with former planters but with their liberators as well. Few Republicans seriously called for land confiscation and distribution and sometimes sought the support of their Democratic rivals to maintain order.[10]

Northern whites who professed their support for the struggles of former slaves were often bound by their own ideologies. In *Free to Work: Labor Law, Emancipation, and Reconstruction, 1815-1880* (1998), James D. Schmidt argued that the Freedmen's Bureau propagated northern conceptions of contract labor law through its work in the South after the war, but the bureau itself could not transform the attitudes of southern whites or blacks. Schmidt built upon the work of Amy Dru Stanley, who asserted that legislators and employers alike demanded that men work during Reconstruction. Schmidt also sharpened scholars' perspective on labor mobility proposed by Cohen. The emerging ideal of "free labor" that permitted "unrestricted movement in the labor market" clashed with an insistence upon "unbreakable, definite contracts between laborer and employer." Schmidt contended that "middle-class northerners had come to see the sanctity of contract as essential to labor discipline, especially in agriculture. Yet they also had begun to define legal rights of workers by class." The state possessed the responsibility to compel people to work, although northern reformers presumed that "the state's regulation of vagrancy must be paternal and reformatory, aimed primarily at establishing bourgeois culture." Vagrants likewise possessed "an obligation to the *state*, which then had a right to their labor," but the Black Codes passed during early Presidential Reconstruction attracted the ire of northern observers, who argued that these measures imposed a new form of slavery upon convicted vagrants. These southern laws required that the Freedmen's Bureau intervene on behalf of the freedpeople. The work of the agency ultimately rested upon the intent of agents and their relations with southern whites. Schmidt navigated the competing interpretations of the bureau's work by suggesting that agents' commitment to free labor and the demands of vagrancy laws reflected contemporary contradictions yet to be resolved. He proposed that this contradiction resulted in a "mutation" of northern principles of free labor. Schmidt also recognized African Americans' experiences in this process: "As Freedmen's Bureau agents of all ideological stripes pointed out repeatedly, the freedpeople often saw any legal restriction on labor as an imposition on their hard-won freedom and their desire for autonomy from white control." The freedpeople sought intervention, but only to protect their rights as laborers, including "basic rights to self-ownership, custodial control of children, and some form of payment." In this sense, the freedpeople contributed immensely to the process of reshaping the southern labor system.

And the northern system simultaneously underwent its own transformation, imposing a degree of labor discipline upon workers while preserving notions of labor mobility.[11]

Historian John C. Rodrigue further illustrated the importance of labor mobility and negotiation in *Reconstruction in the Cane Fields: From Slavery to Free Labor in Louisiana's Sugar Parishes, 1862-1880* (2001), arguing that the freedpeople took advantage of the unique conditions of sugar cultivation to collectively challenge planters' authority. Former slaves contested their housing, supplies, wages, and hours. Their struggles initially received endorsement from General Benjamin Butler, who supervised occupied Louisiana during the war. Although he favored loyal planters in their disputes with freed slaves, Butler recognized the rights of freed laborers and established the precedent of federal intervention on their behalf. According to Rodrigue, freedpeople "refashioned northern free-labor ideology to comport with their own experiences of life and labor on sugar plantations and with the communitarian ethos that had afforded them psychological and spiritual sustenance under slavery." Whereas most freed slaves clamored for land, even if they could only cultivate it as tenants, Rodrigue argued that the practical demands of sugar cultivation and planters' desires to deny their laborers any independence ensured the wage labor system would prevail in the sugar-growing section of Louisiana. Yet the same requirements of sugar cultivation also created conditions favorable to collective action that "enabled freedmen to defend their political rights both during and after Reconstruction." Their most prized benefits of wage labor proved to be the freedom of movement the system provided, a point supporting earlier conclusions by William Cohen and James Schmidt, and the wages that brought "a measure of individual autonomy and the black community's self-determination." Redemption, however, spoiled black autonomy, as planters found the Democratic government much more responsive to their appeals for state-sponsored labor control than Republicans had been during Reconstruction. Rodrigue concluded that black workers continued to resist planter authority, even if the backing of their northern white allies had been lost.[12]

Indeed, as Rebecca Scott observed in her essay "Fault Lines, Color Lines, and Party Lines: Race, Labor, and Collective Action in Louisiana and Cuba, 1862-1912" (2000), sugar workers continued to organize, culminating with a strike in 1887. Blacks demanded higher wages paid in cash. When African Americans went on strike, planters evicted strikers and mobilized the local militia to suppress dissent. Scott attributed this to the "white-line strategy" that cast black strikers as a menace to law and order and their white counterparts as citizens obliged to protect the community from this threat. Although African Americans united with white workers in common economic and political cause on smaller properties and in certain trades, "the sharp distinctions of citizenship imposed throughout the state under Democratic rule helped to reinforce the color line during strikes, for only whites were now eligible for militia service." The Knights of Labor offered support, but the campaign of local whites to suppress the strike assured its defeat.[13]

Some Louisiana sugar planters imagined an alternative to African American laborers after the Civil War. While southern historians have generally overlooked the history of immigration in the region, Moon-Ho Jung explored efforts to secure Chinese replacements in *Coolies and Cane: Race, Labor, and Sugar in the Age of Emancipation* (2006). Sugar growers in the Caribbean turned to Chinese "coolies" in response to emancipation, and the Louisiana planters took notice. Jung explained that former slaveholders in the Caribbean and the U.S. South imagined coolies as "voluntary migrants," whose lack of rights made them ideal replacements for newly freed African American laborers. Yet a combination of economic developments and concerns about the undesirable racial identity of Chinese migrants undermined the shift to coolie labor. Indeed, as southern whites grappled with the idea of free labor, they imagined the workforce in racialized terms. Whites imagined the possibility of replacing black laborers with a more pliable white substitute. For those who feared the influx of supposedly inferior nonwhite immigrants, European laborers represented the more desirable alternative. These advocates imagined an exclusively white labor force, purging the South of its nonwhite population. These immigration proponents imagined a far different South, founded upon the Jeffersonian image of the small farmer. Jung observed, "The capitalization and consolidation of sugar production—made conspicuous by elite planters' consumption of land, machinery, and migrant workers—spawned a countermovement for white immigrants and small farms." The failure of these immigration schemes in part explains why scholars have devoted little attention to them, but as historian Erin Elizabeth Clune argued, efforts to attract foreign laborers to the South were part of whites' strategy for managing the adjustment from slavery to freedom and retaining control over African Americans and therefore deserves more attention.[14]

Amy Dru Stanley also recognized the unique position of freedwomen in the middle of the postbellum labor struggle, and she proposed that scholars must place greater importance upon the labor of formerly enslaved women.[15] In *A Hard Fight for We: Women's Transition from Slavery to Freedom in South Carolina* (1997), historian Leslie A. Schwalm shifted the focus of Reconstruction studies toward the experiences of freedwomen. Schwalm challenged scholars' conclusion that freedwomen simply withdrew their labor at the insistence of their husbands or in mimicry of white women's example. She criticized historians for relying too heavily on unreliable primary sources and limited secondary sources, particularly Ransom and Sutch's *One Kind of Freedom*. In her study of the South Carolina low country, Schwalm instead argued that the freedwomen "attempted to shape their agricultural and domestic employment as well as their social and reproductive labor, according to their own expectations." Schwalm contended that freedwomen resisted any semblance of slavery after emancipation. The unique nature of work and life in the low country undoubtedly shaped freedwomen's activism as they clashed with former masters and northern officials who espoused very different ideas about the appropriate kind of freedom for African Americans. By the early eighteenth century, South Carolina planters were cultivating rice in the coastal section of the colony. They utilized the task labor system, which permitted the enslaved a degree of autonomy depending on the seasonal requirements of the crop. Once freed during the Civil War, African Americans insisted on retaining this labor system to preserve their autonomy. Like former slaves across the South, they identified land ownership as the key to escaping their former masters' authority. By withdrawing their labor in acts of protest, freedwomen proved instrumental in the adoption of the work-rent system, which required that freedpeople complete tasks in the fields for two or three days in exchange for a portion of the harvest and the right to cultivate a small parcel of land on the plantation. According to Schwalm, this system "permitted greater freedom of movement between their household and family economies and the plantation economy, greater insularity from the supervision of overseers and other hated figures from their recent past, and the option of making their own decisions about how best to allocate their time and their labor."[16]

Nancy Bercaw's *Gendered Freedoms: Race, Rights, and the Politics of Household in the Delta, 1861-1875* (2003) continued the theme of creative labor organization, stressing the importance of group labor structures as a response to the disappointments of freedom in the Mississippi Delta. With these arrangements, freedwomen "distanced themselves from wage labor and created a base for economic autonomy." Yet whites insisted that freedom be understood in terms of property rights, which would constrain freedpeople's status in the postbellum South. As public discourse on this point shifted, freedmen demanded the rights entitled to independent heads of households: "their wages, the crop, and their families." Bercaw built on the work of Laura F. Edwards on Reconstruction in Granville County, North Carolina. In *Gendered Strife and Confusion: The Political Culture of Reconstruction* (1997), Edwards proposed that African American men attempted to claim independence and control over their dependent wives and children despite their lack of property. The freedpeople thus resisted the planters' desire for continuity between antebellum conditions that gave absolute authority to former slaveholders and postbellum labor relations. Bercaw argued that freedwomen "ceded this ground to freedmen," but they did not relinquish their "household rights," and they insisted upon their own claims to "social citizenship" that conferred rights as members of a kin group however those groups might be defined. And yet Republicans did not recognize this conception, nor did Mississippi Democrats, who still placed men at the center of the household, thus undermining African American women's appeals.[17]

By turning scholars' gaze to the North in *The Death of Reconstruction: Race, Labor, and Politics in the Post-Civil War North, 1865-1901* (2001), historian Heather Cox Richardson offered further insight into northern white Republicans' eventual abandonment of Reconstruction. Seeking to understand their decision, she concluded that many northern whites "interpreted the demands of the ex-slaves for land, social services, and civil rights as part of an attempt to subvert the American way." Northern whites became increasingly alarmed about labor agitators, particularly in the wake of the Paris Commune in 1871. American labor unions appeared more menacing, becoming symbols of a transatlantic movement to destroy capitalism in the United States. By the 1870s, Richardson maintained, northern whites' antagonism toward organized labor appeared alongside negative depictions of African Americans in the press. Critics equated Republican policies in South Carolina with socialism, as the South Carolina Tax-payers' Association effectively cast freedpeople as usurpers intent upon using political power to redistribute wealth. Northern observers meanwhile praised those freed slaves who labored to provide for themselves, such as those who fled the South for less oppressive environments in the nation's heartland. Yet those African Americans who remained in the South became symbols of the dangers that indigent masses posed to the free labor model. As labor unrest ebbed and flowed at the end of the century, northern whites accepted discriminatory measures to restrict African Americans' rights in light of what those whites considered "the laziness, ignorance, and violence associated with those who rejected the free labor ideal." Jim Crow laws thus became a form of labor control, and northern whites' racism only further exacerbated their negative views of African Americans, further legitimizing violations of their rights.[18]

Yet while some northerners sought to dissociate themselves from African Americans, others, notably northern white and black women, found common cause with the freedpeople. In *Women's Radical*

Reconstruction: The Freedmen's Aid Movement (2004), Carol Faulkner explored the politics of freedmen's aid, illustrating how "abolitionist-feminists," denied influence by their male counterparts, established their own societies. These women "lobbied the government, worked as agents of the Freedmen's Bureau, founded freedmen's relief societies, toured the country raising money for freedmen's aid, bought land to sell and rent to freedpeople, started common and industrial schools for freedpeople, and moved permanently to the South to act on their commitment to justice and equality for former slaves." According to Faulkner, these women, white and black, were among the most radical northerners, imagining the federal government as the great agent of social and economic relief and transformation. Self-interest certainly informed this perspective, as this vision required the federal government to extend the right to vote to women as well as African American men. Although white women sympathized with the plight of the freedwomen and freedchildren, these radical reformers attempted to impose their own conceptions of domestic tasks and wage labor. They encountered the same opposition from freedwomen as did others intent upon dictating the meaning of freedom to former slaves. Faulkner noted that these racial and class biases continued to divide white and black women activists for decades.[19]

Recent scholarship has proposed that the study of Reconstruction should not be confined to an analysis of events between 1865 and 1877. Steven Hahn offered a new chronological framework for understanding the black freedom struggle in *A Nation under Our Feet: Black Political Struggles in the Rural South from Slavery to the Great Migration* (2003). In many ways a successor to Foner's account of Reconstruction, *A Nation under Our Feet* documented struggles from the antebellum period through the migration of African Americans out of the South and the rise of black nationalist Marcus Garvey in the 1910s and 1920s. According to Hahn, "These struggles speak directly to the revolutionary nature of the Civil War and emancipation, to the character and complexities of nineteenth-century southern and American politics, to the process of nation-building and sectional reconciliation, and eventually to the massive remapping of the country's political landscape in the twentieth century." Instead of treating these phases distinctively, Hahn proposed that "freedpeople built and drew on relations, institutions, infrastructures, and aspirations that they and their ancestors had struggled for and constructed as slaves." Hahn linked the historical consensus on slave communities and resistance with the work of Saville, Schwalm, Bercaw, and others who recognized the importance of such community-based organizing during Reconstruction. Hahn thus illustrated the obstacles African Americans faced, making clear that they remained relentless in their struggles for autonomy.[20]

The acquisition of the right to vote granted important sources of power and influence, with Republican officials protecting the interests of black workers in southern courts. These Republican regimes severed ties with the old order, much to the consternation of Democrats, who were determined to retain political, social, and economic power. Hahn acknowledged the limits of Republican influence that he attributed in part to very different interests, even within the African American community. The limits of Republican power were also made evident by the Democratic campaign to reclaim southern states. In the end, Redemption compelled African Americans to decide if they wanted to stand and fight to preserve their rights or flee the South entirely. As Rodrique argued, African Americans in Louisiana's sugar parishes maintained a degree of strength because of the nature of their labor organization. In contrast, those in cotton regions proved far more vulnerable to white control. Beginning with the Exodusters, who migrated to the American heartland starting in the mid-1870s, African Americans began to abandon the South incrementally. Hahn proposed that African American women led the migration debates: "Given their responsibility for many of the activities that maintained and nurtured household and community life—producing market and food crops, cultivating garden plots and caring for livestock, preparing food and making clothing, educating the children, and carrying out many of the obligations of kinship and friendship—black women may have had a more intense interest." Hahn concluded that their investment in the postbellum community-building project and the opportunity to establish an

Gender and Labor

even stronger environment made emigration an attractive alternative. While earlier migrations did not significantly alter the distribution of the nation's black population, the Great Migration that began during World War I marked an exodus as African Americans sought the life denied them in the South.[21]

Hahn's work established the value of exploring events before and after Reconstruction as part of a longer process, a model that historian Susan Eva O'Donovan validated in *Becoming Free in the Cotton South* (2007). O'Donovan began her story of freedpeople's struggle in southwest Georgia before the war, when whites first settled in the region in pursuit of cotton fortunes. She argued that unique conditions in the region ultimately hindered former slaves' pursuit of freedom. O'Donovan contended that "planters pulled out all stops to restore, as they bluntly and repeatedly put it, capital's reign over labor." Like their counterparts elsewhere in the South, planters in southwestern Georgia intended to maintain control of their former slaves. From the beginning of Reconstruction, they relied on violence to supplement the Black Codes. She observed, however, that planters no longer wished to command the labor of African American women. Introducing a new explanation for the withdrawal of freed women's labor, O'Donovan asserted that "planters took special pains to rid their estates of black women, especially those with small children." She argued that landowners only sought labor from those workers capable of the highest levels of productivity; this decision represented a significant departure from the antebellum era, when enslaved women were prized for their reproductive abilities. O'Donovan contended that freedwomen sought reentry into the labor market through their husbands, who proved capable of negotiating contracts for their spouses and demanding redress for poor treatment. Yet she concluded that labor agitation and political upheaval so successful in challenging planter authority elsewhere in the South failed to make inroads in southwest Georgia.[22]

Thavolia Glymph shifted the focus from the field to the "big house" and the struggle between plantation mistresses and freedwomen over domestic labor in *Out of the House of Bondage: The Transformation of the Plantation Household* (2008). Echoing earlier arguments about freedwomen's withdrawal of their labor, she argued, "In leaving white homes and demanding reduced hours and a reorganization of household work, black women accomplished part of the interconnected work of claiming their freedom, and in consequence, reconstructing notions of southern womanhood." According to Glymph, freedwomen's battles to assert greater control over their time and labor served the interests of their families, as they sought "to devote a part of their labor to their families' crops, to work at home for themselves and their families, or simply to have more time for themselves." Glymph proposed that freedwomen did not succeed in securing lasting gains, but also that they did not relent in their fight for their rights as workers.[23]

Freedwomen capitalized on certain resources at their disposal in their struggles against abusive or unfair treatment by their employers. Historians have long focused on the work of the Freedmen's Bureau with freedmen, either neglecting agents' interactions with freedwomen or concluding that these women generally avoided the bureau. Mary Farmer-Kaiser countered this historiographical trend by arguing that freedwomen routinely appealed to bureau agents for support. In *Freedwomen and the Freedmen's Bureau: Race, Gender, and Public Policy in the Age of Emancipation* (2010), Farmer-Kaiser argued that freedwomen were not always beneficiaries of the bureau's rulings, but that they persisted in submitting their "complaints that demanded agents' involvement in a variety of 'public' and 'private' matters." Bureau agents struggled to reconcile their Victorian gender assumptions which demanded that freedwomen deserved "relief as dependents" and the identification of former slaves as laborers who must work. Victorian standards also required freedwomen to conform to agents' conception of womanhood and domesticity, which carried with it certain advantages, but Farmer-Kaiser proposed that freedwomen resisted the dictates of agents and former slaveholders alike, "demonstrat[ing] an intense desire to define the meaning of free labor on their own terms." She concluded that "the bureau sought justice for these women but did so against racial wrongs and only as its agents could enforce the obligations of freedom, the ideals of free labor and contract, black manhood, and northern principles of domesticity and household governance." Even as the agency privileged the needs of freedwomen, officials also recognized the supreme right of freedwomen to control their children's labor in the midst of competing demands by husbands and employers. The bureau thus did not neglect freedwomen, nor did freedwomen avoid the bureau; instead, they struggled against the limits of the bureau's power and agents' Victorian attitudes. Reconstruction was, in Foner's words, "an unfinished revolution" for all.[24]

Assessing the recent wave of publications on Reconstruction, historians Bruce E. Baker and Brian Kelly noted that "the field has seen a steady output of studies emphasizing freedpeople's agency, but little acknowledgment until recently that there were limits to the former slaves' power to remake their world." Baker and Kelly edited a collection of essays as part of the After Slavery Project, a collaboration between American and British universities focused on the transition from enslaved to free labor. Focused on the postwar period at the state and local levels, these essays revealed the complex contest over the meaning of freedom during Reconstruction, the challenges freedpeople faced, and their relentless pursuit of what they believed constituted freedom. At once signaling the current state and the future of the literature, the collection should encourage further study of issues of gender and labor at the state and local levels while reimagining a "long" Reconstruction as Hahn modeled. The next wave of Reconstruction scholarship will also surely continue to balance varying degrees of continuity and change as Eric Foner proposed and redirect understanding of the postwar years in far more dynamic and holistic terms.[25]

Notes

1. Among the most valuable historiographical essays are Vernon L. Wharton, "Reconstruction," in *Writing Southern History: Essays in Historiography in Honor of Fletcher M. Green,* ed. Arthur S. Link and Rembert W. Patrick (Baton Rouge: Louisiana State Univ. Press, 1965), 295-315; Joe Gray Taylor, "The White South from Secession to Redemption," in *Interpreting Southern History:*

Historiographical Essays in Honor of Sanford W. Higginbotham, ed. John B. Boles and Evelyn Thomas Nolen (Baton Rouge: Louisiana State Univ. Press, 1987), 182-98; Eric Foner, "Reconstruction Revisited," *Reviews in American History* 10 (Dec. 1982): 82-100; John C. Rodrigue, "Black Agency after Slavery," in *Reconstructions: New Perspectives on the Postbellum South*, ed. Thomas J. Brown (New York: Oxford Univ. Press, 2006), 40-65; and R. Tracy McKenzie, "Southern Labor and Reconstruction," in *A Companion to the Civil War and Reconstruction*, ed. Lacy K. Ford (Malden, Mass.: Wiley-Blackwell, 2011), 366-85.

2. W. E. B. Du Bois, *Black Reconstruction in America: An Essay toward a History of the Part Which Black Folk Played in the Attempt to Reconstruct Democracy in America, 1860-1880* (1935; repr., New York: Atheneum, 1973), 130, 239, 429, 719; Foner, "Reconstruction Revisited," 82-83. For more on the Dunning School, see John David Smith and J. Vincent Lowery, eds., *The Dunning School: Historians, Race, and the Meaning of Reconstruction* (Lexington: Univ. Press of Kentucky, 2013).

3. Francis B. Simkins, "New Viewpoints of Southern Reconstruction," *Journal of Southern History* 5 (Feb. 1939): 49-61 (quotation, 52); Francis B. Simkins and Robert H. Woody, *South Carolina during Reconstruction* (Chapel Hill: Univ. of North Carolina Press, 1932); Howard K. Beale, "On Rewriting Reconstruction History," *American Historical Review* 45 (July 1940): 807-27 (quotation, 810); Wharton, "Reconstruction," 295-315; Foner, "Reconstruction Revisited," 82-100.

4. Kenneth M. Stampp, *The Era of Reconstruction, 1865-1877* (New York: Alfred A. Knopf, 1966), 78, 80, 82. For a collection of revisionist analyses, see Kenneth M. Stampp and Leon F. Litwack, eds., *Reconstruction: An Anthology of Revisionist Writings* (Baton Rouge: Louisiana State Univ. Press, 1969). For a survey of revisionist works, see Taylor, "The White South from Secession to Redemption," 182-98.

5. Stampp, *Era of Reconstruction*, 78, 80, 82, 123, 133; John Hope Franklin, *Reconstruction: After the Civil War* (1961; repr., Chicago: Univ. of Chicago Press, 1966), 219-20, 223.

6. Roger L. Ransom and Richard Sutch, *One Kind of Freedom: The Economic Consequences of Emancipation* (London: Cambridge Univ. Press, 1977), 2, 6, 36, 70. On econometricians and southern history, see Harold Woodman, "Economic Reconstruction and the Rise of the New South, 1865-1900" in *Interpreting Southern History*, 267-69. For more on the historiography on withdrawal, see Rodrigue, "Black Agency after Slavery," 50-53. For more on the historiographical debate surrounding *One Kind of Freedom*, see Peter A. Coclanis and Scott Marler, "The Economics of Reconstruction" and McKenzie, "Southern Labor and Reconstruction," 352-59, 372-77.

7. Gerald David Jaynes, *Branches without Roots: Genesis of the Black Working Class in the American South, 1862-1882* (New York: Oxford Univ. Press, 1986), 229-30, 232.

8. Eric Foner, *Reconstruction: America's Unfinished Revolution, 1863-1877* (New York: HarperCollins, 1988), 157, 174; Foner, "Reconstruction Revisited," 83-100 (quotations, 84 and 87).

9. William Cohen, *At Freedom's Edge: Black Mobility and the Southern White Quest for Racial Control, 1861-1915* (Baton Rouge: Louisiana State Univ. Press, 1991), 24-25; Jonathan M. Wiener, "Class Structure and Economic Development in the American South, 1865-1955," *American Historical Review* 84 (Oct. 1979): 970-92; Harold D. Woodman, "'Class Structure and Economic Development in the American South, 1865-1955': Comments," *American Historical Review* 84 (Oct. 1979): 997-1001; Gavin Wright, *Old South, New South: Revolutions in the Southern Economy since the Civil War* (New York: Basic Books, 1986). For a valuable survey of this historiographical debate, see Cohen, *At Freedom's Edge*, 24-28.

10. Julie Saville, *The Work of Reconstruction: From Slave to Wage Labor in South Carolina, 1860-1870* (New York: Cambridge Univ. Press, 1994), 2.

11. James D. Schmidt, *Free to Work: Labor Law, Emancipation, and Reconstruction, 1815-1880* (Athens: Univ. of Georgia Press, 1998), 2, 5, 52, 53, 119, 192; Amy Dru Stanley, *From Bondage to Contract: Wage Labor, Marriage, and the Market in the Age of Slave Emancipation* (Cambridge: Cambridge Univ. Press, 1998).

12. John C. Rodrigue, *Reconstruction in the Cane Fields: From Slavery to Free Labor in Louisiana's Sugar Parishes, 1862-1880* (Baton Rouge: Louisiana State Univ. Press, 2001), 3, 103, 140.

13. Frederick Cooper, Thomas C. Holt, and Rebecca J. Scott, *Beyond Slavery: Explorations of Race, Labor, and Citizenship in Postemancipation Societies* (Chapel Hill: Univ. of North Carolina Press, 2000), 82, 102; Rebecca J. Scott, *Degrees of Freedom: Louisiana and Cuba after Slavery* (Cambridge, Mass.: The Belknap Press of Harvard Univ. Press, 2005).

14. Moon-Ho Jung, *Coolies and Cane: Race, Labor, and Sugar in the Age of Emancipation* (Baltimore, Md.: Johns Hopkins Univ. Press, 2006), 4-5, 223; Erin Elizabeth Clune, "Black Workers, White Immigrants, and the Postemancipation Problem of Labor: The New South in Transnational Perspective," in *Global Perspectives on Industrial Transformation in the American South*, ed. Susanna Delfino and Michele Gillespie (Columbia: Univ. of Missouri Press, 2005), 199-228. Essential studies of the immigration movement in the South include Bert James Loewenberg, "Efforts of the South to Encourage Immigration, 1865-1900," *South Atlantic Quarterly* 33 (Oct. 1934): 363-85, and Rowland T. Berthoff, "Southern Attitudes toward Immigration," *Journal of Southern History* 17 (Aug. 1951): 328-60. For state-level studies, see C. G. Belisary, "Tennessee and Immigration, 1865-1880," *Tennessee Historical Quarterly* 7 (Sept. 1948): 229-48; Claude Smith, "Official Efforts of the State of Mississippi to Encourage Immigration, 1868-1886," *Journal of Mississippi History* 32 (Nov. 1970): 327-40; and George E. Pozzetta, "Foreigners in Florida: A Study of Immigration Promotion, 1865-1910," *Florida Historical Quarterly* 53 (Oct. 1974): 164-80.

15. Stanley, *From Bondage to Contract*.

16. Leslie A. Schwalm, *A Hard Fight for We: Women's Transition from Slavery to Freedom in South Carolina* (Urbana: Univ. of Illinois Press, 1997), 7, 232; Rodrigue, "Black Agency after Slavery," 50-53. For more on the gendered dimensions of the historiography of Reconstruction, see Jeannie Whayne, "Southern Women during the Age of Emancipation," in *Companion to the Civil War and Reconstruction*, 403-22.

17. Nancy Bercaw, *Gendered Freedoms: Race, Rights, and the Politics of Household in the Delta, 1861-1875* (Gainesville: Univ. Press of Florida, 2003), 49, 156, 186-87; Laura F. Edwards, *Gendered Strife and Confusion: The Political Culture of Reconstruction* (Urbana: Univ. of Illinois Press, 1997).

18. Heather Cox Richardson, *The Death of Reconstruction: Race, Labor, and Politics in the Post-Civil War North, 1865-1901* (Cambridge, Mass.: Harvard Univ. Press, 2001), xiv, 216; Heather Cox Richardson, "Reconstruction and the Nation," in *Companion to the Civil War and Reconstruction*, 447-67.

19. Carol Faulkner, *Women's Radical Reconstruction: The Freedmen's Aid Movement* (Philadelphia: Univ. of Pennsylvania Press, 2004), 2, 83.

20. Steven Hahn, *A Nation under Our Feet: Black Political Struggles in the Rural South from Slavery to the Great Migration* (Cambridge, Mass.: The Belknap Press of Harvard Univ. Press, 2003), 4, 6. For more on the comparison between the works of Foner and Hahn, see Rodrigue, "Black Agency after Slavery," 63-64.

21. Hahn, *A Nation under Our Feet*, 340-41. For more on the Exodusters, see Nell Irvin Painter, *Exodusters: Black Migration to Kansas after Reconstruction* (New York: Alfred A. Knopf, 1977).

22. Susan Eva O'Donovan, *Becoming Free in the Cotton South* (Cambridge, Mass.: Harvard Univ. Press, 2007), 158, 268.

23. Thavolia Glymph, *Out of the House of Bondage: The Transformation of the Plantation Household* (New York: Cambridge Univ. Press, 2008), 166, 168.

24. Mary Farmer-Kaiser, *Freedwomen and the Freedmen's Bureau: Race, Gender, and Public Policy in the Age of Emancipation* (New York: Fordham Univ. Press, 2010), 8, 67, 169.

25. Bruce E. Baker and Brian Kelly, "Introduction," in *After Slavery: Race, Labor, and Citizenship in the Reconstruction South*, ed. Bruce E. Baker and Brian Kelly (Gainesville: Univ. Press of Florida, 2013), 8. For a survey of the historiography of agency, see Rodrigue, "Black Agency after Slavery."

CHAPTER SEVEN

Reconstruction

Intellectual Life and Historical Memory

K. STEPHEN PRINCE

Since the early twentieth century, political and social methodologies have dominated the historiography of Reconstruction. The first generations of scholarship on the period—notably the work of the Dunning School—focused almost exclusively on the electoral and legislative history of the postwar era. Early revisionist critics like Kenneth Stampp disagreed with Dunningite conclusions but largely maintained a focus on high politics. With the arrival of the Civil Rights Era, practitioners of the new so-called social history revolutionized the study of Reconstruction, putting the experience of emancipated African Americans front and center. To find the deepest significance of Reconstruction, social historians argued, one should not look to Congress and state capitols, but rather to the farms, cities, and plantations of the South. Since the 1960s, much of the best work on Reconstruction has sought to recast the history of the period from the bottom up. Between them, political and social historians have defined the boundaries of Reconstruction studies, influencing research agendas and shaping scholarly understandings of the period.

In this context, it is not unreasonable to ask where one might look to find the cultural and intellectual history of Reconstruction. At first glance, the field seems rather barren. As historian Leslie Butler explains, most "intellectual and cultural historians have not focused specifically on the 'classic' period of Reconstruction or the constitutional, political, or economic processes of Reconstruction."[1] Appearances, however, can be deceiving. If full-fledged intellectual and cultural histories of Reconstruction are relatively rare, scholars working on a wide variety of topics have recognized that the period posed intellectual problems just as surely as political and social ones. Indeed, with a slight shift of perspective, it becomes clear that the history of Reconstruction is, in large measure, a history of ideas. For proof, it is only necessary to ask a simple question: what do historians write about when they write about Reconstruction? The answers to this question—race, region, gender, labor, violence, democracy, power, freedom—are topics with which cultural and intellectual historians of the United States are intimately familiar. Reconstruction was not just about political access or plantation labor relations. It was, at its core, a struggle over meaning, ideology, and narrative. On this level, Reconstruction offers fertile ground for intellectual and cultural historians.

Before proceeding further, some definitions are in order. Though they are related, intellectual history and cultural history are not synonymous. While intellectual history focuses on the works of an elite group of writers and thinkers, cultural historians tend to take a much more democratic approach with regard to subjects and sources. In fact, cultural history might be fruitfully understood as intellectual history written from the bottom up. Beyond this, cultural historians tend to concern themselves not merely with the history of ideas, but with the ways in which regimes of knowledge have been created, disseminated, and contested in the past. In recent decades, the field of cultural history has grown in prominence and visibility, while the influence of intellectual history has waned.[2] For those interested in the intellectual life of Reconstruction, however, an awareness of both methodologies is essential. A unifying principle connects the two approaches: ideas matter and they die slowly. Intellectual and cultural historians agree that history is more than the study of past events. It is also the study of the way that people have imagined, understood, and explained their world. Cultural and intellectual productions are not simply reflections of the past. They form an essential component of it.

Taking these definitions as a starting point, it is possible to sketch out a historiography of intellectual life during Reconstruction. It must be admitted at the outset that most of the authors of the works cited in this essay did not consider themselves intellectual or cultural historians or intend to write studies in these genres. Most, in fact, were explicitly engaged in different projects: political history, social history, gender history, biography, memory studies. Even so, a recognition of the significance of ideas and ideology pervades all of the volumes enumerated here. Significantly, the history of Reconstruction provides an ideal canvas on which to explore the shifting relationship between intellectual work (both elite and popular) and on-the-ground social realities. Far from a lacuna or a blind spot in the historiography, the intellectual and cultural history of Reconstruction represents a rich and significant site of scholarly inquiry.

Before addressing more recent publications, it will be helpful to turn briefly to a trio of earlier works that made significant contributions to the study of intellectual life during Reconstruction. Two books that appeared in the mid-1960s—Willie Lee Rose's *Rehearsal for Reconstruction: The Port Royal Experiment* (1964) and George M. Fredrickson's *The Inner Civil War: Northern Intellectuals and the Crisis of the Union* (1965)—map the intellectual world of the early Reconstruction period. Rose's book explores the ways in which the racial and religious expectations of northern missionaries shaped their experience working with emancipated African Americans during the wartime Reconstruction of South Carolina's Sea Islands.[3] Fredrickson argues that the experience of war fundamentally changed the way that the northern intellectual elite understood democracy, civic engagement, and the role of government. These reconfigured ideas, in turn, shaped their approach to the problem of Reconstruction.[4] Though it is not primarily a work of intellectual history, Leon Litwack's *Been in the Storm So Long: The Aftermath of Slavery* (1979) offers an important commentary on the multiple and conflicting meanings of free labor in the postemancipation South. African

Americans tended to assume that freedom meant the right to control one's labor, while white former masters expected to preserve the compulsions of the slave system in a postemancipation world. The social tumult of Reconstruction, Litwack suggests, contributed significantly to the persistence of these incommensurable worldviews.[5]

The publication of Eric Foner's *Reconstruction: America's Unfinished Revolution, 1863-1877* (1988) marked a turning point in the historiography. Foner's book offers a synthesis of revisionist and postrevisionist scholarship on Reconstruction. At the same time, it presents a compelling reinterpretation of the period. Though the book draws inspiration from several genres—political history, social history, and economic history—Foner's work reflects a willingness to take ideas seriously as a motive force of historical change. Indeed, his Reconstruction is both a fundamentally ideological struggle and a deeply transformative intellectual moment. Foner explores the political ideals that unified and divided the northern Republican coalition; he describes the long-term reconfiguration of categories of race and citizenship in the North and the South; he narrates a larger transformation in the relationship of the citizenry to a newly expansive federal government. However, it is the concept of freedom that is at the heart of Foner's analysis. In *Reconstruction,* he presents freedom as a complex and variable notion whose ambiguities defined both the possibilities and limitations of the postwar period.[6]

Building on the work of Litwack and Foner, a number of books published since the mid-1990s analyze the contested meanings of freedom and labor in the plantation South. Julie Saville's *The Work of Reconstruction: From Slave to Wage Laborer in South Carolina, 1860-1870* (1994), John C. Rodrigue's *Reconstruction in the Cane Fields: From Slavery to Free Labor in Louisiana's Sugar Parishes, 1862-1880* (2001), and Susan Eva O'Donovan's *Becoming Free in the Cotton South* (2007) are powerful and deeply researched social histories that skillfully detail the transition from slavery to wage labor.[7] At the same time, each book explores the ways in which a broad range of historical actors, black and white, female and male, debated and renegotiated ideas of race, gender, labor, and freedom in the cotton and cane fields of the Reconstruction South. In *From Bondage to Contract: Wage Labor, Marriage, and the Market in the Age of Slave Emancipation* (1998), Amy Dru Stanley argues that debates over slavery and emancipation encouraged a movement toward contractual relationships as a general means of organizing American society. From wage labor to marriage, contract was a cornerstone of emerging late-nineteenth-century notions of freedom.[8] Scholars who employ a comparative lens have shed important light on the transnational character of debates over slavery and freedom. In *Degrees of Freedom: Louisiana and Cuba after Slavery* (2005), Rebecca J. Scott explores the meaning and legacies of emancipation in two plantation societies, while Demetrius L. Eudell's *Political Languages of Emancipation in the British Caribbean and the U.S. South* (2001) analyzes the rhetoric and reality of freedom, race, and labor in Jamaica and the southern United States.[9]

Political historians have produced a number of important works relating to intellectual life during the Reconstruction period. Kate Masur's *An Example for All the Land: Emancipation and the Struggle over Equality in Washington, D.C.* (2010) is more than a study of Reconstruction in the nation's capital; it is a careful exploration of the meaning of race, democracy, and citizenship in the postwar United States. Masur's work foregrounds the political activism of black Washingtonians while highlighting the conflicts and contradictions that marked congressional rule in the District.[10] Carole Emberton's *Beyond Redemption: Race, Violence, and the American South after the Civil War* (2013) turns to popular politics in the South. Violence, Emberton argues, was the lingua franca of postwar politics, with abstract notions of freedom, manhood, and citizenship made real through the threat of violence.[11] Hannah Rosen's *Terror in the Heart of Freedom: Citizenship, Sexual Violence, and the Meaning of Race in the Postemancipation South* (2008) makes similar claims, focusing on the role that sexual violence against black women played in the maintenance of southern white supremacy. Even as white-on-black rape bolstered white male power, African American women employed a variety of discursive strategies to defend their bodies and their rights.[12] In *Iron Confederacies: Southern Railways, Klan Violence, and Reconstruction* (1999), Scott Reynolds Nelson connects the ascendancy of white supremacist Democrats to the politics of railroad construction in the postwar South. In so doing, Nelson adds an important figure—the northern capitalist—to the cast of characters responsible for the overthrow of Reconstruction.[13] Finally, Susanna Michele Lee's *Claiming the Union: Citizenship in the Post-Civil War South* (2014) uses southerners' postwar claims of wartime loyalty to explore the politics of citizenship.[14] In each of these works, the history of ideas plays a prominent role. They remind us that political ideology is not only a product of learned treatises and congressional legislation. It can also arise from the day-to-day practice of popular politics.

Historians of gender have placed questions of language and ideology at the center of Reconstruction studies. Laura F. Edwards's *Gendered Strife and Confusion: The Political Culture of Reconstruction* (1997) uses legal documentation and court records to connect public and private life in Granville County, North Carolina. Edwards convincingly argues that gender—specifically conceptions of manliness, femininity, marriage, and domesticity—animated political struggle at the local level.[15] In *Out of the House of Bondage: The Transformation of the Plantation Household* (2008), Thavolia Glymph insists that both before and after emancipation, white women of the planter class exercised extraordinary—and frequently violent—coercive power over black women, in spite of their own subordination to patriarchal authority.[16] Nancy Bercaw's *Gendered Freedoms: Race, Rights, and the Politics of Household in the Delta, 1861-1875* (2003), covers similar ground, using the idea of the "household" to explore the gendered meaning of emancipation in the Mississippi Delta.[17] Leslie A. Schwalm's *A Hard Fight for We: Women's Transition from Slavery to Freedom in South Carolina* (1997) places the productive and reproductive work of black women at the center of Reconstruction in the low country. Schwalm's work offers a new perspective on labor relations, black agency and resistance, and the role of the federal government (specifically the Freedmen's Bureau).[18] Perhaps because gender history has been so directly influenced by critical theory, historians working in this subfield have been uniquely situated to introduce a cultural and intellectual approach to the study of Reconstruction. In so doing, they have reframed some of the central questions of the period, shedding new light on all that was at stake during Reconstruction.

In recent years, many historians have turned away from the traditional binaries—North/South, black/white—that have long structured Reconstruction historiography. The decade and a half following the Civil War witnessed a sustained reconsideration of issues of race, citizenship, and freedom. An awareness of the way that these conversations played out beyond the South immeasurably strengthens our understanding of the era's main intellectual currents. Western historians have played an important role in this process. Adam Arenson's *The Great Heart of the Republic: St. Louis and the Cultural Civil War* (2011) uses a major urban center located in a border state to explore issues of nation and region in the Civil War era.[19] Stacey L. Smith's *Freedom's Frontier: California and the Struggle over Unfree Labor, Emancipation, and Reconstruction* (2013) challenges traditional narratives of Reconstruction through an interrogation of servile labor in the postwar West.[20] In multiracial California—a "free" state that supported a variety of unfree labor regimes throughout the Civil War Era—struggles over emancipation followed a very different path than in the South. Native American historians have also helped to expand the geographical and intellectual scope of Reconstruction historiography. Though it is not a study of Reconstruction, per se, C. Joseph Genetin-Pilawa's *Crooked Paths to Allotment: The Fight over Federal Indian Policy after the Civil War* (2012) analyzes postwar debates over race and citizenship that provide a helpful counterpoint to those produced in the South.[21] In a similar vein, Elliot West's *The Last Indian War: The Nez Perce Story* (2011) sets the Nez Perce War of 1877 in the context of a national project of Reconstruction and racial reorganization.[22] On the basis of this flurry of scholarship, students of Reconstruction now ignore the West at their own peril. Precisely because they decenter the South, these works help historians to recognize the larger intellectual frameworks that structured Reconstruction—within the South and beyond it.

A number of works have sought to internationalize the study of Reconstruction. An early pioneer was Philip M. Katz's *From Appomattox to Montmartre: Americans and the Paris Commune* (1998), which uses popular responses to the Paris Commune of 1871 to track shifting patterns of thought with regard to labor, government, and social protest.[23] In *Fenians, Freedmen, and Southern Whites: Race and Nationality in the Era of Reconstruction* (2007), Mitchell Snay compares the political ideologies of three Reconstruction Era organizations: the Union League; the Ku Klux Klan; and the Fenians, an Irish nationalist society. Though the first two groups are familiar players in the historiography of Reconstruction, Snay's inclusion of the Fenians allows him to reframe scholarly debates over race and nationalism in the postwar United States.[24] Matthew Pratt Guterl's *American Mediterranean: Southern Slaveholders in the Age of Emancipation* (2009) imaginatively connects the South's planter class with a hemispheric community of slaveholders. The challenge of emancipation was not one that defeated Confederates faced alone, Guterl argues. They turned, with surprising frequency, to an international elite familiar with the experience of mastery.[25] In *Coolies and Cane: Race, Labor, and Sugar in the Age of Emancipation* (2008), Moon-Ho Jung uses the presence of Chinese laborers in the sugar cane fields of Louisiana and the Caribbean to reframe debates over race, work, immigration, and freedom in the postwar era.[26] As such volumes suggest, nineteenth-century Americans frequently looked beyond national borders in their attempts to grapple with the intellectual challenges of Reconstruction. Historians, it is clear, must follow their lead.

The expansion of the chronological bounds of Reconstruction has been a hallmark of recent historiography. Scholars have proven increasingly willing to ignore the traditional endpoint of the Reconstruction period, 1877, instead offering studies that extend into the 1880s, 1890s, and beyond. It is no coincidence that historians who engage with the cultural and intellectual life of the era have been at the forefront of this movement. While 1877 retains its significance as a political turning point, marking the ascendancy of the Democratic Party in the entirety of the former Confederacy, cultural and intellectual historians have insisted that the "redemption" of South Carolina, Louisiana, and Florida left many of the most pressing problems of the Reconstruction period unresolved. Indeed, the twelve years between 1865 and 1877—a period we might term the "short Reconstruction" to distinguish it from the "long Reconstruction" that many works now adopt as their chronological frame— marked only the opening salvo in longer-term struggles over issues of race, violence, citizenship, and democracy. As a political program, Reconstruction may have come to an end in 1877. As a cultural and intellectual process, however, it was only just beginning.

Among proponents of a long Reconstruction, Heather Cox Richardson merits special mention. In *The Death of Reconstruction: Race, Labor, and Politics in the Post-Civil War North* (2004), Richardson ties declining support for southern African American rights to rising conflicts between labor and capital in the Gilded Age North. During Reconstruction, the northern public imagined the freedpeople as idealized free laborers, but as time passed, popular portrayals of southern black people grew more negative. Northern media sources began to depict a disaffected labor force inappropriately reliant on federal assistance. It is in this context, Richardson argues, that the northern public lost its appetite for federal involvement in southern racial affairs.[27] In another work, *West from Appomattox: The Reconstruction of America after the Civil War* (2008), Richardson embraces an even broader perspective, placing southern Reconstruction into a longer history of nation building in the late nineteenth century. In the decades following the Civil War, Americans—northern, southern, and western—struggled over the proper place of the federal government in the reunited nation. While labor leaders, feminists, and black activists called for an enlarged federal government responsive to the needs of its citizenry, many Americans preferred a smaller state with more carefully delineated responsibilities.[28] In both books, Richardson's focus on shifting patterns of thought—political economy in *The Death of Reconstruction*, the role of the state in *West from Appomattox*—benefits from an extended chronology. The dozen years after the Civil War raised as many questions as they answered, Richardson suggests. To write the intellectual history of the period, it is necessary to adopt a more expansive view.

A similar logic runs through *Declarations of Dependence: The Long Reconstruction of Popular Politics in the South, 1861-1908* (2011), by Gregory P. Downs. In his study of political thought in North Carolina, Downs explores the ways that the Civil War and Reconstruction forced black and white southerners to reimagine their relationship to government. Belying notions of American independence, average southerners consistently appealed to the state and federal governments for support, protection, and favor.[29] Mark Elliot's *Color-blind Justice: Albion Tourgée and the Quest for Racial Equality from the Civil War to* Plessy v. Ferguson (2006) falls into the long Reconstruction camp largely due to the fact that its protagonist, the neoabolitionist jurist and lawyer Albion W. Tourgée, lived until the early twentieth century. Even so, Elliot's masterful intellectual biography of the best-selling author and outspoken racial egalitarian makes the most of its expansive canvas, using Tourgée's writing and activism to track shifting patterns of popular thought from Reconstruction to Jim Crow.[30]

Another important biography, Stephen Kantrowitz's *Ben Tillman and the Reconstruction of White Supremacy* (2000), uses the life of South Carolina governor and senator Benjamin Tillman to reframe issues of manhood, whiteness, and democracy in the postwar South. Though Reconstruction proper occupies only a small portion of the narrative, the book's chronological sweep allows Kantrowitz to highlight intellectual continuities across the nineteenth century and into the twentieth. Historians working in women's history have also embraced the long Reconstruction model.[31] Jane Turner Censer's *The Reconstruction of White Southern Womanhood, 1865-1915* (2003), for instance, explores the experiences of elite white women in the Upper South in the fifty years after the Civil War. Rich in insights in social history, Censer's work also focuses on the evolution of gender roles across the Reconstruction and post-Reconstruction decades.[32]

Shifting ideas of region and nation have attracted a number of scholars writing in the long Reconstruction tradition. In *Reforging the White Republic: Race, Religion, and American Nationalism, 1865-1898* (2005), Edward J. Blum argues that a vision of white, Protestant, American nationalism was central to the reunion of the sections in the aftermath of the Civil War. As Blum notes, this intellectual alliance between white northerners and white southerners left little room for notions of racial democracy and concern over African American civil rights.[33] Literary scholar Jennifer Rae Greeson's *Our South: Geographic Fantasy and the Rise of National Literature* (2010) argues that visions of the exotic, foreign South were a staple of the American literary tradition for much of the nineteenth century. The Civil War and Reconstruction challenged inherited patterns of thought but did not displace them entirely.[34] In a similar vein, Natalie J. Ring's *The Problem South: Region, Empire, and the New Liberal State, 1880-1930* (2012) reminds readers that the formal end of Reconstruction in 1877 did little to weaken northern cultural chauvinism with regard to southern affairs.[35] My own book, *Stories of the South: Race and the Reconstruction of Southern Identity, 1865-1915* (2014), uses shifting definitions of the South in print, visual, and performance culture to trace the nation's retreat from racial egalitarianism in the five decades after the Civil War.[36] Though their approaches vary, all of these works engage with popular debates over the nature of the South and the character of a reunited nation. Recognizing that such questions refuse to abide by traditional structures of periodization, each adopts a chronological framing that extends the Reconstruction story beyond 1877.

Scholars working in memory studies have produced some of the most significant cultural and intellectual histories of the postwar period. The study of historical memory begins with the premise that historians are not the only people who lay claim on the past. Americans of all stripes have turned to the past—or, more accurately, to their impression of it—in an attempt to shape the present and the future. Indeed, history has always been a site of power, contestation, and debate. Popular responses to the Civil War offer a case in point. From the close of hostilities onward, Americans struggled for the right to define the conflict in the realms of culture and memory. The power to tell the story of the Civil War, commentators recognized, conferred very real powers and privileges in the postwar era. Rather than segregating studies of Civil War memory from the historiography of Reconstruction, it is helpful to put these literatures in conversation. Though many of the works cited below address the traditional or short Reconstruction only in passing, they are included here because they offer an important new perspective on the intellectual and cultural world of the late nineteenth century.

Any discussion of Civil War memory must begin with David Blight's *Race and Reunion: The Civil War in American Memory* (2001). Blight argues that in the aftermath of the Civil War, three possible understandings of the war's meaning were open to the American people: a reconciliationist vision of the war that focused on the survival of the Union and demanded postwar sectional reunion; a white supremacist vision of the war that emphasized the martial valor of northern and southern whites; and an emancipationist memory of the war that foregrounded the African American experience of freedom. Blight argues that over a fifty-year span, the reconciliationist imperative combined with a white supremacist rendering of the war to overawe and erase the drama of emancipation from white Americans' memory of the Civil War. The nation's retreat from racial egalitarianism, Blight suggests, was in large part a matter of remembrance and forgetting.[37] Though Blight's thesis has been extraordinarily influential, it has not gone unchallenged. Caroline Janney's *Remembering the Civil War: Reunion and the Limits of Reconciliation* (2013) offers a revision of some of Blight's claims. Drawing a helpful distinction between "reunion" (defined as a political act) and "reconciliation" (a matter of sentiment and emotion), Janney argues that northerners and southerners of both races held onto distinctive and contradictory visions of the war well into the twentieth century. The South's Lost Cause and the North's Union Cause retained their salience for decades after the war. Janney's work celebrates the diversity and variability of popular memory, arguing that the impulse toward sentimental reconciliation always coexisted with strains of memorial partisanship.[38]

The sweeping overviews presented by Blight and Janney have helped to define the field of Civil War memory studies, but a number of historians have produced significant works that explore the process of historical memory and memorialization on a smaller scale. Anne E. Marshall's *Creating a Confederate Kentucky: The Lost Cause and Civil War Memory in a Border State* (2010) uses the case of Kentucky to explore the relationship between race, politics, and popular memory. Marshall argues that although the Bluegrass State stayed loyal to the Union during the Civil War, many white Kentuckians aligned themselves with the South in the postwar era, inventing a mythic Confederate past in the process.[39] Joan Waugh's *U. S. Grant: American Hero, American Myth* (2009) treats Ulysses S. Grant as both an active participant in postwar memory struggles and an important topic of memorialization in his own right.[40] Grant was not the only Civil War veteran to grapple with issues of memory. Historians Stuart McConnell, James Marten, and Barbara Gannon have analyzed the memorial activities of Civil War veterans' groups, including the Grand Army of the Republic and the United Confederate Veterans.[41] Donald R. Shaffer's work, notably *After the Glory: The Struggles of Black Civil War Veterans* (2004) and *Voices of Emancipation: Understanding Slavery, the Civil War, and Reconstruction through the U.S Pension Bureau* (coedited with Elizabeth A. Regosin, 2008), focuses on the commemorative agenda and political activism of African American Union veterans.[42]

A number of authors have turned to death and mourning as sites of memory. Drew Gilpin Faust's *This Republic of Suffering: Death and the American Civil War* (2008) argues that the unprecedented devastation of the Civil War fundamentally changed the nation's relationship to death and dying.[43] In his book *Awaiting the Heavenly Country: The Civil War and America's Culture of Death* (2008), Mark A. Schantz argues that contemporary notions of death and the afterlife helped to prepare soldiers and civilians for the bloodshed of the Civil War.[44] John R. Neff and William A. Blair have each suggested that staggering wartime death tolls posed a problem of commemoration and reunion in the war's aftermath. Neff's *Honoring the Civil War Dead: Commemoration and the Problem of Reconciliation* (2005) largely focuses on northern debates and practices, while Blair's *Cities of the Dead: Contesting the Memory of the Civil War in the South, 1865-1914* (2004) explores memorial practices in the former Confederacy.[45] Given the extraordinary death tolls of the Civil War, such studies offer an invaluable glimpse into the intellectual life of the postwar era.

As a number of historians have shown, northern and southern women were key players in Civil War commemoration. Karen L. Cox's *Dixie's Daughters: The United Daughters of the Confederacy and the Preservation of Confederate Culture* (2004) and Caroline E. Janney's *Burying the Dead but Not the Past: Ladies' Memorial Associations and the Lost Cause* (2007) put Confederate women at the center of the Lost Cause.[46] Through memorial celebrations, textbook campaigns, and monument building, the women of the postwar South worked unceasingly to enshrine their vision of the Civil War at the heart of regional and national memory. Turning to the written word, Lyde Cullen Sizer and Sarah E. Gardner track depictions of the Civil War in the postwar work of (respectively) northern and southern female authors.[47] Though it is not strictly a work of women's history, Nina Silber's *The Romance of Reunion: Northerners and the South, 1865-1900* (1993) puts questions of gender at the center of postwar sectional reunion. More specifically, Silber argues that the northerners seeking reconciliation recast the South as feminine, alluring, and unthreatening. The popular romance novels of the period—which invariably paired a northern man and a southern woman—offer a key to the larger cultural processes that produced reunion.[48]

Several important works address the place of African Americans within the commemorative landscape of the postwar era. Kirk Savage's *Standing Soldiers, Kneeling Slaves: Race, War, and Monument in Nineteenth-Century America* (1997) studies public monuments of the Civil War Era, noting the ways in which commemorative art tended to reinforce rather than challenge antebellum racial stereotypes.[49] In a similar vein, Micki McElya's *Clinging to Mammy: The Faithful Slave in Twentieth-Century America* (2007) notes the persistence of "faithful slave" iconography long after the advent of black freedom.[50]

John David Smith's *An Old Creed for the New South: Proslavery Ideology and Historiography, 1865-1918* (1985; 3rd ed., 2008) explores the treatment of slavery and emancipation in popular and professional history writing.[51] Other historians have emphasized patterns of memorialization and commemoration within the black community. Mitch Kachun's *Festivals of Freedom: Memory and Meaning in African American Emancipation Celebrations, 1809-1915* (2003) and Kathleen Ann Clark's *Defining Moments: African American Commemoration and Political Culture in the South, 1863-1913* (2005) argue that public celebrations of emancipation served as important sites of community building, identity formation, and political education among freedpeople. As northern and southern whites endeavored to whitewash the history of slavery in the interest of sectional unity, African American commemorations of emancipation made an important statement indeed.[52] Kidada E. Williams's *They Left Great Marks on Me: African American Testimonies of Racial Violence from Emancipation to World War I* (2012) offers a different perspective on black commemoration, analyzing African American attempts to grapple with the long shadow of racial violence in the postwar United States.[53]

Memory, then, deserves a central place in our understanding of the Reconstruction process. The questions that the literature on Civil War memory raises—What was the lasting meaning of the war? Which groups would guide the course of a postwar United States? How were the imperatives of racial justice and regional reunion to be balanced?—are, in large measure, the same questions that concern all historians of Reconstruction. Without an awareness of the intellectual world of the postwar era, it is impossible to understand the political and social history of Reconstruction. The ways in which Americans understood the Civil War—their generation's defining experience—indelibly shaped the political events that would follow. For this reason, the study of memory has proven an extraordinarily fruitful area of inquiry for scholars of the postwar United States.

In closing, it seems appropriate to point out a few areas for further study. First, given the remarkable depth and breadth of the historiography of Civil War memory, the comparative absence of work addressing how Americans remembered Reconstruction is quite striking. In the years after 1877, Americans continued to debate the meaning and legacy of Reconstruction. Such discussions held deep political significance. And yet, the modern historiography of Reconstruction memory amounts to a single monograph and a collection of essays: Bruce E. Baker's *What Reconstruction Meant: Historical Memory in the American South* (2007) and *The Dunning School: Historians, Race, and the Meaning of Reconstruction*, edited by John David Smith and J. Vincent Lowery (2013). If the memory of the Civil War indelibly shaped the political world of Reconstruction, it is equally clear that popular memories of Reconstruction helped to structure race and regional politics from the 1880s on. Though Baker's book and the collection of essays on the Dunning School have begun this work, much more remains to be said.[54]

Second, historians of popular culture continue to occupy a somewhat tenuous place in the historiography of Reconstruction. The field would benefit immeasurably from a more sustained engagement with the way that popular culture shaped and reflected the politics of the period. Elaine Frantz Parsons's work on the Ku Klux Klan provides a model here, as do a pair of monographs that apply cultural studies to a slightly later period in southern history: Grace Elizabeth Hale's *Making Whiteness: The Culture of Segregation in the South, 1890–1940* (1998) and Amy Louise Wood's *Lynching and Spectacle: Witnessing Racial Violence in America, 1890–1940* (2009).[55]

Finally, scholars working in the up-and-coming fields of sense history and sound studies might turn their attention to the Reconstruction period. In helping to uncover the ways that average Americans of both races experienced Reconstruction, sense history promises to advance scholarly understanding of the period on a deeply human level. Research in these areas will build upon many of the works cited in this essay, advancing the study of intellectual life and historical memory in the postwar period.

Notes

1. Leslie Butler, "Reconstructions in Intellectual and Cultural Life," in *Reconstructions: New Perspectives on the Postbellum United States*, ed. Thomas Brown (New York: Oxford Univ. Press, 2008), 173.

2. For more on this distinction, see Thomas Bender, "Intellectual and Cultural History," in *The New American History, Revised and Expanded Edition*, ed. Eric Foner (Philadelphia: Temple Univ. Press, 1997), 181-202.

3. Willie Lee Rose, *Rehearsal for Reconstruction: The Port Royal Experiment* (Indianapolis, Ind.: Bobbs-Merrill, 1964).

4. George M. Fredrickson, *The Inner Civil War: Northern Intellectuals and the Crisis of the Union* (New York: Harper and Row, 1965).

5. Leon F. Litwack, *Been in the Storm so Long: The Aftermath of Slavery* (New York: Alfred A. Knopf, 1979).

6. Eric Foner, *Reconstruction: America's Unfinished Revolution, 1863-1877* (New York: Harper and Row, 1988).

7. Julie Saville, *The Work of Reconstruction: From Slave to Wage Laborer in South Carolina, 1860-1870* (New York: Cambridge Univ. Press, 1994); John C. Rodrigue, *Reconstruction in the Cane Fields: From Slavery to Free Labor in Louisiana's Sugar Parishes, 1862-1880* (Baton Rouge: Louisiana State Univ. Press, 2001); Susan Eva O'Donovan, *Becoming Free in the Cotton South* (Cambridge, Mass.: Harvard Univ. Press, 2007).

8. Amy Dru Stanley, *From Bondage to Contract: Wage Labor, Marriage, and the Market in the Age of Slave Emancipation* (New York: Cambridge Univ. Press, 1998).

9. Rebecca J. Scott, *Degrees of Freedom: Louisiana and Cuba after Slavery* (Cambridge, Mass.: Harvard Univ. Press, 2005); Demetrius L. Eudell, *The Political Languages of Emancipation in the British Caribbean and the U.S. South* (Chapel Hill: Univ. of North Carolina Press, 2002).

10. Kate Masur, *An Example for All the Land: Emancipation and the Struggle over Equality in Washington, D.C.* (Chapel Hill: Univ. of North Carolina Press, 2010).

11. Carole Emberton, *Beyond Redemption: Race, Violence, and the American South after the Civil War* (Chicago: Univ. of Chicago Press, 2013).

12. Hannah Rosen, *Terror in the Heart of Freedom: Citizenship, Sexual Violence, and the Meaning of Race in the Postemancipation South* (Chapel Hill: Univ. of North Carolina Press, 2009).

13. Scott Reynolds Nelson, *Iron Confederacies: Southern Railways, Klan Violence, and Reconstruction* (Chapel Hill: Univ. of North Carolina Press, 1999).

14. Susanna Michelle Lee, *Claiming the Union: Citizenship in the Post-Civil War South* (New York: Cambridge Univ. Press, 2014).

15. Laura Edwards, *Gendered Strife and Confusion: The Political Culture of Reconstruction* (Urbana: Univ. of Illinois Press, 1997).

16. Thavolia Glymph, *Out of the House of Bondage: The Transformation of the Plantation Household* (New York: Cambridge Univ. Press, 2008).

17. Nancy Bercaw, *Gendered Freedoms: Race, Rights, and the Politics of Household in the Delta, 1861-1875* (Gainesville: Univ. Press of Florida, 2003).

18. Leslie A. Schwalm, *A Hard Fight for We: Women's Transition from Slavery to Freedom in South Carolina* (Urbana: Univ. of Illinois Press, 1997).

19. Adam Arenson, *The Great Heart of the Republic: St. Louis and the Cultural Civil War* (Cambridge, Mass.: Harvard Univ. Press, 2011).

20. Stacey L. Smith, *Freedom's Frontier: California and the Struggle over Unfree Labor, Emancipation, and Reconstruction* (Chapel Hill: Univ. of North Carolina Press, 2013).

21. C. Joseph Genetin-Pilawa, *Crooked Paths to Allotment: The Fight over Federal Indian Policy after the Civil War* (Chapel Hill: Univ. of North Carolina Press, 2012).

22. Elliott West, *The Last Indian War: The Nez Perce Story* (New York: Oxford Univ. Press, 2009).

23. Philip M. Katz, *From Appomattox to Montmartre: Americans and the Paris Commune* (Cambridge, Mass.: Harvard Univ. Press, 1998).

24. Mitchell Snay, *Fenians, Freedmen, and Southern Whites: Race and Nationality in the Era of Reconstruction* (Baton Rouge: Louisiana State Univ. Press, 2007).

25. Matthew Pratt Guterl, *American Mediterranean: Southern Slaveholders in the Age of Emancipation* (Cambridge, Mass.: Harvard Univ. Press, 2008).

26. Moon-Ho Jung, *Coolies and Cane: Race, Labor, and Sugar in the Age of Emancipation* (Baltimore: Johns Hopkins Univ. Press, 2006).

27. Heather Cox Richardson, *The Death of Reconstruction: Race, Labor, and Politics in the Post-Civil War North, 1865-1901* (Cambridge, Mass.: Harvard Univ. Press, 2001).

28. Heather Cox Richardson, *West from Appomattox: The Reconstruction of America after the Civil War* (New Haven, Conn.: Yale Univ. Press, 2007).

29. Gregory P. Downs, *Declarations of Dependence: The Long Reconstruction of Popular Politics in the South, 1861-1908* (Chapel Hill: Univ. of North Carolina Press, 2011).

30. Mark Elliott, *Color-blind Justice: Albion Tourgée and the Quest for Racial Equality from the Civil War to* Plessy v. Ferguson (New York: Oxford Univ. Press, 2006).

31. Stephen Kantrowitz, *Ben Tillman and the Reconstruction of White Supremacy* (Chapel Hill: Univ. of North Carolina Press, 2000).

32. Jane Turner Censer, *The Reconstruction of White Southern Womanhood, 1865-1895* (Baton Rouge: Louisiana State Univ. Press, 2003).

33. Edward J. Blum, *Reforging the White Republic: Race, Religion, and American Nationalism, 1865-1898* (Baton Rouge: Louisiana State Univ. Press, 2005).

34. Jennifer Rae Greeson, *Our South: Geographic Fantasy and the Rise of National Literature* (Cambridge, Mass.: Harvard Univ. Press, 2010).

35. Natalie J. Ring, *The Problem South: Region, Empire, and the New Liberal State, 1880-1930* (Athens: Univ. of Georgia Press, 2012).
36. K. Stephen Prince, *Stories of the South: Race and the Reconstruction of Southern Identity, 1865-1915* (Chapel Hill: Univ. of North Carolina Press, 2014).
37. David W. Blight, *Race and Reunion: The Civil War in American Memory* (Cambridge, Mass.: Harvard Univ. Press, 2001).
38. Caroline E. Janney, *Remembering the Civil War: Reunion and the Limits of Reconciliation* (Chapel Hill: Univ. of North Carolina Press, 2013).
39. Anne E. Marshall, *Creating a Confederate Kentucky: The Lost Cause and Civil War Memory in a Border State* (Chapel Hill: Univ. of North Carolina Press, 2010).
40. Joan Waugh, *U. S. Grant: American Hero, American Myth* (Chapel Hill: Univ. of North Carolina Press, 2009).
41. Stuart McConnell, *Glorious Contentment: The Grand Army of the Republic, 1865-1900* (Chapel Hill: Univ. of North Carolina Press, 1992); James Marten, *Sing Not War: The Life of Union and Confederate Veterans in Gilded Age America* (Chapel Hill: Univ. of North Carolina Press, 2011); Barbara A. Gannon, *The Won Cause: Black and White Comradeship in the Grand Army of the Republic* (Chapel Hill: Univ. of North Carolina Press, 2011).
42. Donald R. Shaffer, *After the Glory: The Struggles of Black Civil War Veterans* (Lawrence: Univ. Press of Kansas, 2004); Elizabeth A. Regosin and Donald R. Shaffer, eds., *Voices of Emancipation: Understanding Slavery, the Civil War, and Reconstruction through the U.S. Pension Bureau Files* (New York: New York Univ. Press, 2008).
43. Drew Gilpin Faust, *This Republic of Suffering: Death and the American Civil War* (New York: Alfred A. Knopf, 2008).
44. Mark S. Schantz, *Awaiting the Heavenly Country: The Civil War and America's Culture of Death* (Ithaca, N.Y.: Cornell Univ. Press, 2008).
45. William A. Blair, *Cities of the Dead: Contesting the Memory of the Civil War in the South, 1865-1914* (Chapel Hill: Univ. of North Carolina Press, 2004); John R. Neff, *Honoring the Civil War Dead: Commemoration and the Problem of Reconciliation* (Lawrence: Univ. Press of Kansas, 2005).
46. Karen L. Cox, *Dixie's Daughters: The United Daughters of the Confederacy and the Preservation of Confederate Culture* (Gainesville: Univ. Press of Florida, 2003); Caroline E. Janney, *Burying the Dead but Not the Past: Ladies' Memorial Associations and the Lost Cause* (Chapel Hill: Univ. of North Carolina Press, 2008).
47. Lyde Cullen Sizer, *The Political Work of Northern Women Writers and the Civil War, 1850-1872* (Chapel Hill: Univ. of North Carolina Press, 2000); Sarah E. Gardner, *Blood and Irony: Southern White Women's Narratives of the Civil War, 1861-1937* (Chapel Hill: Univ. of North Carolina Press, 2003).
48. Nina Silber, *The Romance of Reunion: Northerners and the South, 1865-1900* (Chapel Hill: Univ. of North Carolina Press, 1993).

49. Kirk Savage, *Standing Soldiers, Kneeling Slaves: Race, War, and Monument in Nineteenth-Century America* (Princeton, N.J.: Princeton Univ. Press, 1997).

50. Micki McElya, *Clinging to Mammy: The Faithful Slave in Twentieth-Century America* (Cambridge, Mass.: Harvard Univ. Press, 2007).

51. John David Smith, *An Old Creed for the New South: Proslavery Ideology and Historiography, 1865-1918* (1985; repr., Carbondale: Southern Illinois Univ. Press, 2008).

52. Mitch Kachun, *Festivals of Freedom: Memory and Meaning in African American Emancipation Celebrations* (Amherst: Univ. of Massachusetts Press, 2003); Kathleen Ann Clark, *Defining Moments: African American Commemoration and Political Culture in the South, 1863-1913* (Chapel Hill: Univ. of North Carolina Press, 2005).

53. Kidada E. Williams, *They Left Great Marks on Me: African American Testimonies of Racial Violence from Emancipation to World War I* (New York: New York Univ. Press, 2012).

54. Bruce E. Baker, *What Reconstruction Meant: Historical Memory in the American South* (Charlottesville: Univ. of Virginia Press, 2007); John David Smith and J. Vincent Lowery, eds., *The Dunning School: Historians, Race, and the Meaning of Reconstruction* (Lexington: Univ. Press of Kentucky, 2013).

55. Elaine Frantz Parsons, "Midnight Rangers: Costume and Performance in the Reconstruction-Era Ku Klux Klan," *Journal of American History* 92 (Dec. 2005): 811-36; Grace Elizabeth Hale, *Making Whiteness: The Culture of Segregation in the South* (New York: Pantheon Books, 1998); Amy Louise Wood, *Lynching and Spectacle: Witnessing Racial Violence in America, 1890-1940* (Chapel Hill: Univ. of North Carolina Press, 2009).

CHAPTER EIGHT

Reconstruction

Transnational History

ANDREW ZIMMERMAN

Among the most important periods in U.S. history, Reconstruction might appear too narrowly national to reward an international approach.[1] But viewed from such a perspective, Reconstruction appears as a particularly influential instance in a number of interrelated worldwide processes of the nineteenth century. These include (1) the shift of much agricultural production away from unfree labor, especially slavery in the Americas and serfdom in Eastern Europe; (2) the shift of manufacturing from self-employed craft labor to hired industrial labor; (3) a renewed importance of race, racial hierarchies, and white supremacy, even after the end of slavery, in the organization of economic production and political power at the local, national, and supranational levels; and (4) a resumption of colonial expansion, especially in Africa and the Pacific islands. While all four processes resulted in new concentrations of power and wealth, elites did not simply impose them on a passive world: these processes were rather crossproducts of popular struggles for democracy and autonomy with opposing elite struggles for state power and capital accumulation. Taken together, the four processes made up a new phase in the history of global capitalism, not capitalism as imagined in economics textbooks but capitalism as lived in workshops and factories, on farms and plantations. They helped create the world we still live in today, structured by what W. E. B.

Du Bois identified as "the problem of the color line, the question as to how far differences of race... will hereafter be made the basis of denying to over half the world the right of sharing to their utmost ability the opportunities and privileges of modern civilization."[2]

Historians interested in studying phenomena extending beyond the boundaries of the nation-state now have at least three options. The oldest is *international history*, which looks at contacts among nation-states, especially through diplomacy and war. Somewhat more recent is *global history*, which seeks to discern processes affecting people in every nation, including environmental change, technological innovations, and even cultural and intellectual transformations. The most recent is transnational history. This looks at processes on many different scales, some confined to nations, some specific only to subnational groups like classes or races, some broadly global, and some narrowly regional. Transnational history does not operate in a predefined geography, as national and global history do, but rather follows its subjects wherever they may go. It is impossible to research any one of these types of history in isolation from the other two. Nonetheless, this essay on Reconstruction will take a more transnational approach. Its losses in geographic and temporal boundedness will be recouped, I hope, by new approaches to U.S. history that it opens.

Viewing Reconstruction as a contested set of global political and economic processes dissolves many of the boundaries that commonly define Reconstruction as a twelve-year period in the history of the U.S. South. The final withdrawal of federal troops from the former Confederacy in 1877, the moment commonly deemed the end of Reconstruction, marked a major shift, but by no means brought to a halt, the contest over capitalism, democracy, and racial hierarchies in the United States or around the world. We might also trace the search for a post-slavery capitalist world order as far back as the founding of Liberia in 1822 as a place to settle manumitted U.S. slaves. Popular struggles against slavery and other forms of political and economic domination emerged even earlier in Europe, Africa, and the Americas. Historians Peter Linebaugh and Marcus Rediker have characterized this broad set of movements as a "many-sided struggle against confinement—on ships, in workshops, in prisons, or even in empires—and the simultaneous search for autonomy."[3] Studying the end of slavery as a component of this broader set of popular struggles challenges conventional approaches to labor history that take free white craft and wage workers as the norm and cast enslaved black workers or indentured Asian workers as challenges to, rather than as participant in their own right in, working-class politics. At issue in global Reconstruction was not only the existence of slavery but also the meaning of freedom in a world in which a broadly defined democracy stood against dominant plans for economic development.

Reconstruction, viewed transnationally, was thus not only an incomplete transition to freedom in the United States, what Eric Foner called "America's unfinished revolution," but also a deep conflict about what freedom would mean regionally, nationally, and globally.[4] Many groups, above all the formerly enslaved, had far different visions from economic and political elites of what economic, social, and political order might follow the destruction of slave society. At every turn, they contested racial stratification and the concentration of production in hierarchical plantations and firms dominated by the wealthy. Many slaves in the United States fought for a type of freedom for which slaves elsewhere in the Americas and also many formally free workers struggled: economic independence and personal autonomy.[5] The enslaved of the Americas, whether in Haiti, Santo Domingo, Jamaica, Cuba, Brazil, or the United States, sought this independence not simply in legal freedom but also in independent smallhold farms, sometimes carved out of the plantations of their erstwhile masters.[6] Many whites in the United States similarly pursued homesteads as an escape from wage dependency.[7] A variety of socialisms popular in Europe and the United States similarly promised ways of organizing production on an individual or a cooperative basis that would free workers from the dependency of wage labor.[8] In the antebellum period, the division of the U.S. working class between free white workers and enslaved black workers masked these common aspirations, which extended back to popular democratic Atlantic traditions. Reconstruction would begin to reawaken them.

Former slaves and former slaveholders had struggled over the meaning of emancipation in other parts of the Americas well before Civil War broke out in the United States. The movement of freedpeople in the Americas toward autonomous farming prompted plantation owners to devise methods of compelling them to perform for wages the work they had performed as slaves. Historians have produced a rich comparative picture of these coercive postemancipation labor regimes.[9] Perhaps the paradigmatic example was the short-lived "apprenticeship system" applied in the British West Indies after the passage of the British Emancipation Act in 1833. The act bound former slaves as "apprentices" to their former masters for a period of four to six years. These ex-slaves had worked for years on the plantations to which they were apprenticed, and the function of the act was not to train them in any particular skill but rather to continue coercion after slavery. A combination of labor actions by former slaves in the West Indies and sympathetic protests by abolitionists in Britain brought the apprenticeship system to an end in 1838.[10] For governments considering how to manage abolition, as well as for historians studying this process, the British apprenticeship system has remained a paradigm.[11]

Emancipation did not occur against a static political and economic background, and former slaves were just one group that had to work out its fate in the face of an increasingly all-encompassing system of capitalist production. Capitalist production rests on a separation between those who own the means of production, like factories and farmland, and those who, because they do not own the means of production, even to provide for their own subsistence, must work for these owners.[12] This system was new enough in the mid-nineteenth century that historian Eric Hobsbawm has dubbed the period the "age of capital" and noted that even the word *capitalism* only came into regular use in the 1860s.[13] At the beginning of the nineteenth century, in both Europe and the United States, manufacturing occurred on such a small scale that many white workers could aspire to own their own shops, making the compulsion to work for wages only a passing phase in the life of an individual. The growth of the scale of industry meant that the dream of economic independence remained unattainable for nearly all workers, who now faced the prospect of a lifetime of labor under the supervision of an employer.[14] This process of proletarianization concerned many groups, from workers dismayed by their declining independence to elites repulsed by urban squalor and political radicalization. A wealth of comparative work puts the American Civil War and Reconstruction in the center of this widespread political-economic reorientation.[15]

The racial self-conceptions of many white workers and the most basic political ideas of the United States depended on denying an increasingly obvious similarity—but not identity—between proletarianized and enslaved workers.[16] Well before the wage system compelled free workers to serve employers, enslaved individuals had been compelled to work for owners of the means of production. For this reason, many historians consider plantation slavery, at least in the nineteenth century, to be a form of capitalism. The highly organized labor of the plantation preceded and even prefigured the highly organized labor of the modern factory.[17] President Abraham Lincoln, in his first annual message to Congress, acknowledged the problematic similarity of slavery and wage labor when he rejected the view that economic conditions meant that most Americans would have to become "either hired laborers, or what we call slaves."[18] The diminishing prospects of economic independence for the majority in an expanding capitalist economy concerned not only those directly affected by proletarianization but those who praised the independent yeoman farmer and craftsman as the foundation of a republican social order. The perceived similarities of wage, or "hireling," labor and slave labor also threatened racial distinctions between white and black workers. Many working-class whites responded to this perceived threat to their racial status with antiblack racism. Some historians have also detected white working-class identification with their enslaved black counterparts.[19]

A common struggle against slavery in the United States temporarily united groups with fundamentally opposed views of wage labor. Many of the European immigrants who joined the fight against slavery in the decade before the Civil War were political refugees who had responded to the declining independence of craft workers by flocking to the growing communist and socialist movements and taking part in unsuccessful revolutions of 1848-1849.[20] They would become important leaders and rank-and-file members of the Union army and of the radical labor movement, thus intertwining the European with the U.S. response to capitalism.[21] Many blacks looked to longer Atlantic traditions of economic self-sufficiency and autonomy. Against these two traditions, many elite opponents of slavery came to praise wage labor, that is, work for an employer expected to exercise control and management, as an alternate to slavery. In doing so, they rejected the older connection of slave and wage labor as dependent labor. This was in part a defense against proponents of slavery who pointed to the miserable condition of northern wage workers to argue that slavery was a more humane form of dependency.[22] Many abolitionists in the United States thus made an argument that would have great consequences not only for Reconstruction and the lives of freedpeople, but for all American workers: they argued that wage labor, rather threatening individual freedom, was in fact was basic to human freedom.[23] In doing so, some may have intended only to condemn slavery in the age of capitalism, but they also threatened many other visions of economic freedom that might have been more beneficial to black and white workers alike.[24]

It was the anti-wage-labor branch of antislavery that informed what was perhaps the first great account of this period, *Black Reconstruction* (1935), by the African American historian W. E. B. Du Bois.[25] For Du Bois, emancipation began with a "general strike" of enslaved "black workers" against their own bondage. He recounted how, with the approach of Union soldiers, thousands of slaves brought about their own emancipation by ceasing to work for slaveholders, fleeing their plantations to Union lines, and eventually taking up arms against slavery in the United States Colored Troops. He thus challenged common presentations of emancipation as something granted to slaves from above by the federal government. Few historians today would deny that state policy played an important role in emancipation, but most have also accepted some version of what scholars now call the self-emancipation thesis put forward by Du Bois. Du Bois characterized emancipation as a type of political action with which readers in the militant days of the labor movement in the 1930s would have been familiar: the general strike. Du Bois would join the Communist Party of the United States later in his life, but already in the 1930s he, like many, saw Marxism and Communism as welcome allies in the long struggle against racism in the United States and imperialism abroad. If he perhaps spoke too enthusiastically when he called Reconstruction "one of the most extraordinary experiments of Marxism that the world, before the Russian revolution, had seen," his assessment does reflect what was at stake for many in the overthrow of slavery in the United States.[26] By placing emancipation in the context of the labor movement, Du Bois inserted it in a broader democratic struggle of workers, white and black, enslaved and free. Indeed, the radical labor context from which Du Bois wrote *Black Reconstruction* was itself one of the outcomes of the multiracial labor movement that had lain dormant in the antebellum United States and that had been reawakened in the Civil War.

The sharecropping system that emerged in much of the South after the Civil War, though not entirely original to the United States, became an influential model around the world. Even with all its obviously oppressive features, it represented a kind of compromise between the demands of planters for gangs of wage workers and the demands of freedpeople for the economic independence of small landholdings. In this system, plantations were divided into small farms, much as freedpeople had demanded. Farmers were not, however, granted title to this land, which remained the property of former masters. Sharecroppers were thus subjected to a rental agreement that did not simply take a share of the yearly produce but subjected growers to highly coercive systematic management and extraordinary economic exploitation.[27] Agrarian capitalists from eastern Germany to colonial Africa gradually embraced this combination of landlord supervision with family farming, for it gave a sense of autonomy to farmers, prevented the proletarianization that many feared would lead to more radical politics, and still rendered agricultural surpluses to landlords. In some cases southern sharecropping was an explicit model for foreign economic thinkers and policy makers.[28]

For all the limitations of the freedom won by the enslaved in the postwar U.S. South, Du Bois's example of the massive worker uprising that led to emancipation also offered encouragement and inspiration to predominantly white labor movements in the United States and in Europe. Socialists and other labor radicals around the world had paid close attention to the progress of the American Civil War, concerned as they were with the fate of one of the world's only democratic republics; interested in the war against slaveholders as a kind of proxy battle against their own aristocracy; and opposed to slavery as a grievous injury to workers, both enslaved and free. Karl Marx and Friedrich Engels, living in exile in London, followed the Civil War closely and wrote extensively about the American conflict.[29] Many of their socialist comrades, having been forced into exile in the United States, participated in the Civil War on the side of the Union. Organized workers also arguably kept Britain from intervening to support the Confederacy, and no other European power would have dared offer support to secession on its own.[30] This working-class intervention in British foreign policy, as well as the victories of the Union against Confederate slaveholders, gave working-class radicals in Europe new confidence. In 1864 they founded the International Working Men's Association, with Karl Marx as its intellectual leader.[31] Today known as the First International, the organization brought together British trade unionists with the many radical workers already living in exile in London. Its purpose was to help coordinate the activities of socialist, anarchist, and trade unionist movements in Europe and the United States. Marx's most thorough analysis of capitalism, *Capital* (1867), contained numerous references to the American Civil War. Its preface also declared that the American conflict had "sounded the alarm bell" for the "European working class."[32] Emancipation in the United States gave hope to many that other forms of exploitative labor, including wage labor, might also be abolished. As Marx offered in his inaugural address to the First International, "Like slave labour, like serf labour, hired labour is but a transitory and inferior form, destined to disappear before associated labour plying its toil with a willing hand, a ready mind, and a joyous heart."[33]

The postwar U.S. labor movement, and especially the movement for the legal limitation of the working day to eight hours without a corresponding decrease in wages, also inspired European socialists and trade unionists. As historian David Montgomery has emphasized, the war to end slavery gave way to a U.S. labor movement that, on the one hand, continued the struggle against inequality that antislavery had begun, but on the other hand, challenged the support for wage labor that prevailed in Reconstruction policy.[34] White workers in the United States continued to express many of their class anxieties in racist terms and often remained violently hostile to black competitors, but an ideal of interracial class solidarity emerged from the war that, according to historian David Roediger, had not existed in the antebellum period.[35] Many advocated the eight-hour day in order to limit the control of employers over the entire waking lives of their employees, much as slaveholders had claimed control over the entire lives of their human chattel. The eight-hours movement achieved some victories in state law and a national victory in 1868 when Congress granted the eight-hour day to all federal employees.

Yet, while the Civil War, emancipation, and the postwar U.S. labor movement inspired Marx and other European working-class and socialist revolutionaries, no mass socialist party emerged in the United States to match those in Europe. A National Labor Union (NLU), founded in 1866, became a political labor party, the National Labor Reform Party, but it collapsed in the 1870s. In Europe, meanwhile, workers and their political allies founded labor and socialist parties in the 1870s and 1880s, slightly later but also with much greater longevity than the NLU.[36] There were chapters of the First International inside the United States, but conflicts between working-class and often foreign-born revolutionaries on the one hand, and middle-class reformers for whom socialist politics had less appeal on the other, hindered their success.³⁷ In 1906, the German sociologist Werner Sombart posed one of the longest-standing puzzles of comparative history: Why is there no socialism in the United States?³⁸ Though this question has prompted important research, it is also, as Eric Foner has argued, somewhat misleading, because there has in fact been a great deal of resistance to the power of the bourgeoisie in the United States, even if this has rarely employed the rhetoric of socialism or taken the form of a labor party.³⁹ Still, U.S. emancipation perhaps had a greater influence in international socialist and labor movements than it did in the U.S. labor movement itself.

If the Civil War seemed in retrospect to have been a bourgeois revolution, it was because of the partial victory of liberals in defining the postwar U.S. political scene, not because of anything inherent in the end of slavery itself. If many workers and their political leaders considered the eight-hour movement, other legal protections for workers, and the growing international union and socialist movements as fruits of the northern victory, many bourgeois, including erstwhile radicals, considered the labor movement as a threat to the economic freedom for which they thought the war had been fought.⁴⁰ The United States thus experienced what European historians refer to as a "split of proletarian and bourgeois democracy," one that typically emerged on the continent earlier in the nineteenth century.⁴¹ Their opposed positions on the legally mandated eight-hour day illustrate the incompatibility between bourgeois-liberal and working-class attitudes toward the legacy of the Civil War and toward democracy more broadly. Workers and their political allies argued that limitations to the working day continued the process of emancipation by helping to free wage laborers from the domination by their employers. Liberals, by contrast, interpreted emancipation as a blow against outside interference over individual economic freedom. They thus rejected attempts by the state to regulate the hours of labor or virtually any other aspect of private business, whether through legislation or through collective bargaining, as a continuation of an economic slavery. It was a great victory for these liberals when the Fourteenth Amendment, designed originally to protect the individual rights of former slaves against political persecution, came to protect the supposed rights of corporations, defined legally as individuals, from much legal regulation.[42]

Liberalism was the bourgeois counterpart of the trade unionism, socialism, and anarchism that emerged as working-class ideologies in the United States and internationally. The Liberal Republican Party, whose candidate, Horace Greeley, unsuccessfully challenged Ulysses S. Grant's reelection in 1872, represented many of the attitudes of U.S. liberals, but liberalism as a political orientation was also much broader and long lasting than this short-lived party. While contemporary U.S. parlance uses liberalism and leftism synonymously, no nineteenth-century thinker would have confused the two. U.S. liberals, like their European counterparts, considered themselves as upright men of property and as bulwarks against what they perceived as mob rule. Divided responses to the 1871 Paris Commune, a short-lived revolutionary socialist government suppressed violently by the French state, revealed the split of working-class and bourgeois conceptions of democracy in the United States. The Left in the United States feted the Commune in parades and in the press while liberals condemned it as an example of the worst excesses of the mob.[43] Many bourgeois elites in the United States also came to look with the same disdain upon the demands of freedpeople in the South for state protection of their freedom as they did on demands of workers in the North for an eight-hour day and other legal safeguards.[44] European scholars have long looked critically at this elitist form of liberalism whose promises of rights and equality excluded— some would even say depended on excluding—those defined as inferior, often because of their class, race, gender, or all three.[45] This was a liberalism that enthusiastically embraced empire as an opportunity for a supposedly humanitarian elite to impart their universal values on the world.[46] Like their European counterparts, many bourgeois liberals in the United States came to suspect democracy itself, and in New York they even attempted—unsuccessfully in the end—to place property limitations on universal manhood suffrage in city elections.[47]

Whiteness played a role in perhaps every national variant of liberalism, but it played it with particular strength in the United States. Liberalism allowed for a reconciliation between white elites in the North and the South by minimizing emancipation along with a whole range of emancipatory efforts by black and white workers. Historian David W. Blight has analyzed how white elites in the North and the South commemorated the Civil War as a tragic conflict and thereby suggested that black emancipation was secondary or even a mixed blessing.[48] This white bourgeois sectional reconciliation lay at the foundation of an ideology of a so-called New South that presented blacks not as an awkward reminder of a defunct slave system but rather as an especially docile and efficient agricultural working class. Racism, as historians beginning perhaps with C. Vann Woodward have shown, was not simply a holdover from slavery, but was rather a development of practices and ideas of race that emerged globally in the wake of slavery.[49] While the Old South elites had justified slavery with reference to racial hierarchies, elites in the New South and in the Gilded Age North made racial hierarchies themselves political and economic institutions. New systems of labor placed various ethnicities, not only people of African descent but also many other groups defined as nonwhite, in various relations of political and economic subordination.[50] As such the United States, or at least the Jim Crow South, for as much as a century after the Civil War, had the dubious distinction, along with Apartheid South Africa and Nazi Germany, of being a relatively unique racial state. While many, if not all, European states had strong racist currents in their foreign and domestic economics and politics, whites in these three racial states organized political, social, and economic life around white hegemony and the subordination of those deemed racially inferior by the state and by elite classes.[51]

As the earliest of the three racial states, the New South became a model for many Europeans establishing and expanding colonial empires in the late nineteenth century. To support the proposition that white people should rule not only their own countries, but also much of the globe, political thinkers could turn to the critical narrative of Reconstruction that the political scientist John W.

Burgess and the historian William Archibald Dunning crafted at Columbia University. The central tenet of the so-called Dunning School was the proposition that Republicans had erred in allowing African Americans to vote and serve in governments during Reconstruction. To cast doubt on all democratic social change, Dunning even compared Reconstruction to the French Revolution: "The enfranchisement of the freedmen and their enthronement in political power was as reckless a species of statecraft," he explained, as the French Revolution.[52]

John W. Burgess brought such concerns about democracy and race to the fields of political science and international relations when he founded the *Political Science Quarterly* in 1886. In an article that Burgess contributed to the first volume, he warned that legal equality between "the superior race and the inferior"—he specified blacks and Asians as "inferior"—threated the political unity of the state, the very foundation of political science.[53] James Bryce of Oxford University played an especially important role in disseminating Dunning's and Burgess's frankly racist assessments of black political enfranchisement around the world, thereby internationalizing white solidarity against peoples of color, who were seen as potential economic assets as workers but also as political threats to dominant whites.[54] The journal *Foreign Affairs,* today one of the major publications in the United States devoted to the topic, began in 1910 as the *Journal of Race Development.* One of its purposes, as its cofounder George H. Blakeslee explained, was to deal with "the negro problem" in the United States and the similar problems facing European nations colonizing territories of the Pacific Ocean, "inhabited, for the most part, by nations of a more primitive culture than our own."[55] Although it is rarely acknowledged today, the fields of political science and international relations emerged in part from concerns about race and empire prevalent in the United States following Reconstruction.[56]

Such concerns about race and empire also shaped global economic practices, much as they had influenced imperial and international policy. Through the nineteenth century, the large-scale plantation spread from the Americas, where it had been a central component of slave economies, to much of the tropic world; there it became a central component of colonial economies.[57] While these new plantations employed mostly wage labor, they continued to subject their workers, whom they often defined as racially inferior to whites, to high levels of coercion and paid them poorly. Contract laborers from China and India, commonly called coolies, became one of the most important new plantation labor forces in the age of emancipation. Although Americans tend to identify coolies from China for their work beginning in the 1840s in California, they also worked in the United States on sugar plantations, much as they did in the rest of the world, from Cuba to Samoa. Contracts bound coolies to work far from home for a set number of years. There was a great deal of deception in the contracts and great privations awaited those workers who signed them. Historian Moon-Ho Jung has studied Chinese coolies who worked in the sugar plantations of Reconstruction Louisiana. Abolitionists had long decried coolie labor as a form of slavery, and supporters of the Chinese Exclusion Act of 1881 equated the measure to earlier prohibitions on the slave trade. At the same time, images of servile Asians helped shore up racial concepts of whiteness in the era of emancipation and wage labor. Even dependent white wage workers seemed free in comparison to servile Asians, while blacks were easily condemned as insolent and unruly when compared to hardworking, docile Asians in this early use of the "model minority" argument.[58]

The global expansion of plantation and other large-scale forms of agriculture also transformed the production and consumption of food staples and raw materials. Both the general expansion of the textile industry and a desire to break the United States's near monopoly of industrial-grade cotton production prompted a global expansion of cotton growing. Many of these new cotton efforts followed the example of the New South in its coercive treatment of formally free growers.[59] The ongoing growth of industrial production also led to a search for global sources for other commodities, including tropical rubber, West African palm oil (which had a range of industrial uses), and even foodstuffs common today like pineapples and bananas.⁶⁰ The globalization of agricultural production not only brought new supplies of foods and raw materials to powerful nations but also took these goods from less powerful nations. The expansion of Russian and especially U.S. wheat production challenged Central European agriculture to such an extent that it helped spark the international Panic of 1873.⁶¹ The globalization of agricultural production could also have tragic consequences for exporting nations. Scholar Mike Davis has discerned what he calls "late Victorian holocausts" when global traders exported food from areas already suffering from widespread famine, causing millions of deaths in Brazil, India, and elsewhere.⁶²

The end of slavery in the Americas, including in the United States, played an important role in the so-called Scramble for Africa, when European powers established colonial states over most of the continent between 1884 and 1914.⁶³ Africa became the main theater of what historians describe as a new imperialism beginning in the later nineteenth century, a resumption of formal colonial expansion after the loss of the European slave-labor empires founded in the Americas after the sixteenth century. Antislavery, in fact, had played a central role in the colonial conquest of Africa even before the new imperialism. Britain had established Sierra Leone in 1787 to settle manumitted slaves and, after Britain outlawed the slave trade in 1807, so-called recaptives, that is, Africans freed by the British navy from illegal slavers. In 1822, the American Colonization Society (ACS) followed the British example in founding Liberia as a settlement for slaves manumitted in the United States. The members of the ACS acted out of a range of motives, from genuine opposition to slavery to a desire to expel free blacks from the United States. Most black abolitionists and many white abolitionists opposed colonization because they believed it was motivated by racism and by a desire to protect the institution of slavery from the influence of free blacks opposed to human bondage.⁶⁴

Still, some African Americans did detect emancipatory possibilities in Africa that went beyond, or even directly opposed, white domination and exploitation. In 1859, the African American abolitionist Martin Delany traveled to Abeokuta, in present-day Nigeria, to establish African American cotton farms that would compete with, and he hoped undermine, the cotton-producing slave plantations in the United States.[65] Nothing came of this scheme, but the interesting mix of Pan-African solidarity, antislavery, and the prevalent assumption that African Americans could "improve" Africans reveals an interesting mix of colonialism and antislavery. Such missions of African Americans to Africa continued throughout the periods of Reconstruction and the New South and beyond.[66] After the Civil War, African intellectuals also looked to the postslavery American South, even with all the obvious shortcomings of black life there, as a model of black self-help, in which people of African descent made their own political and economic fortunes without waiting for whites to overcome their own racism. Though the conservative African American educator and principal of Tuskegee Institute, Booker T. Washington, often supported European colonial efforts in Africa, many anticolonial Africans admired him. These included E. W. Blyden of Liberia, J. E. Casely Hayford of Gold Coast, and John Dube of South Africa.[67] The Jamaican black nationalist Marcus Garvey had a similarly high opinion of Tuskegee Institute.[68]

The U.S. federal government also played a direct role in the new imperialism, especially in the Caribbean and the Pacific.[69] In the first wave of imperialism, the British had founded, among other colonies, those in North America that would become the United States. Imperial expansion in North America continued apace after the Civil War. The United States employed its army, which had grown massively during the Civil War, in a new wave of conquest of autonomous Native American nations. Some Native American societies, including the so-called Five Civilized Tribes, held slaves, and emancipation and birthright citizenship became one of the means by which the United States diminished Indian sovereignty. Historian Claudio Saunt has highlighted how difficult it is to draw easy moral or political lessons from this reconfiguration of politics and economics in westward expansion.[70] Concerns about race, emancipation, and citizenship also shaped U.S. overseas expansion. Often, as historian Eric T. Love has argued, certain forms of antiracism could motivate imperialism as much as forms of racism did.[71] Thus, in his finally unsuccessful efforts to annex Santo Domingo (today the Dominican Republic) to the United States, President Ulysses S. Grant hoped, as he wrote privately, that the island might serve as a refuge for African Americans suffering gross economic, political, and personal oppression. He also speculated that the threat of African American workers relocating to the Caribbean island might prompt whites to improve their own behavior. Grant, however, could not make this claim publically, because many whites were loath to do anything for African Americans or to expand the United States to include more people of color. The Grant administration negotiated a treaty to annex Santo Domingo in 1870 but the Senate refused to ratify it. Questions about race, emancipation, and the value and purpose of overseas expansion also played important roles in the U.S. occupation of Cuba, Puerto Rico, and the Philippines after the Spanish-American War of 1898 and the gradual acquisition of Hawaii as a U.S. territory in 1900.[72] The decades-long process of locating and building a canal to connect the Caribbean to the Pacific, culminating in the opening of the Panama Canal in 1914, included similar complex entanglements of race, labor, and empire.[73]

Historians incur obvious costs and gain obvious benefits from taking a transnational perspective on Reconstruction. The most obvious cost is that its defining boundaries, like those of nations viewed from outer space, disappear. The transnational history of Reconstruction extends beyond the geographical borders of the United States and outside the temporal limits of 1865-1877. Indeed, this essay will appear both in this volume devoted to Reconstruction and in another dedicated to the New South. The political movements of the Reconstruction Era of the United States blend into long histories of African and African American antislavery; European and Euro-American opposition to wage labor; postemancipation plantation labor regimes; bourgeois liberalism; and overseas colonization. Yet this very breakdown of national distinctions is also an advantage. Without gainsaying the reality of boundaries of nations and even historical periods, these boundaries are porous, and what crosses them is often as important and interesting as what they keep in and keep out.

Those conducting original transnational historical research on Reconstruction, the New South, or any other period would do well to focus on a few, or even just one, of these border crossers, whether individuals, social groups, or commodities.[74] The goal is not to narrow the transnational to a single perspective, but rather to expand the single perspective to the transnational. This will in no way obviate the need for traditionally bounded national and regional studies—indeed, students pursuing transnational history will find themselves all the more grateful for national and regional studies. But transnational history will also provide new insights into traditionally bounded topics, including Reconstruction and the New South.

Notes

1. For an exemplary international treatment of Reconstruction, see Mark Smith, "The Past as a Foreign Country: Reconstruction, Inside and Out," in *Reconstructions: New Perspectives on the Postbellum United States,* ed. Thomas J. Brown (New York: Oxford Univ. Press, 2006), 117-40.

2. Alexander Walters, Henry B. Brown, H. Sylvester Williams, and W. E. B. Du Bois, "To the Nations of the World" (1900), in *An ABC of Color: Selections Chosen by the Author from Over a Half Century of His Writings,* by W. E. B. Du Bois (New York: International Publishers, 1969), 20. On race as a component of capitalism, see esp. Cedric J. Robinson, *Black Marxism: The Making of the Black Radical Tradition,* 2nd ed. (Chapel Hill: Univ. of North Carolina Press, 2000); and David R. Roediger and Elizabeth D. Esch, *The Production of Difference: Race and the Management of Labor in U.S. History* (New York: Oxford Univ. Press, 2012).

3. Peter Linebaugh and Marcus Rediker, "The Many-Headed Hydra: Sailors, Slaves, and the Atlantic Working Class in the Eighteenth Century," *Journal of Historical Sociology* 3 (Sept. 1990): 225-52, 244. See also their magisterial *The Many-Headed Hydra: Sailors, Slaves, Commoners, and the Hidden History of the Revolutionary Atlantic* (London: Verso Books, 2002). The work on popular and working-class revolutionary traditions in the Atlantic world is too rich to cover in a single endnote. One place to start is work on the Haitian Revolu-

tion, from C. L. R. James, *The Black Jacobins: Toussaint L'Ouverture and the San Domingo Revolution*, (1938; 2nd rev. ed., New York: Vintage, 1963), to Laurent Dubois, *Avengers of the New World: The Story of the Haitian Revolution* (Cambridge, Mass.: Harvard Univ. Press, 2004). Another place to begin the study of popular politics in the Atlantic world is the literature on Africans in the Americas, perhaps especially J. Lorand Matory, *Black Atlantic Religion: Tradition, Transnationalism, and Matriarchy in the Afro-Brazilian Candomblé* (Princeton, N.J.: Princeton Univ. Press, 2005); Stephan Palmié, *Wizards and Scientists: Explorations in Afro-Cuban Modernity and Tradition* (Durham, N.C.: Duke Univ. Press, 2002); and John Thornton, *Africa and Africans in the Making of the Atlantic World, 1400-1800*, 2nd ed. (New York: Cambridge Univ. Press, 1998).

4. Eric Foner, *Reconstruction: America's Unfinished Revolution, 1863-1877* (New York: Harper and Row, 1988).

5. Barbara Jeanne Fields, *Slavery and Freedom on the Middle Ground: Maryland during the Nineteenth Century* (New Haven, Conn.: Yale Univ. Press, 1985); Julie Saville, *The Work of Reconstruction: From Slave to Wage Laborer in South Carolina, 1860-1870* (New York: Cambridge Univ. Press, 1994); Amy Dru Stanley, *From Bondage to Contract: Wage Labor, Marriage, and the Market in the Age of Slave Emancipation* (New York: Cambridge Univ. Press, 1998).

6. Carolyn Fick, "Emancipation in Haiti: From Plantation Labour to Peasant Proprietorship," *Slavery & Abolition* 21 (Aug. 2000): 11-40; Eric Foner, *Nothing but Freedom: Emancipation and Its Legacy* (Baton Rouge: Louisiana State Univ. Press, 1983); Thomas C. Holt, *The Problem of Freedom: Race, Labor, and Politics in Jamaica and Britain, 1832-1938* (Baltimore: Johns Hopkins Univ. Press, 1992); Stuart B. Schwartz, *Slaves, Peasants, and Rebels: Reconsidering Brazilian Slavery* (Urbana: Univ. of Illinois Press, 1992), esp. chapter 4, "Rethinking Palmares: Slave Resistance in Colonial Brazil," 103-36.

7. Eric Foner, *Free Soil, Free Labor, Free Men: The Ideology of the Republican Party before the Civil War* (New York: Oxford Univ. Press, 1970).

8. For a good introduction to utopian socialisms in the United States, see Daniel Walker Howe, "Pursuing the Millennium," in his *What Hath God Wrought: The Transformation of America, 1815-1848* (New York: Oxford Univ. Press, 2007), 285-327. For a challenging and inspiring approach to artisan socialism in France, see Jacques Rancière, *The Nights of Labor: The Workers' Dream in Nineteenth-Century France* (Philadelphia: Temple Univ. Press, 1989).

9. An excellent introduction to this work is Frederick Cooper, Thomas C. Holt, and Rebecca J. Scott, *Beyond Slavery: Explorations of Race, Labor, and Citizenship* (Chapel Hill: Univ. of North Carolina Press, 2000).

10. Holt, *Problem of Freedom*. See also the essays collected in Mary Turner, ed., *From Chattel Slaves to Wage Slaves: The Dynamics of Labour Bargaining in the Americas* (Bloomington: Indiana Univ. Press, 1995).

11. Seymour Drescher, *The Mighty Experiment: Free Labor vs. Slavery in British Emancipation* (New York: Oxford Univ. Press, 2002). On the influence of

this experiment, and of British abolition more broadly, on U.S. abolition, see Edward Bartlett Rugemer, *The Problem of Emancipation: The Caribbean Roots of the American Civil War* (Baton Rouge: Louisiana State Univ. Press, 2008).

12. The common definition of capitalism as a "market economy" is misleading, since markets are not particular to capitalism or any other system. The nineteenth-century "market revolution" identified by historian Charles Sellers was, as Sellers notes, a consequence of a more fundamental transformation in the way people produced goods in a class society that compelled most people to work for owners of the means of production. See Sellers, *The Market Revolution: Jacksonian America, 1815-1846* (New York: Oxford Univ. Press, 1991).

13. Eric J. Hobsbawm, *The Age of Capital: 1848-1875* (1975; repr., New York: Vintage, 1996), 1.

14. Alfred D. Chandler, *The Visible Hand: The Managerial Revolution in American Business* (Cambridge, Mass.: Harvard Univ. Press, 1977); Sean Wilentz, *Chants Democratic: New York City and the Rise of the American Working Class, 1788-1850* (New York: Oxford Univ. Press, 1984). The southern case was made more complicated by the fact that many in manufacturing were enslaved. For an important study of free white immigrant and enslaved southern urban workers, see Ira Berlin and Herbert G. Gutman, "Natives and Immigrants, Free Men and Slaves: Urban Workingmen in the Antebellum American South," *American Historical Review* 88 (Dec. 1983): 1175-1200. Robert J. Steinfeld has shown how a variety of legal sanctions around the world compelled ostensibly free workers to obey their employers as paternal authorities in a household rather than as partners in a free contract. See Steinfeld, *The Invention of Free Labor: The Employment Relation in English and American Law and Culture, 1350-1870* (Chapel Hill: Univ. of North Carolina Press, 1991), and Steinfeld, *Coercion, Contract, and Free Labor in the Nineteenth Century* (New York: Cambridge Univ. Press, 2001). For the colonial context, see Paul Craven and Douglas Hay, eds., *Masters, Servants, and Magistrates in Britain and the Empire, 1562-1955* (Chapel Hill: Univ. of North Carolina Press, 2004).

15. The greatest comparative study placing the Civil War in the context of bourgeois revolutions and the transition to capitalism remains perhaps Barrington Moore, *Social Origins of Dictatorship and Democracy: Lord and Peasant in the Making of the Modern World* (1966; repr., Boston: Beacon Press, 1993).

16. For a related argument, see John Ashworth, "Towards a Bourgeois Revolution? Explaining the American Civil War," *Historical Materialism* 19, no. 4 (2011): 193-205. This condenses aspects of John Ashworth, *Slavery, Capitalism, and Politics in the Antebellum Republic,* 2 vols. (New York: Cambridge Univ. Press, 1995, 2007).

17. One of the most important works making this case is Sidney W. Mintz, *Sweetness and Power: The Place of Sugar in Modern History* (New York: Viking, 1985). More recently, scholars have begun developing a notion of an especially advanced capitalist "second slavery" in Cuba, Brazil, and the

Mississippi Valley. For a good introduction, see Anthony E. Kaye, "The Second Slavery: Modernity in the Nineteenth-Century South and the Atlantic World," *Journal of Southern History* 75 (Aug. 2009): 627-50. The literature on comparative slavery and emancipation is vast. A good place to start is Enrico Dal Lago, *American Slavery, Atlantic Slavery, and Beyond: The U.S. "Peculiar Institution" in International Perspective* (Boulder, Colo.: Paradigm Publishers, 2012). Also important is Peter Kolchin, *A Sphinx on the American Land: The Nineteenth-Century South in Comparative Perspective* (Baton Rouge: Louisiana State Univ. Press, 2003). Most recently, see Walter Johnson, *River of Dark Dreams: Slavery and Empire in the Cotton Kingdom* (Cambridge, Mass.: Harvard Univ. Press, 2013), and Edward E. Baptist, *The Half Has Never Been Told: Slavery and the Making of American Capitalism* (New York: Basic Books, 2014). The journal *Slavery & Abolition* (1980-) remains indispensable.

18. Abraham Lincoln, "Annual Message to Congress," December 3, 1861, in *The Collected Works of Abraham Lincoln*, ed. Roy P. Basler, 8 vols. (New Brunswick, N.J.: Rutgers Univ. Press, 1953), 5: 35-53.

19. Noel Ignatiev, *How the Irish Became White* (1995; repr., New York: Routledge, 2009); Eric Lott, *Love and Theft: Blackface Minstrelsy and the American Working Class* (New York: Oxford Univ. Press, 1993); David R. Roediger, *The Wages of Whiteness: Race and the Making of the American Working Class* (1991; rev. ed., New York: Verso, 1999); Alexander Saxton, *The Rise and Fall of the White Republic: Class Politics and Mass Culture in Nineteenth-Century America* (London: Verso, 2003). For an important critique of the field of whiteness studies, see Eric Arnesen, "Whiteness and the Historians' Imagination," *International Labor and Working-Class History* 60 (2001): 3-32.

20. The greatest study of the European labor movement remains E. P. Thompson, *The Making of the English Working Class* (1964; repr., New York: Vintage, 1966), even if scholars have continued to develop and apply Thompson's insights. For an important study revealing how foundational gender was to class formation, see Anna Clark, *The Struggle for the Breeches: Gender and the Making of the British Working Class* (Berkeley: Univ. of California Press, 1995).

21. On these '48ers in the Civil War, see Alison Clark Efford, *German Immigrants, Race, and Citizenship in the Civil War Era* (New York: Cambridge Univ. Press, 2013); Mischa Honeck, *We Are the Revolutionists: German-Speaking Immigrants and American Abolitionists after 1848* (Athens: Univ. of Georgia Press, 2011); Bruce Levine, *The Spirit of 1848: German Immigrants, Labor Conflict, and the Coming of the Civil War* (Urbana: Univ. of Illinois Press, 1992); Martin W. Öfele, *German-Speaking Officers in the United States Colored Troops, 1863-1867* (Gainesville: Univ. Press of Florida, 2004); Martin W. Öfele, *True Sons of the Republic: European Immigrants in the Union Army* (Westport, Conn.: Praeger, 2008); Andrew Zimmerman, "From the Rhine to the Mississippi: Property, Democracy, and Socialism in the American Civil War," *Journal of the Civil War Era* 5 (Mar. 2015): 3-37.

22. Elizabeth Fox-Genovese and Eugene D. Genovese, *Slavery in White and Black: Class and Race in the Southern Slaveholders' New World Order* (New York: Cambridge Univ. Press, 2008).

23. Marcus Cunliffe, *Chattel Slavery and Wage Slavery: The Anglo-American Context, 1830-1860* (Athens: Univ. of Georgia Press, 1979); Foner, *Free Soil, Free Labor, Free Men.*

24. Jonathan H. Earle, *Jacksonian Antislavery and the Politics of Free Soil, 1824-1854* (Chapel Hill: Univ. of North Carolina Press, 2004).

25. W. E. B. Du Bois, *Black Reconstruction: An Essay toward a History of the Part Which Black Folk Played in the Attempt to Reconstruct Democracy in America, 1860-1880* (1935; repr., New York: Free Press, 1998).

26. Ibid., 319.

27. On sharecropping, see Barbara Jeanne Fields, "The Advent of Capitalist Agriculture: The New South in a Bourgeois World," in *Essays on the Postbellum Southern Economy*, ed. Thavolia Glymph and John J. Kushma (College Station: Texas A&M Univ. Press, 1985), 73-94; Roger L. Ransom and Richard Sutch, *One Kind of Freedom: The Economic Consequences of Emancipation*, (1977; 2nd rev. ed., New York: Cambridge Univ. Press, 2001); and Gavin Wright, *Old South, New South: Revolutions in the Southern Economy since the Civil War* (New York: Basic Books, 1986).

28. Andrew Zimmerman, *Alabama in Africa: Booker T. Washington, the German Empire, and the Globalization of the New South* (Princeton, N.J.: Princeton Univ. Press, 2010).

29. Andrew Zimmerman, ed., *Marx, Engels, and the Civil War in the United States* (New York: International Publishers, forthcoming in 2016).

30. There has been some debate about the support of British workers for the Union. The consensus is that they did support the Union collectively, although the opinions of individual workers of course varied greatly. See R. J. M. Blackett, *Divided Hearts: Britain and the American Civil War* (Baton Rouge: Louisiana State Univ. Press, 2001).

31. David Fernbach, "Introduction," in *The First International and After*, ed. David Fernbach, in *Marx's Political Writings* (new ed., 1973; London: Verso, 2010), 3:9-71.

32. Karl Marx, *Capital*, vol. 1, trans. Ben Fowkes (1867; New York: Penguin Classics, 1976), 91. Translation modified.

33. Marx, "Inaugural Address of the Working Men's International Association" London, September 28, 1864, in Zimmerman, *Marx, Engels, and the Civil War in the United States,* forthcoming.

34. David Montgomery, *Beyond Equality: Labor and the Radical Republicans, 1862-1872* (1967; repr., Urbana: Univ. of Illinois Press, 1981).

35. Roediger, *Wages of Whiteness.* For an important case study, see Eric Arnesen, *Waterfront Workers of New Orleans: Race, Class, and Politics, 1863-1923*, Illini Books ed. (1991; Urbana: Univ. of Illinois Press, 1994).

36. Geoff Ely, *Forging Democracy: The History of the Left in Europe, 1850-2000* (New York: Oxford Univ. Press, 2002).

37. See Robin Blackburn, *An Unfinished Revolution: Karl Marx and Abraham Lincoln* (London: Verso, 2011). Well researched but finally too condemning of the foreign-born sections of the International to serve as a useful introduction is Timothy Messer-Kruse, *The Yankee International: Marxism and the American Reform Tradition, 1848-1876* (Chapel Hill: Univ. of North Carolina Press, 1998).

38. Werner Sombart, *Warum gibt es in den Vereinigten Staaten keinen Sozialismus?* (Tübingen, Germany: J. C. B. Mohr, 1906).

39. Eric Foner, "Why Is There No Socialism in the United States?" *History Workshop* no. 17 (Spring 1984): 57-80.

40. On this individualistic conception of freedom and the limitations it placed on Reconstruction, see Foner, *Free Soil, Free Labor, Free Men*.

41. Gustav Mayer, "Die Trennung der proletarischen von der bürgerlichen Demokratie in Deutschland 1863-1870," in *Radikalismus, Sozialismus und bürgerliche Demokratie*, ed. Hans Ulrich Wehler (Frankfurt am Main, Federal Republic of Germany: Suhrkamp, 1969), 108-78.

42. Amy Dru Stanley, *From Bondage to Contract: Wage Labor, Marriage, and the Market in the Age of Slave Emancipation* (New York: Cambridge Univ. Press, 1998).

43. Philip M. Katz, *From Appomattox to Montmartre: Americans and the Paris Commune* (Cambridge, Mass.: Harvard Univ. Press, 1998).

44. See Nancy Cohen, *The Reconstruction of American Liberalism, 1865-1914* (Chapel Hill: Univ. of North Carolina Press, 2002); Heather Cox Richardson, *The Death of Reconstruction: Race, Labor, and Politics in the Post-Civil War North, 1865-1901* (Cambridge, Mass.: Harvard Univ. Press, 2001); and John G. Sproat, *"The Best Men": Liberal Reformers in the Gilded Age* (New York: Oxford Univ. Press, 1968). Sproat's view has been challenged by Andrew L. Slap, *The Doom of Reconstruction: The Liberal Republicans in the Civil War Era* (New York: Fordham Univ. Press, 2006). For a similar twentieth-century elitist liberalism, see Brett Gary, *The Nervous Liberals: Propaganda Anxieties from World War I to the Cold War* (New York: Columbia Univ. Press, 1999).

45. For a good overview, which begins with a discussion of South Carolinian John C. Calhoun, see Domenico Losurdo, *Liberalism: A Counter-History*, trans. Gregory Elliott (London: Verso Books, 2011).

46. Nobody has analyzed this attitude for the United States better than William Appleman Williams, *The Tragedy of American Diplomacy* (1959; repr., New York: W. W. Norton, 2009). For the European counterpart, see Uday Singh Mehta, *Liberalism and Empire: A Study in Nineteenth-Century British Liberal Thought* (Chicago: Univ. of Chicago Press, 1999). For an especially sophisticated study connecting liberalism in colony and metropole, see Anne McClintock, *Imperial Leather: Race, Gender, and Sexuality in the Colonial Contest* (New York: Routledge, 1995).

47. Sven Beckert, *The Monied Metropolis: New York City and the Consolidation of the American Bourgeoisie, 1850-1896* (New York: Cambridge Univ. Press, 2001).

48. David W. Blight, *Race and Reunion: The Civil War in American Memory* (Cambridge, Mass.: Harvard Univ. Press, 2001).

49. See C. Vann Woodward, *Origins of the New South, 1877-1913* (1951; Baton Rouge: Louisiana State Univ. Press, 1972), and his *The Strange Career of Jim Crow* (1955; New York: Oxford Univ. Press, 1974). On the historiographical debate following Woodward's work, see John David Smith, *When Did Southern Segregation Begin?* (New York: Bedford/St. Martin's, 2002). See also George M. Fredrickson, *The Black Image in the White Mind: The Debate on Afro-American Character and Destiny, 1817-1914* (New York: Harper and Row, 1971).

50. Roediger and Esch, *Production of Difference*.

51. There has been much interesting comparative work on racisms, and much more needs to be done. See George M. Fredrickson, *White Supremacy: A Comparative Study in American and South African History* (New York: Oxford Univ. Press, 1981); David Theo Goldberg, *The Racial State* (Malden, Mass.: Blackwell Publishers, 2002); and Stanley B. Greenberg, *Race and State in Capitalist Development: Comparative Perspectives* (New Haven, Conn.: Yale Univ. Press, 1980).

52. William Archibald Dunning, "The Process of Reconstruction," in his *Essays on the Civil War and Reconstruction and Related Topics* (New York: Macmillan, 1897), 176-252, 250-251; John David Smith and J. Vincent Lowery, eds., *The Dunning School: Historians, Race, and the Meaning of Reconstruction* (Lexington: Univ. Press of Kentucky, 2013).

53. John W. Burgess, "The American Commonwealth: Changes in Its Relation to the Nation," *Political Science Quarterly* 1 (Mar. 1886): 9-35, 16.

54. Marilyn Lake and Henry Reynolds, *Drawing the Global Colour Line: White Men's Countries and the International Challenge of Racial Equality* (New York: Cambridge Univ. Press, 2008).

55. George H. Blakeslee, "Introduction," *Journal of Race Development* 1 (1910-1911): 1-4; quotation, 2.

56. On race and empire and the birth of the field of international relations, see Robert Vitalis, "The Noble American Science of Imperial Relations and Its Laws of Race Development," *Comparative Studies in Society and History* 52 (Oct. 2010): 909-38, and the essays in David Long and Brian C. Schmidt, eds. *Imperialism and Internationalism in the Discipline of International Relations* (Albany: State Univ. of New York Press, 2005).

57. Philip D. Curtin, *The Rise and Fall of the Plantation Complex: Essays in Atlantic History* (New York: Cambridge Univ. Press, 1990).

58. Moon-Ho Jung, *Coolies and Cane: Race, Labor, and Sugar in the Age of Emancipation* (Baltimore: Johns Hopkins Univ. Press, 2006).

59. Sven Beckert, "Emancipation and Empire: Reconstructing the Worldwide Web of Cotton Production in the Age of the American Civil War," *American Historical Review* 109 (Dec. 2004): 1405-38; Allen Isaacman and Rich-

ard Roberts, eds., *Cotton, Colonialism, and Social History in Sub-Saharan Africa* (Portsmouth, N.H.: Heinemann, 1995); Zimmerman, *Alabama in Africa*.

60. See, for example, Greg Grandin, *Fordlandia: The Rise and Fall of Henry Ford's Forgotten Jungle City* (New York: Metropolitan Books, 2009); Martin Lynn, *Commerce and Economic Change in West Africa: The Palm Oil Trade in the Nineteenth Century* (New York: Cambridge Univ. Press, 1997); Gary Y. Okihiro, *Pineapple Culture: A History of the Tropical and Temperate Zones* (Berkeley: Univ. of California Press, 2009).

61. Scott Reynolds Nelson, *A Nation of Deadbeats: An Uncommon History of America's Financial Disasters* (New York: Alfred A. Knopf, 2012). On U.S. wheat production and exports, see William Cronon, *Nature's Metropolis: Chicago and the Great West* (New York: W. W. Norton, 1991).

62. Mike Davis, *Late Victorian Holocausts: El Niño Famines and the Making of the Third World* (London: Verso, 2001).

63. Kevin Grant, *A Civilised Savagery: Britain and the New Slaveries in Africa, 1884-1926* (New York: Routledge, 2005); Paul E. Lovejoy, *Transformations in Slavery: A History of Slavery in Africa*, 2nd ed. (New York: Cambridge Univ. Press, 2000).

64. On the American Colonization Society, see Eric Burin, *Slavery and the Peculiar Solution: A History of the American Colonization Society* (Gainesville: Univ. Press of Florida, 2005). On abolitionist opposition to the American Colonization Society, see Paul Goodman, *Of One Blood: Abolitionism and the Origins of Racial Equality* (Berkeley: Univ. of California Press, 1998).

65. See Richard Blackett, "Martin R. Delany and Robert Campbell: Black Americans in Search of an African Colony," *Journal of Negro History* 62 (Jan. 1977): 1-25; James T. Campbell, "Redeeming the Race: Martin Delany and the Niger Valley Exploring Party, 1859-60," *New Formations* 45 (Winter 2001-2002): 125-49.

66. For an especially critical perspective, see Tunde Adeleke, *UnAfrican Americans: Nineteenth-Century Black Nationalists and the Civilizing Mission* (Lexington: Univ. Press of Kentucky, 1998). For a broad history, see James T. Campbell, *Middle Passages: African American Journeys to Africa, 1787-2005* (New York: Penguin, 2006). For more specific studies, see James T. Campbell, *Songs of Zion: The African Methodist Episcopal Church in the United States and South Africa* (New York: Oxford Univ. Press, 1995); Kevin K. Gaines, *Uplifting the Race: Black Leadership, Politics, and Culture in the Twentieth Century* (Chapel Hill: Univ. of North Carolina Press, 1996); and Robert Trent Vinson, *The Americans Are Coming! Dreams of African American Liberation in Segregationist South Africa* (Athens: Ohio Univ. Press, 2012).

67. Imanuel Geiss, *The Pan-African Movement; a History of Pan-Africanism in America, Europe, and Africa* (New York: Africana Publishing, 1974); Zimmerman, *Alabama in Africa*.

68. Judith Stein, *The World of Marcus Garvey: Race and Class in Modern Society* (Baton Rouge: Louisiana State Univ. Press, 1986).

69. For an overview of work on U.S. foreign policy, including imperial policy, at this time, see Jay Sexton, "Toward a Synthesis of Foreign Relations in the Civil War Era, 1848-77," *American Nineteenth Century History* 5 (Fall 2004): 50-73. The classic work remains Williams, *Tragedy of American Diplomacy*. Important recent works include Charles Soutter Campbell, *The Transformation of American Foreign Relations, 1865-1900* (New York: Harper and Row, 1976); Matthew Frye Jacobson, *Barbarian Virtues: The United States Encounters Foreign Peoples at Home and Abroad, 1876-1917* (New York: Hill and Wang, 2000); Jay Sexton, *Debtor Diplomacy: Finance and American Foreign Relations in the Civil War Era, 1837-1873* (Oxford, U.K.: Clarendon, 2005); and Jay Sexton, *The Monroe Doctrine: Empire and Nation in Nineteenth-Century America* (New York: Hill and Wang, 2011).

70. See Claudio Saunt, "The Paradox of Freedom: Tribal Sovereignty and Emancipation during the Reconstruction of Indian Territory," *Journal of Southern History* 70 (Feb. 2004): 63-94. See also Smith, "Past as a Foreign Country," 136-39.

71. Eric T. Love, *Race over Empire: Racism and U.S. Imperialism, 1865-1900* (Chapel Hill: Univ. of North Carolina Press, 2004). See also Amy Kaplan, *The Anarchy of Empire in the Making of U.S. Culture* (Cambridge, Mass.: Harvard Univ. Press, 2002).

72. For an excellent analysis of the complex dynamics of race and empire in the Philippines, see Paul A. Kramer, *The Blood of Government: Race, Empire, the United States, and the Philippines* (Chapel Hill: Univ. of North Carolina Press, 2006). On Santo Domingo, Hawaii, and the Philippines, see Love, *Race over Empire*.

73. Julie Greene, *The Canal Builders: Making America's Empire at the Panama Canal* (New York: Penguin Press, 2009).

74. For an exemplary study of individuals, see James H. Sweet, *Domingos Álvares, African Healing, and the Intellectual History of the Atlantic World* (Chapel Hill: Univ. of North Carolina Press, 2011); of social groups, see Jung, *Coolies and Cane;* of commodities, see the literature cited in notes 59 and 60.

Bibliography

PRIMARY SOURCES

Carter Godwin Woodson Papers, Library of Congress, Washington, D.C.
Howard K. Beale Papers, Wisconsin Historical Society, Madison

SECONDARY SOURCES

Adams, Kevin, and Khal Schneider. "'Washington Is a Long Way Off': The Round Valley War and the Limits of Federal Power on a California Indian Reservation." *Pacific Historical Review* 80 (Dec. 2011): 557-96.
Adeleke, Tunde. *UnAfrican Americans: Nineteenth-Century Black Nationalists and the Civilizing Mission.* Lexington: Univ. Press of Kentucky, 1998.
Allen, James S. (Sol Auerbach). *Reconstruction: The Battle for Democracy, 1865-1876.* New York: International Publishers, 1937.
Anderson, Eric, and Alfred A. Moss Jr., eds. *The Facts of Reconstruction: Essays in Honor of John Hope Franklin.* Baton Rouge: Louisiana State Univ. Press, 1991.
Andrews, E. Benjamin. Review of *Reconstruction, Political and Economic, 1865-1877,* by William A. Dunning. *American Historical Review* 13 (Jan. 1908): 371.
Archer, William. *Through Afro-America: An English Reading of the Race Problem.* New York: E. P. Dutton, 1910.
Arenson, Adam. *The Great Heart of the Republic: St. Louis and the Cultural Civil War.* Cambridge, Mass.: Harvard Univ. Press, 2001.
Arneson, Eric. "Towards a Bourgeois Revolution? Explaining the American Civil War." *Historical Materialism* 19, no. 4 (2011): 193-205.

———. *Waterfront Workers of New Orleans: Race, Class, and Politics, 1863-1923.* Illini Books ed. 1991. Reprint, Urbana: Univ. of Illinois Press, 1994.

———. "Whiteness and the Historians' Imagination." *International Labor and Working-Class History* 60 (2001): 3-32.

Ashworth, John. *Slavery, Capitalism, and Politics in the Antebellum Republic.* 2 vols. New York: Cambridge Univ. Press, 1995, 2007.

Astor, Aaron. *Rebels on the Border: Civil War, Emancipation, and the Reconstruction of Kentucky and Missouri.* Baton Rouge: Louisiana State Univ. Press, 2012.

Ayers, Edward. "The First Occupation." *New York Times Magazine,* May 29, 2005.

Baggett, James Alex. *The Scalawags: Southern Dissenters in the Civil War and Reconstruction.* Baton Rouge: Louisiana State Univ. Press, 2003.

Baker, Bruce. *What Reconstruction Meant: Historical Memory in the American South.* Charlottesville: Univ. of Virginia Press, 2007.

———, and Brian Kelly, eds. *After Slavery: Race, Labor, and Citizenship in the Reconstruction South.* Gainesville: Univ. Press of Florida, 2013.

Baker, Jean. *Affairs of Party: The Political Culture of Northern Democrats in the Mid-Nineteenth Century.* Ithaca, N.Y.: Cornell Univ. Press, 1983.

Balogh, Brian. *A Government Out of Sight: The Mystery of Authority in Nineteenth-Century America.* New York: Cambridge Univ. Press, 2009.

Bardaglio, Peter W. *Reconstructing the Household: Families, Sex, and the Law in the Nineteenth-Century South.* Chapel Hill: Univ. of North Carolina Press, 1995.

Barreyre, Nicolas. "The Politics of Economic Crises: The Panic of 1873, the End of Reconstruction, and the Realignment of American Politics." *Journal of the Gilded Age and Progressive Era* 10 (Oct. 2011): 403-23.

Basler, Roy P., ed. *The Collected Works of Abraham Lincoln,* 8 vols. New Brunswick, N.J.: Rutgers Univ. Press, 1953.

Beale, Howard K. *The Critical Year: A Study of Reconstruction.* New York: Harcourt, Brace, 1930.

———. "On Rewriting Reconstruction History." *American Historical Review* 45 (July 1940): 807-27.

Beckert, Sven. "Emancipation and Empire: Reconstructing the Worldwide Web of Cotton Production in the Age of the American Civil War." *American Historical Review* 109 (Dec. 2004): 1405-38.

———. *The Monied Metropolis: New York City and the Consolidation of the American Bourgeoisie, 1850-1896.* New York: Cambridge Univ. Press, 2001.

Belisary, C. G. "Tennessee and Immigration, 1865-1880." *Tennessee Historical Quarterly* 7 (Sept. 1948): 229-48.

Belz, Herman. "The New Orthodoxy in Reconstruction Historiography." *Reviews in American History* 1 (Mar. 1973): 106-7.

Benedict, Michael Les. *A Compromise of Principle: Congressional Republicans and Reconstruction, 1863-1869*. New York: W. W. Norton, 1974.
———. *The Fruits of Victory: Alternatives in Restoring the Union, 1865-1877*. Lanham, Md.: Univ. Press of America, 1986.
Bennett, Lerone, Jr. *Black Power U.S.A.: The Human Side of Reconstruction, 1867-1877*. New York: Johnson Publishing, 1967.
Bercaw, Nancy. *Gendered Freedoms: Race, Rights, and the Politics of the Household in the Delta, 1861-1875*. Gainesville: Univ. Press of Florida, 2003.
Bergeron, Paul. *Andrew Johnson's Civil War and Reconstruction*. Knoxville: Univ. of Tennessee Press, 2012.
Berlin, Ira, and Herbert G. Gutman. "Natives and Immigrants, Free Men and Slaves: Urban Workingmen in the Antebellum American South." *American Historical Review* 88 (Dec. 1983): 1175-1200.
Berlin, Ira, Joseph P. Reidy, Leslie S. Rowland, and Barbara J. Fields, eds. *Freedom: A Documentary History of Emancipation, 1861-1867*. 6 vols. New York: Cambridge Univ. Press, 1982-2013.
Berthoff, Rowland T. "Southern Attitudes toward Immigration." *Journal of Southern History* 17 (Aug. 1951): 328-60.
Blackburn, Robin. *An Unfinished Revolution: Karl Marx and Abraham Lincoln*. London: Verso, 2011.
Blackett, R. J. M. *Divided Hearts: Britain and the American Civil War*. Baton Rouge: Louisiana State Univ. Press, 2001.
Blackett, Richard. "Martin R. Delany and Robert Campbell: Black Americans in Search of an African Colony." *Journal of Negro History* 62 (Jan. 1977): 1-25.
Blackmon, Douglas A. *Slavery by Another Name: The Re-Enslavement of Black Americans from the Civil War to World War II*. New York: Random House, 2008.
Blaine, James G. *Twenty Years of Congress: From Lincoln to Garfield, with a Review of the Events which led to the Political Revolution of 1860*. 2 vols. Norwich, Conn.: Henry Hill Publishing, 1884, 1893.
Blair, William. *Cities of the Dead: Contesting the Memory of the Civil War in the South, 1865-1914*. Chapel Hill: Univ. of North Carolina Press, 2004.
Blakeslee, George H. "Introduction." *Journal of Race Development* 1 (1910-1911): 1-4.
Blight, David W. *Race and Reunion: The Civil War in American Memory*. Cambridge, Mass.: Harvard Univ. Press, 2001.
Blum, Edward J. *Reforging the White Republic: Race, Religion, and American Nationalism, 1865-1898*. Baton Rouge: Louisiana State Univ. Press, 2005.
———, and W. Scott Poole, eds. *Vale of Tears: New Essays on Religion and Reconstruction*. Macon, Ga.: Mercer Univ. Press, 2005.

Boles, John B., ed. *A Companion to the American South*. Malden, Mass.: Blackwell Publishers, 2002.

———, and Evelyn Thomas Nolen, eds. *Interpreting Southern History: Historiographical Essays in Honor of Sanford W. Higginbotham*. Baton Rouge: Louisiana State Univ. Press, 1987.

Bottoms, D. Michael. *An Aristocracy of Color: Race and Reconstruction in California and the West, 1850-1890*. Norman: Univ. of Oklahoma Press, 2013.

Bowers, Claude. *The Tragic Era: The Revolution after Lincoln*. Cambridge, Mass.: Literary Guild of America, 1929.

Bradley, Mark. *Bluecoats and Tarheels: Soldiers and Civilians in Reconstruction North Carolina*. Lexington: Univ. Press of Kentucky, 2009.

Brands, H. W. *The Man Who Saved the Union: Ulysses Grant in War and Peace*. New York: Doubleday, 2012.

Brandwein, Pamela. "A Judicial Abandonment of Blacks? Rethinking the 'State Action' Cases of the Waite Court." *Law & Society Review* 41 (June 2007): 343-86.

———. *Reconstructing Reconstruction: The Supreme Court and the Production of Historical Truth*. Durham, N.C.: Duke Univ. Press, 1999.

———. *Rethinking the Judicial Settlement of Reconstruction*. Cambridge: Cambridge Univ. Press, 2011.

Brodie, Fawn. *Thaddeus Stevens: Scourge of the South*. New York: W. W. Norton, 1959.

Brown, Thomas J., ed. *Reconstructions: New Perspectives on the Postbellum United States*. New York: Oxford Univ. Press, 2006.

Brown, William Garrott. Review of *History of the United States from the Compromise of 1850 to the Final Restoration of Home Rule in the South in 1877*, by James Ford Rhodes. *American Historical Review* 12 (Apr. 1907): 681-82.

Browning, Judkin. *Shifting Loyalties: The Union Occupation of Eastern North Carolina*. Chapel Hill: Univ. of North Carolina Press, 2011.

Budiansky, Stephen. *The Bloody Shirt: Terror after Appomattox*. New York: Viking, 2008.

Burgess, John W. "The American Commonwealth: Changes in Its Relation to the Nation." *Political Science Quarterly* 1 (Mar. 1886): 9-35.

———. *Reconstruction and the Constitution 1866-1876*. New York: Scribner, 1902.

———. Review of *History of the United States, from the Compromise of 1850 to the Final Restoration of Home at the South in 1877*. Vols. I and II, *1850-1860*, by James Ford Rhodes. *Political Science Quarterly* 8 (June 1893): 342-46.

Burin, Eric. *Slavery and the Peculiar Solution: A History of the American Colonization Society*. Gainesville: Univ. Press of Florida, 2005.

Burton, Vernon. Review of *Reconstruction: America's Unfinished Revolution*,

1863-1877, by Eric Foner. *South Carolina Historical Magazine* 91 (July 1990): 217-20.

Butchart, Ronald E. *Schooling for the Freed People: Teaching, Learning, and the Struggle for Black Freedom, 1861-1876*. Chapel Hill: Univ. of North Carolina Press, 2010.

Calhoun, Charles W. *Conceiving a New Republic: The Republican Party and the Southern Question, 1869-1900*. Lawrence: Univ. Press of Kansas, 2006.

———. *From Bloody Shirt to Full Dinner Pail: The Transformation of Politics and Governance in the Gilded Age*. New York: Hill and Wang, 2010.

Campbell, Charles Soutter. *The Transformation of American Foreign Relations, 1865-1900*. New York: Harper and Row, 1976.

Campbell, James T. *Middle Passages: African American Journeys to Africa, 1787-2005*. New York: Penguin, 2006.

———. "Redeeming the Race: Martin Delany and the Niger Valley Exploring Party, 1859-60." *New Formations* 45 (Winter 2001-2002): 125-49.

———. *Songs of Zion: The African Methodist Episcopal Church in the United States and South Africa*. New York: Oxford Univ. Press, 1995.

Carter, Dan T. *When the War Was Over: The Failure of Self-Reconstruction in the South, 1865-1867*. Baton Rouge: Louisiana State Univ. Press, 1985.

Censer, Jane Turner. *The Reconstruction of White Southern Womanhood, 1865-1895*. Baton Rouge: Louisiana State Univ. Press, 2003.

Chandler, Alfred D. *The Visible Hand: The Managerial Revolution in American Business*. Cambridge, Mass.: Harvard Univ. Press, 1977.

Chang, David. *The Color of the Land: Race, Nation, and the Politics of Landownership in Oklahoma, 1832-1929*. Chapel Hill: Univ. of North Carolina Press, 2010.

Cimbala, Paul A. *The Great Task Remaining Before Us: Reconstruction as America's Continuing Civil War*. New York: Fordham Univ. Press, 2011.

———. *Under the Guardianship of the Nation: The Freedmen's Bureau and the Reconstruction of Georgia, 1865-1870*. Athens: Univ. of Georgia Press, 1997.

———, and Randall M. Miller, eds. *The Freedmen's Bureau and Reconstruction: Reconsiderations*. New York: Fordham Univ. Press, 1999.

Clark, Anna. *The Struggle for the Breeches: Gender and the Making of the British Working Class*. Berkeley: Univ. of California Press, 1995.

Clark, Kathleen Ann. *Defining Moments: African American Commemoration and Political Culture in the South, 1863-1913*. Chapel Hill: Univ. of North Carolina Press, 2005.

Clayton, Nicholas. "Managing the Transition to a Free Labor Society: American Interpretations of the British West Indies during the Civil War and Reconstruction." *American Nineteenth Century History* 7 (Feb. 2006): 89-108.

Clement, Elizabeth. Review of *Moral Reconstruction: Christian Lobbyists and the Federal Legislation of Morality, 1865-1920,* by Gaines M. Foster. *New York History* 85 (Winter 2004): 71-73.

Click, Patricia C. *Time Full of Trial: The Roanoke Island Freedmen's Colony, 1862-1867.* Chapel Hill: Univ. of North Carolina Press, 2001.

Cohen, Nancy. *The Reconstruction of American Liberalism, 1865-1914.* Chapel Hill: Univ. of North Carolina Press, 2002.

Cohen, William. *At Freedom's Edge: Black Mobility and the Southern White Quest for Racial Control, 1861-1915.* Baton Rouge: Louisiana State Univ. Press, 1991.

Conner, Frank. *The South under Siege.* Newman, Ga.: Collards Publishing, 2002.

Cook, Robert J. *Troubled Commemoration: The American Civil War Centennial, 1961-1965.* Baton Rouge: Louisiana State Univ. Press, 2007.

Cooper, Frederick, Thomas C. Holt, and Rebecca J. Scott. *Beyond Slavery: Explorations of Race, Labor, and Citizenship in Postemancipation Societies.* Chapel Hill: Univ. of North Carolina Press, 2000.

Coulter, E. Merton. *The South during Reconstruction, 1865-1877.* Baton Rouge: Louisiana State Univ. Press, 1947.

Cox, John H., and LaWanda Cox. "General O. O. Howard and the Misrepresented Bureau." *Journal of Southern History* 19 (Nov. 1953): 427-56.

———. "Negro Suffrage and Republican Politics: The Problem of Motivation in Reconstruction Historiography." *Journal of Southern History* 33 (Aug. 1967): 303-30.

———. *Politics, Principle, and Prejudice, 1865-1866: Dilemma of Reconstruction America.* New York: Free Press of Glencoe, 1963.

Cox, Karen L. *Dixie's Daughters: The United Daughters of the Confederacy and the Preservation of Confederate Culture.* Gainesville: Univ. Press of Florida, 2003.

Cox, LaWanda. "Reconstruction Foredoomed? The Policy of Southern Consent." *Reviews in American History* 1 (Dec. 1973): 541-47.

Craven, Avery. Review of *Reconstruction: After the Civil War,* by John Hope Franklin. *Journal of Southern History* 28 (May 1962): 255-56.

Craven, Paul, and Douglas Hay, eds. *Masters, Servants, and Magistrates in Britain and the Empire, 1562-1955.* Chapel Hill: Univ. of North Carolina Press, 2004.

Cronon, William. *Nature's Metropolis: Chicago and the Great West.* New York: W. W. Norton, 1991.

Cruden, Robert. *James Ford Rhodes: The Man, The Historian, and His Work.* Cleveland, Ohio: Press of Western Reserve Univ., 1961.

Cunliffe, Marcus. *Chattel Slavery and Wage Slavery: The Anglo-American Context, 1830-1860.* Athens: Univ. of Georgia Press, 1979.

Current, Richard N., ed. *Reconstruction in Retrospect: Views from the Turn of the Century*. Baton Rouge: Louisiana State Univ. Press, 1969.

Curry, Richard O. "The Civil War and Reconstruction, 1861-1877: A Critical Overview of Recent Trends and Interpretations." *Civil War History* 20 (Sept. 1974): 215-38.

Curtin, Philip D. *The Rise and Fall of the Plantation Complex: Essays in Atlantic History*. New York: Cambridge Univ. Press, 1990.

Curtis, Michael Kent. Review of *Rethinking the Judicial Settlement of Reconstruction*, by Pamela Brandwein. *American Political Thought* 1 (Spring 2012): 161-65.

Dailey, Jane. *Before Jim Crow: The Politics of Race in Postemancipation Virginia*. Chapel Hill: Univ. of North Carolina Press, 2000.

Dal Lago, Enrico. *American Slavery, Atlantic Slavery, and Beyond: The U.S. "Peculiar Institution" in International Perspective*. Boulder, Colo.: Paradigm Publishers, 2012.

Daly, John Patrick. Review of *Vale of Tears: New Essays on Religion and Reconstruction*, ed. Edward J. Blum and W. Scott Poole. *South Carolina Historical Magazine* 109 (Oct. 2008): 322-23.

Davis, David Brion. *The Problem of Slavery in the Age of Emancipation*. New York: Alfred A. Knopf, 2014.

Davis, Hugh. *We Will Be Satisfied with Nothing Less: The African American Struggle for Equal Rights in the North during Reconstruction*. Ithaca, N.Y.: Cornell Univ. Press, 2011.

Davis, Mike. *Late Victorian Holocausts: El Niño Famines and the Making of the Third World*. London: Verso, 2001.

Davis, William Watson. *The Civil War and Reconstruction in Florida*. 1913. Reprint, Gainesville: Univ. of Florida Press, 1964.

Degler, Carl N. Letter to the editor, *New York Times Book Review*, July 13, 2008, 6.

Delfino, Susanna, and Michele Gillespie, eds. *Global Perspectives on Industrial Transformation in the American South*. Columbia: Univ. of Missouri Press, 2005.

Dodd, William E. Review of *The Sequel of Appomattox: A Chronicle of the Reunion of the States*, by Walter Lynwood Fleming. *Mississippi Valley Historical Review* 7 (Dec. 1920): 279-81.

Downs, Gregory P. *Declarations of Dependence: The Long Reconstruction of Popular Politics in the South, 1861-1908*. Chapel Hill: Univ. of North Carolina Press, 2011.

Dray, Philip. *At the Hands of Persons Unknown: The Lynching of Black America*. New York: Modern Library, 2002.

———. *Capitol Men: The Epic Story of Reconstruction through the Lives of the First Black Congressmen*. New York: Houghton Mifflin, 2008.

Drescher, Seymour. *The Mighty Experiment: Free Labor vs. Slavery in British Emancipation.* New York: Oxford Univ. Press, 2002.

Du Bois, W. E. B. *An ABC of Color: Selections Chosen by the Author from Over a Half Century of His Writings.* New York: International Publishers, 1969.

———. *Black Reconstruction in America: An Essay towards a History of the Part Which Black Folk Played in the Attempt to Reconstruct Democracy in America, 1860-1880.* 1935. Reprint, New York: Atheneum, 1973. Reprint, New York: The Free Press, 1992.

———. "Open Letter to Woodrow Wilson." *The Crisis* 5 (March 1913): 236.

———. "Reconstruction and Its Benefits." *American Historical Review* 15 (July 1910): 781-99.

———. *The Souls of Black Folk: Essays and Sketches.* Chicago: A. C. McClurg, 1903.

Dubois, Laurent. *Avengers of the New World: The Story of the Haitian Revolution.* Cambridge, Mass: Harvard Univ. Press, 2004.

Dunn, Joe P. Review of *The Scalawags: Southern Dissenters in the Civil War and Reconstruction,* by James Alex Baggett. *South Carolina Historical Magazine* 104 (Oct. 2003): 281-83.

Dunning, William A. *Essays on the Civil War and Reconstruction and Related Topics.* 1897. Reprint, New York: Harper Torchbook, 1965.

———. *Reconstruction, Political and Economic, 1865-1877.* New York: Harper and Brothers, 1907.

Dutton, Faye E. *Fighting Chance: The Struggle over Woman Suffrage and Black Suffrage in Reconstruction America.* New York: Oxford Univ. Press, 2011.

Dykstra, Robert R. *Bright Radical Star: Black Freedom and White Supremacy on the Hawkeye Frontier.* Cambridge, Mass.: Harvard Univ. Press, 1993.

Earle, Jonathan H. *Jacksonian Antislavery and the Politics of Free Soil, 1824-1854.* Chapel Hill: Univ. of North Carolina Press, 2004.

Edwards, Laura F. *Gendered Strife and Confusion: The Political Culture of Reconstruction.* Urbana: Univ. of Illinois Press, 1997.

———. *The People and Their Peace: Legal Culture and the Transformation of Inequality in the Post-Revolutionary South.* Chapel Hill: Univ. of North Carolina Press, 2009.

Edwards, Rebecca. *Angels in the Machinery: Gender in American Party Politics from the Civil War to the Progressive Era.* New York: Oxford Univ. Press, 1997.

Efford, Alison Clark. *German Immigrants, Race, and Citizenship in the Civil War Era.* New York: Cambridge Univ. Press, 2013.

Egerton, Douglas R. *The Wars of Reconstruction: The Brief, Violent History of America's Most Progressive Era.* New York: Bloomsbury Press, 2014.

Elliott, Mark. *Color-blind Justice: Albion Tourgée and the Quest for Racial Equality from the Civil War to Plessy v. Ferguson*. New York: Oxford Univ. Press, 2006.

———. "Nation-Building Begins at Home." *Reviews in American History* 35 (June 2007): 239-46.

Ely, Geoff. *Forging Democracy: The History of the Left in Europe, 1850-2000*. New York: Oxford Univ. Press, 2002.

Emberton, Carole. *Beyond Redemption: Race, Violence, and the American South after the Civil War*. Chicago: Univ. of Chicago Press, 2013.

Eudell, Demetrius L. *The Political Languages of Emancipation in the British Caribbean and the U.S. South*. Chapel Hill: Univ. of North Carolina Press, 2002.

Fabre, Geneviève, and Robert O'Meally, eds. *History and Memory in African-American Culture*. New York: Oxford Univ. Press, 1994.

Fairclough, Adam. "Congressional Reconstruction: A Catastrophic Failure." *Journal of the Historical Society* 12 (Sept. 2012): 271-82.

———. "Was the Grant of Black Suffrage a Political Error? Reconsidering the Views of John W. Burgess, William A. Dunning, and Eric Foner on Congressional Reconstruction." *Journal of the Historical Society* 12 (June 2012): 155-88.

Farmer-Kaiser, Mary. *Freedwomen and the Freedmen's Bureau: Race, Gender, and Public Policy in the Age of Emancipation*. New York: Fordham Univ. Press, 2010.

Faulkner, Carol. *Women's Radical Reconstruction: The Freedmen's Aid Movement*. Philadelphia: Univ. of Pennsylvania Press, 2004.

Faust, Drew Gilpin. *This Republic of Suffering: Death and the American Civil War*. New York: Alfred A. Knopf, 2008.

Feimster, Crystal. *Southern Horrors: Women and the Politics of Rape and Lynching*. Cambridge, Mass.: Harvard Univ. Press, 2009.

Feldman, Glenn, ed. *Reading Southern History: Essays on Interpreters and Interpretations*. Tuscaloosa: Univ. of Alabama Press, 2001.

Fellman, Michael. *In the Name of God and Country: Reconsidering Terrorism in American History*. New Haven, Conn.: Yale Univ. Press, 2010.

Fernbach, David. *Marx's Political Writings*. Vol. 3. 1973. Reprint, London: Verso, 2010.

Fick, Carolyn. "Emancipation in Haiti: From Plantation Labour to Peasant Proprietorship." *Slavery & Abolition* 21 (Aug. 2000): 11-40.

Fields, Barbara Jeanne. *Slavery and Freedom on the Middle Ground: Maryland during the Nineteenth Century*. New Haven, Conn.: Yale Univ. Press, 1985.

Fitzgerald Michael W. "Reconstruction Reengineered: Or, Is Doubting Black Suffrage a Mistake?" *Journal of the Historical Society* 12 (Sept. 2012): 241-47.

———. Review of *The Bloody Shirt: Terror after Appomattox*, by Stephen Budiansky, in H-Law (June 2008). http://www.h-net.org/reviews/showrev.php?id=14581 (accessed July 1, 2008).
———. *Splendid Failure: Postwar Reconstruction in the American South*. Chicago: Ivan R. Dee, 2007.
———. *The Union League Movement in the Deep South: Politics and Agricultural Change during Reconstruction*. Baton Rouge: Louisiana State Univ. Press, 1989.
———. *Urban Emancipation: Popular Politics in Reconstruction Mobile*. Baton Rouge: Louisiana State Univ. Press, 2002.
Fleming, Walter Lynwood. *The Sequel of Appomattox: A Chronicle of the Reunion of the States*. New Haven, Conn.: Yale Univ. Press, 1919.
Follett, Richard, Eric Foner, and Walter Johnson. *Slavery's Ghost: The Problem of Freedom in the Age of Emancipation*. Baltimore: Johns Hopkins Univ. Press, 2011.
Foner, Eric. *The Fiery Trial: Abraham Lincoln and American Slavery*. New York: Norton, 2010.
———. *Forever Free: The Story of Emancipation and Reconstruction*. New York: Alfred A. Knopf, 2005.
———. *Free Soil, Free Labor, Free Men: The Ideology of the Republican Party before the Civil War*. New York: Oxford Univ. Press, 1970.
———. *Freedom's Lawmakers: A Directory of Black Officeholders during Reconstruction*. New York: Oxford Univ. Press, 1993.
———. *Give Me Liberty! An American History*. 3rd ed. Vol. 1. New York: W. W. Norton, 2011.
———. Interview with Catherine Clinton. *Civil War Times* 52 (June 2013): 25.
———. *Nothing but Freedom: Emancipation and Its Legacy*. Baton Rouge: Louisiana State Univ. Press, 1983.
———. *Our Lincoln: New Perspectives on Lincoln and His World*. New York: W. W. Norton, 2008.
———. *Politics and Ideology in the Age of the Civil War*. New York: Oxford Univ. Press, 1980.
———. *Reconstruction: America's Unfinished Revolution, 1863–1877*. New York: Harper and Row, 1988.
———. "Reconstruction Revisited." *Reviews in American History* 10 (Dec. 1982): 82–100.
———. Review of *When the War Was Over*, by Dan T. Carter. *Georgia Historical Quarterly* 69 (June 1985): 258–61.
———. *A Short History of Reconstruction*. New York: Harper and Row, 1988.
———. *Slavery and Freedom in Nineteenth-Century America*. New York: Oxford Univ. Press, 1994.

———. "The Supreme Court and the History of Reconstruction—And Vice-Versa." *Columbia Law Review* 112 (Nov. 2012): 1585-1606.
———. *Who Owns History? Rethinking the Past in a Changing World*. New York: Hill and Wang, 2002.
———. "Why Is There No Socialism in the United States?" *History Workshop* no. 17 (Spring 1984): 57-80.
———, and Olivia Mahoney. *America's Reconstruction: People and Politics after the Civil War*. New York: Harper Perennial, 1994.
———, ed. *A House Divided: America in the Age of Lincoln*. New York: W. W. Norton, 1990.
———, ed. *The New American History: Revised and Expanded Edition*. Philadelphia: Temple Univ. Press, 1997.
———, and Lisa McGirr, eds. *American History Now*. Philadelphia: Temple Univ. Press, 2011.
Ford, Lacy K., ed. *A Companion to the Civil War and Reconstruction*. Malden, Mass.: Blackwell Publishers, 2005.
Foster, Gaines M. *Moral Reconstruction: Christian Lobbyists and the Federal Legislation of Morality, 1865-1920*. Chapel Hill: Univ. of North Carolina Press, 2002.
Fox-Genovese, Elizabeth, and Eugene D. Genovese. *Slavery in White and Black: Class and Race in the Southern Slaveholders' New World Order*. New York: Cambridge Univ. Press, 2008.
Frankel, Noralee. *Freedom's Women: Black Women and Families in Civil War Era Mississippi*. Bloomington: Indiana Univ. Press, 1999.
Franklin, John Hope. *From Slavery to Freedom: A History of American Negroes*. New York: Alfred A. Knopf, 1956.
———. "Mirror for Americans: A Century of Reconstruction History." *American Historical Review* 85 (Feb. 1980): 1-14.
———. *Reconstruction: After the Civil War*. 1961. 2nd ed., 1994; 3rd ed., Chicago: Univ. of Chicago Press, 2013.
———. Review of *The Era of Reconstruction, 1865-1877*, by Kenneth M. Stampp. *Journal of Negro History* 50 (Oct. 1965): 286-88.
———. "Whither Reconstruction Historiography?" *Journal of Negro Education* 17 (Autumn 1948): 446-61.
———, and Evelyn Higginbotham. *From Slavery to Freedom: A History of African Americans*. 9th ed. New York: McGraw-Hill, 2011.
Fredrickson, George M. *The Black Image in the White Mind: The Debate on Afro-American Character and Destiny, 1817-1914*. New York: Harper and Row, 1971.
———. *The Inner Civil War: Northern Intellectuals and the Crisis of the Union*. New York: Harper and Row, 1965.

———. *White Supremacy: A Comparative Study in American and South African History.* New York: Oxford Univ. Press, 1981.

Gaines, Kevin K. *Uplifting the Race: Black Leadership, Politics, and Culture in the Twentieth Century.* Chapel Hill: Univ. of North Carolina Press, 1996.

Gannon, Barbara A. *The Won Cause: Black and White Comradeship in the Grand Army of the Republic.* Chapel Hill: Univ. of North Carolina Press, 2011.

Gardner, Sarah E. *Blood and Irony: Southern White Women's Narratives of the Civil War, 1861-1937.* Chapel Hill: Univ. of North Carolina Press, 2003.

Garner, James W. *Reconstruction in Mississippi.* 1901. Reprint, Baton Rouge: Louisiana State Univ. Press, 1968.

Gary, Brett. *The Nervous Liberals: Propaganda Anxieties from World War I to the Cold War.* New York: Columbia Univ. Press, 1999.

Geiss, Imanuel. *The Pan-African Movement: A History of Pan-Africanism in America, Europe, and Africa.* New York: Africana Publishing, 1974.

Genetin-Pilawa, C. Joseph. *Crooked Paths to Allotment: The Fight over Federal Indian Policy after the Civil War.* Chapel Hill: Univ. of North Carolina Press, 2012.

Giggie, John M. "Rethinking Reconstruction." *Reviews in American History* 35 (Dec. 2007): 545-55.

Gillette, William. *Retreat from Reconstruction, 1869-1879.* Baton Rouge: Louisiana State Univ. Press, 1979.

———. *The Right to Vote: Politics and the Passage of the Fifteenth Amendment.* Baltimore: Johns Hopkins Univ. Press, 1965.

Gilmore, Glenda. *Gender and Jim Crow: Women and the Politics of White Supremacy in North Carolina, 1896-1920.* Chapel Hill: Univ. of North Carolina Press, 1996.

———. "Which Southerners? Which Southern Historians? A Century of Southern History at Yale." *Yale Review* 99 (Jan. 2011): 56-69.

Ginsburg, Benjamin. *Moses of South Carolina: A Jewish Scalawag during Reconstruction.* Baltimore: Johns Hopkins Univ. Press, 2010.

Glymph, Thavolia. *Out of the House of Bondage: The Transformation of the Plantation Household.* New York: Cambridge Univ. Press, 2008.

———, and Jon J. Kushma, eds. *Essays on the Postbellum Southern Economy.* College Station: Texas A&M Univ. Press, 1985.

Goldberg, David Theo. *The Racial State.* Malden, Mass.: Blackwell Publishers, 2002.

Goodman, Paul. *Of One Blood: Abolitionism and the Origins of Racial Equality.* Berkeley: Univ. of California Press, 1998.

Gordon-Reed, Annette. *Andrew Johnson.* New York: Times Books/Henry Holt, 2001.

Grandin, Greg. *Fordlandia: The Rise and Fall of Henry Ford's Forgotten Jungle City.* New York: Metropolitan Books, 2009.

Grant, Kevin. *A Civilised Savagery: Britain and the New Slaveries in Africa, 1884-1926*. New York: Routledge, 2005.

Green, Michael. *Freedom, Union, and Power: Lincoln and His Party in the Civil War North*. New York: Fordham Univ. Press, 2004.

Greenberg, Stanley B. *Race and State in Capitalist Development: Comparative Perspectives*. New Haven, Conn.: Yale Univ. Press, 1980.

Greene, Julie. *The Canal Builders: Making America's Empire at the Panama Canal*. New York: Penguin Press, 2009.

Greenwood, Janette Thomas. *First Fruits of Freedom: The Migration of Former Slaves and Their Search for Equality in Worcester, Massachusetts, 1862-1900*. Chapel Hill: Univ. of North Carolina Press, 2009.

Greeson, Jennifer Rae. *Our South: Geographic Fantasy and the Rise of National Literature*. Cambridge, Mass.: Harvard Univ. Press, 2010.

Grimsley, Mark. "Wars for the American South: The First and Second Reconstructions Considered as Insurgencies." *Civil War History* 58 (Mar. 2012): 6-36.

Guterl, Matthew Pratt. *American Mediterranean: Southern Slaveholders in the Age of Emancipation*. Cambridge, Mass.: Harvard Univ. Press, 2008.

Guyat, Nicholas. "America's Conservatory: Race, Reconstruction, and the Santo Domingo Debate." *Journal of American History* 97 (Mar. 2011): 974-1000.

Hahn, Steven. *A Nation under Our Feet: Black Political Struggles in the Rural South from Slavery to the Great Migration*. Cambridge, Mass.: Harvard Univ. Press, 2003.

———. *The Roots of Southern Populism: Yeoman Farmers and the Transformation of the Georgia Upcountry, 1850-1890*. New York: Oxford Univ. Press, 1983.

Hale, Grace Elizabeth. *Making Whiteness: The Culture of Segregation in the South*. New York: Pantheon Books, 1998.

Hamilton, Peter Joseph. *The Reconstruction Period: The History of North America*. Philadelphia: G. Barrie and Sons, 1906.

Harris, J. William. *Deep Souths: Delta, Piedmont, and Sea Island Society in the Age of Segregation*. Baltimore: Johns Hopkins Univ. Press, 2001.

Harris, William C. *Lincoln's Last Months*. Cambridge, Mass.: Harvard Univ. Press, 2004.

———. *With Charity for All: Lincoln and the Restoration of the Union*. Lexington: Univ. Press of Kentucky, 1997.

Hart, Albert Bushnell. "The Realities of Negro Suffrage." *Proceedings of the American Political Science Association* 2 (1906): 149-65.

Harvey, Paul. Review of *Rebuilding Zion: The Religious Reconstruction of the South, 1863-1877*, by Daniel W. Stowell. *Journal of Southern History* 65 (Nov. 1999): 887-88.

Haworth, Paul L. *Reconstruction and Union, 1865-1912.* New York: Henry Holt, 1912.
Hesseltine, William B. Review of *Andrew Johnson and Reconstruction*, by Eric McKitrick. *Journal of Southern History* 27 (Feb. 1961): 110-11.
Hobsbawm, Eric J. *The Age of Capital, 1848-1875.* 1975. Reprint, New York: Vintage, 1996.
Hogue, James K. *Uncivil War: Five New Orleans Street Battles and the Rise and Fall of Radical Reconstruction.* Baton Rouge: Louisiana State Univ. Press, 2006.
Holden, Charles J. Review of *What Reconstruction Meant: Historical Memory in the American South*, by Bruce E. Baker. *South Carolina Historical Magazine* 111 (July-Oct. 2010): 181-82.
Holt, Michael. *By One Vote: The Disputed Presidential Election of 1876.* Lawrence: Univ. Press of Kansas, 2008.
———. *The Political Crisis of the 1850s.* New York: Wiley, 1978.
Holt, Sharon Ann. *Making Freedom Pay: North Carolina Freedwomen Working for Themselves, 1865-1900.* Athens: Univ. of Georgia Press, 2000.
Holt, Thomas. *Black over White: Negro Political Leadership in South Carolina during Reconstruction.* Urbana: Univ. of Illinois Press, 1977.
Holt, Thomas C. *The Problem of Freedom: Race, Labor, and Politics in Jamaica and Britain, 1832-1938.* Baltimore: Johns Hopkins Univ. Press, 1992.
Honeck, Mischa. *We Are the Revolutionists: German-Speaking Immigrants and American Abolitionists after 1848.* Athens: Univ. of Georgia Press, 2011.
Hoogenboom, Ari A. *Rutherford B. Hayes: Warrior and President.* Lawrence: Univ. Press of Kansas, 1995.
Howard, Victor B. *Religion and the Radical Republican Movement, 1860-1870.* Lexington: Univ. Press of Kentucky, 1990.
Howe, Daniel Walker. *What Hath God Wrought: The Transformation of America, 1815-1848.* New York: Oxford Univ. Press, 2007.
Hume, Richard L., and Jerry B. Gough. *Blacks, Carpetbaggers, and Scalawags: The Constitutional Conventions of Reconstruction.* Baton Rouge: Louisiana State Univ. Press, 2008.
Hunter, Tera. *To Joy My Freedom: Southern Black Women's Lives and Labors after the Civil War.* Cambridge, Mass.: Harvard Univ. Press, 2003.
Hyman, Harold M. *A More Perfect Union: The Impact of the Civil War and Reconstruction on the Constitution.* New York: Alfred A. Knopf, 1973.
Ignatiev, Noel. "'The American Blindspot': Reconstruction according to Eric Foner and W. E. B. Du Bois." *Labour/Le Travail* 31 (Spring 1993): 246-47.
———. *How the Irish Became White.* 1995. Reprint, New York: Routledge, 2009.
Isaacman, Allen, and Richard Roberts, eds. *Cotton, Colonialism, and Social History in Sub-Saharan Africa.* Portsmouth, N.H.: Heinemann, 1995.

Jacobson, Matthew Frye. *Barbarian Virtues: The United States Encounters Foreign Peoples at Home and Abroad, 1876-1917.* New York: Hill and Wang, 2000.

James, C. L. R. *The Black Jacobins: Toussaint L'Ouverture and the San Domingo Revolution.* 1938. Reprint, New York: Vintage, 1989.

Janney, Caroline E. *Burying the Dead but Not the Past: Ladies' Memorial Associations and the Lost Cause.* Chapel Hill: Univ. of North Carolina Press, 2008.

———. *Remembering the Civil War: Reunion and the Limits of Reconciliation.* Chapel Hill: Univ. of North Carolina Press, 2013.

Jaynes, Gerald David. *Branches without Roots: Genesis of the Black Working Class in the American South, 1862-1882.* New York: Oxford Univ. Press, 1986.

Jung, Moon-Ho. *Coolies and Cane: Race, Labor, and Sugar in the Age of Emancipation.* Baltimore: Johns Hopkins Univ. Press, 2006.

Kachun, Mitch. *Festivals of Freedom: Memory and Meaning in African American Emancipation Celebrations.* Amherst: Univ. of Massachusetts Press, 2003.

Kaczorowski, Robert J. *The Politics of Judicial Interpretation: The Federal Courts, Department of Justice, and Civil Rights, 1866-1876.* Dobbs Ferry, N.Y.: Oceana Publications, 1985.

Kantrowitz, Stephen. *Ben Tillman and the Reconstruction of White Supremacy.* Chapel Hill: Univ. of North Carolina Press, 2000.

———. *More Than Freedom: Fighting for Black Citizenship in a White Republic, 1829-1889.* New York: Penguin, 2012.

Kaplan, Amy. *The Anarchy of Empire in the Making of U.S. Culture.* Cambridge, Mass.: Harvard Univ. Press, 2002.

Katz, Philip M. *From Appomattox to Montmartre: Americans and the Paris Commune.* Cambridge, Mass.: Harvard Univ. Press, 1998.

Kaye, Anthony E. "The Second Slavery: Modernity in the Nineteenth-Century South and the Atlantic World." *Journal of Southern History* 75 (Aug. 2009): 627-50.

Kennedy, Ross A., ed. *A Companion to Woodrow Wilson.* London: John Wiley, 2013.

Kerr-Ritchie, Jeffrey R. *Freedpeople in the Tobacco South, Virginia, 1860-1900.* Chapel Hill: Univ. of North Carolina Press, 1999.

Kolchin, Peter. "Comparative Perspectives on Emancipation in the U.S. South: Reconstruction, Radicalism, and Russia." *Journal of the Civil War Era* 2 (June 2012): 203-32.

———. *A Sphinx on the American Land: The Nineteenth-Century South in Comparative Perspective.* Baton Rouge: Louisiana State Univ. Press, 2003.

Kramer, Paul A. *The Blood of Government: Race, Empire, the United States, and the Philippines.* Chapel Hill: Univ. of North Carolina Press, 2006.

Lake, Marilyn, and Henry Reynolds. *Drawing the Global Colour Line: White Men's Countries and the International Challenge of Racial Equality.* New York: Cambridge Univ. Press, 2008.

Lears, Jackson. *Rebirth of a Nation: The Making of Modern America, 1877-1920.* New York: Harper Perennial, 2010.

Lee, Susanna Michelle. *Claiming the Union: Citizenship in the Post-Civil War South.* New York: Cambridge Univ. Press, 2014.

Lemann, Nicholas. *Redemption: The Last Battle of the Civil War.* New York: Farrar, Straus and Giroux, 2006.

Levine, Bruce. *The Spirit of 1848: German Immigrants, Labor Conflict, and the Coming of the Civil War.* Urbana: Univ. of Illinois Press, 1992.

Lincove, David, comp. *Reconstruction in the United States: An Annotated Bibliography.* Westport, Conn.: Greenwood Press, 2000.

Linebaugh, Peter, and Marcus Rediker. "The Many-Headed Hydra: Sailors, Slaves, and the Atlantic Working Class in the Eighteenth Century." *Journal of Historical Sociology* 3 (Sept. 1990): 225-52.

———. *The Many-Headed Hydra: Sailors, Slaves, Commoners, and the Hidden History of the Revolutionary Atlantic.* London: Verso Books, 2002.

Link, Arthur S., and Rembert W. Patrick, eds. *Writing Southern History: Essays in Historiography in Honor of Fletcher M. Green.* Baton Rouge: Louisiana State Univ. Press, 1965.

Litwack, Leon F. *Been in the Storm So Long: The Aftermath of Slavery.* New York: Alfred A. Knopf, 1979.

Loewen, James W., and Edward H. Sebesta, eds. *The Confederate and Neo-Confederate Reader: The "Great Truth" and the "Lost Cause."* Jackson: Univ. Press of Mississippi, 2010.

Loewenberg, Bert James. "Efforts of the South to Encourage Immigration, 1865-1900." *South Atlantic Quarterly* 33 (Oct. 1934): 363-85.

Logan, Rayford W. *The Negro in American Life and Thought: The Nadir.* New York: Dial Press, 1954.

Long, David, and Brian C. Schmidt, eds. *Imperialism and Internationalism in the Discipline of International Relations.* Albany: State Univ. of New York Press, 2005.

Losurdo, Domenico. *Liberalism: A Counter-History.* Translated by Gregory Elliott. London: Verso Books, 2011.

Lott, Eric. *Love and Theft: Blackface Minstrelsy and the American Working Class.* New York: Oxford Univ. Press, 1993.

Love, Eric T. *Race over Empire: Racism and U.S. Imperialism, 1865-1900.* Chapel Hill: Univ. of North Carolina Press, 2004.

Lovejoy, Paul E. *Transformations in Slavery: A History of Slavery in Africa.* 2nd ed. New York: Cambridge Univ. Press, 2000.

Lynch, John R. *The Facts of Reconstruction.* New York: Neale Publishing, 1913.

Lynn, Martin. *Commerce and Economic Change in West Africa: The Palm Oil Trade in the Nineteenth Century.* New York: Cambridge Univ. Press, 1997.

Marshall, Anne E. *Creating a Confederate Kentucky: The Lost Cause and Civil War Memory in a Border State.* Chapel Hill: Univ. of North Carolina Press, 2010.

Marten, James. *Sing Not War: The Life of Union and Confederate Veterans in Gilded Age America.* Chapel Hill: Univ. of North Carolina Press, 2011.

Marx, Karl. *Capital.* Vol. 1. Translated by Ben Fowkes. 1867. Reprint, New York: Penguin Classics, 1976.

Mashaw, Jerry. *Creating the Administrative Constitution: The Lost One Hundred Years of American Administrative Law.* New Haven, Conn.: Yale Univ. Press, 2012.

Masur, Kate. *An Example for All the Land: Emancipation and the Struggle over Equality in Washington D.C.* Chapel Hill: Univ. of North Carolina Press, 2010.

———. Review of *Reconstructions: New Perspectives on the Postbellum United States.* Edited by Thomas J. Brown. H-CivWar (October 2007). http://www.h-net.org/reviews/showrev.php?id=13650 (accessed July 3, 2013).

Matory, J. Lorand. *Black Atlantic Religion: Tradition, Transnationalism, and Matriarchy in the Afro-Brazilian Candomblé.* Princeton, N.J.: Princeton Univ. Press, 2005.

McClintock, Anne. *Imperial Leather: Race, Gender, and Sexuality in the Colonial Contest.* New York: Routledge, 1995.

McConnell, Stuart. *Glorious Contentment: The Grand Army of the Republic, 1865-1900.* Chapel Hill: Univ. of North Carolina Press, 1992.

McElya, Micki. *Clinging to Mammy: The Faithful Slave in Twentieth-Century America.* Cambridge, Mass.: Harvard Univ. Press, 2007.

McFeely, William S. *Yankee Stepfather: General O. O. Howard and the Freedmen.* New Haven, Conn.: Yale Univ. Press, 1968.

McKitrick, Eric. *Andrew Johnson and Reconstruction.* 1960. Reprint, New York: Oxford Univ. Press, 1988.

———. Review of *Reconstruction: After the Civil War,* by John Hope Franklin. *Mississippi Valley Historical Review* 49 (June 1962): 153-54.

McPherson, James. "Reconstruction Reconsidered." *The Atlantic* 261 (Apr. 1988): 75-77.

Mehta, Uday Singh. *Liberalism and Empire: A Study in Nineteenth-Century British Liberal Thought.* Chicago: Univ. of Chicago Press, 1999.

Meier, August. "An Epitaph for the Writing of Reconstruction History?" *Reviews in American History* 9 (Mar. 1981): 82-87.

Messer-Kruse, Timothy. *The Yankee International: Marxism and the American Reform Tradition, 1848-1876.* Chapel Hill: Univ. of North Carolina Press, 1998.

Milton, George Fort. *The Age of Hate: Andrew Johnson and the Radicals.* New York: Coward-McCann, 1930.

Mintz, Sidney W. *Sweetness and Power: The Place of Sugar in Modern History.* New York: Viking, 1985.

Moneyhon, Carl H. *The Impact of the Civil War on Reconstruction in Arkansas: Persistence in the Midst of Ruin.* Baton Rouge: Louisiana State Univ. Press, 1994.

———. *Republicanism in Reconstruction Texas.* Austin: Univ. of Texas Press, 1980.

Montgomery, David. *Beyond Equality: Labor and the Radical Republicans, 1862-1872.* New York: Alfred A. Knopf, 1967.

Moore, Barrington. *Social Origins of Dictatorship and Democracy: Lord and Peasant in the Making of the Modern World.* 1966. Reprint, Boston: Beacon Press, 1993.

Morgan, Lynda J. *Emancipation in Virginia's Tobacco Belt, 1850-1870.* Athens: Univ. of Georgia Press, 1992.

Neff, John R. *Honoring the Civil War Dead: Commemoration and the Problem of Reconciliation.* Lawrence: Univ. Press of Kansas, 2005.

Nelson, Scott Reynolds. *Iron Confederacies: Southern Railways, Klan Violence, and Reconstruction.* Chapel Hill: Univ. of North Carolina Press, 1999.

———. *A Nation of Deadbeats: An Uncommon History of America's Financial Disasters.* New York: Alfred A. Knopf, 2012.

Nelson, William E. *The Fourteenth Amendment: From Political Principle to Judicial Doctrine.* Cambridge, Mass.: Harvard Univ. Press, 1998.

Newman, Louise. Review of *Women's Radical Reconstruction: The Freedmen's Aid Movement,* by Carol Faulkner. *Journal of Southern History* 71 (Feb. 2005): 177-78.

Novick, Peter. *That Noble Dream: The "Objectivity Question" and the American Historical Profession.* Cambridge: Cambridge Univ. Press, 1988.

Nystrom, Justin A. *New Orleans after the Civil War: Race, Politics, and a New Birth of Freedom.* Baltimore: Johns Hopkins Univ. Press, 2010.

Oakes, James. *Freedom National: The Destruction of Slavery in the United States.* New York: W. W. Norton, 2013.

Oberholtzer, Ellis P. Review of *The Sequel of Appomattox: A Chronicle of the Reunion of the States,* by Walter Lynwood Fleming; *The Cleveland Era: A Chronicle of the New Order in Politics,* by Henry Jones Ford; and *The Boss and the Machine: A Chronicle of the Politicians and the Party Organization,* by Samuel P. Orth. All in *American Historical Review* 25 (Apr. 1920): 519-22.

O'Donovan, Susan Eva. *Becoming Free in the Cotton South.* Cambridge, Mass.: Harvard Univ. Press, 2007.

Öfele, Martin W. *German-Speaking Officers in the United States Colored Troops, 1863-1867.* Gainesville: Univ. Press of Florida, 2004.

———. *True Sons of the Republic: European Immigrants in the Union Army.* Westport, Conn.: Praeger, 2008.

Okihiro, Gary Y. *Pineapple Culture: A History of the Tropical and Temperate Zones.* Berkeley: Univ. of California Press, 2009.

Ostler, Jeffrey. *The Plains Sioux and U.S. Colonialism from Lewis and Clark to Wounded Knee.* New York: Cambridge Univ. Press, 2004.

Paddison, Joshua. *American Heathens: Religion, Race, and Reconstruction in California.* Berkeley: Huntington/USC Institute on California and the West and the Univ. of California Press, 2012.

Painter, Nell Irvin. *Exodusters: Black Migration to Kansas after Reconstruction.* New York: Alfred A. Knopf, 1977.

Palmié, Stephan. *Wizards and Scientists: Explorations in Afro-Cuban Modernity and Tradition.* Durham, N.C.: Duke Univ. Press, 2002.

Parsons, Elaine Frantz. "Midnight Rangers: Costume and Performance in the Reconstruction-Era Ku Klux Klan." *Journal of American History* 92 (Dec. 2005): 811-36.

Paxon, Frederic L. Review of *A History of the United States since the Civil War.* Volume II: *1868-1872*, by Ellis Paxson Oberholtzer. *Mississippi Valley Historical Review* 9 (Dec. 1922): 254.

Payne, Charles M. *I've Got the Light of Freedom: The Organizing Tradition and the Mississippi Freedom Struggle.* Berkeley: Univ. of California Press, 2005.

Perman, Michael. "An Autopsy for Reconstruction." *Reviews in American History* 30 (June 2002): 252-54.

———. *Emancipation and Reconstruction.* 2nd ed. Wheeling, Ill.: Harlan Davidson, 2003.

———. "Eric Foner's Reconstruction: A Finished Revolution." *Reviews in American History* 17 (Mar. 1989): 73-78.

———. *Reunion without Compromise: The South and Reconstruction, 1865-1868.* Cambridge: Cambridge Univ. Press, 1973.

———. *The Road to Redemption: Southern Politics, 1869-1879.* Chapel Hill: Univ. of North Carolina Press, 1984.

Phillips, Jason. *Diehard Rebels: The Confederate Culture of Invincibility.* Athens: Univ. of Georgia Press, 2007.

Phillips, Ulrich Bonnell. *American Negro Slavery.* New York: D. Appleton, 1918.

Potter, David M. *Division and the Stress of Reunion, 1845-1876.* Glenview, Ill.: Scott, Foreman, 1973.

Pozzetta, George E. "Foreigners in Florida: A Study of Immigration Promotion, 1865-1910." *Florida Historical Quarterly* 53 (Oct. 1974): 164-80.

Prince, K. Stephen. *Stories of the South: Race and the Reconstruction of Southern Identity, 1865-1915*. Chapel Hill: Univ. of North Carolina Press, 2014.

Rable, George C. *But There Was No Peace: The Role of Violence in the Politics of Reconstruction*. Athens: Univ. of Georgia Press, 1984.

Rancière, Jacques. *The Nights of Labor: The Workers' Dream in Nineteenth-Century France*. Philadelphia: Temple Univ. Press, 1989.

Ranney, Joseph A. *In the Wake of Slavery: Civil War, Civil Rights, and the Reconstruction of Southern Law*. New York: Praeger, 2006.

Ransom, Roger L. "Reconstructing Reconstruction: Options and Limitations to Federal Politics on Land Distribution in 1866-67." *Civil War History* 51 (Dec. 2005): 364-77.

———, and Richard Sutch. *One Kind of Freedom: The Economic Consequences of Emancipation*. 1977. 2nd ed., New York: Cambridge Univ. Press, 2001.

Regosin, Elizabeth A., and Donald R. Shaffer, eds. *Voices of Emancipation: Understanding Slavery, the Civil War, and Reconstruction through the U.S. Pension Bureau Files*. New York: New York Univ. Press, 2008.

Reidy, Joseph P. *From Slavery to Agrarian Capitalism in the Cotton Plantation South: Central Georgia, 1800-1880*. Chapel Hill: Univ. of North Carolina Press, 1992.

Review of *Lincoln's Plan of Reconstruction*, by Charles H. McCarthy. *Southern History Association Publications* 6 (Mar. 1902): 173-74.

Rhodes, James Ford. *History of the United States from the Compromise of 1850*. 7 vols. New York: Macmillan, 1892-1906.

Richardson, Heather Cox. *The Death of Reconstruction: Race, Labor, and Politics in the Post-Civil War North, 1865-1901*. Cambridge, Mass.: Harvard Univ. Press, 2001.

———. *The Greatest Nation of the Earth: Republican Economic Policies during the Civil War*. Cambridge, Mass.: Harvard Univ. Press, 1997.

———. *West from Appomattox: The Reconstruction of America after the Civil War*. New Haven, Conn.: Yale Univ. Press, 2007.

———. *Wounded Knee: Party Politics and the Road to an American Massacre*. New York: Basic Books, 2010.

Ring, Natalie J. *The Problem South: Region, Empire, and the New Liberal State, 1880-1930*. Athens: Univ. of Georgia Press, 2012.

Robinson, Cedric J. *Black Marxism: The Making of the Black Radical Tradition*. 1983. Reprint, Chapel Hill: Univ. of North Carolina Press, 2000.

Rodrigue, John C. *Lincoln and Reconstruction*. Carbondale: Southern Illinois Univ. Press, 2013.

———. *Reconstruction in the Cane Fields: From Slavery to Free Labor in Louisiana's Sugar Parishes, 1862-1880*. Baton Rouge: Louisiana State Univ. Press, 2001.

———. Review of *The Edge of the Sword: The Ordeal of Carpetbagger Marshall H. Twitchell in the Civil War and Reconstruction*, by Ted Tunnell. *Georgia Historical Quarterly* 85 (Winter 2001): 651-53.

Roediger, David R. *The Wages of Whiteness: Race and the Making of the American Working Class.* 1991. Rev. ed. London: Verso, 2007.

———, and Elizabeth D. Esch. *The Production of Difference: Race and the Management of Labor in U.S. History.* New York: Oxford Univ. Press, 2012.

Rogers, William Warren, Jr. *Black Belt Scalawag: Charles Hays and the Southern Republicans in the Era of Reconstruction.* Athens: Univ. of Georgia Press, 1993.

Rose, Willie Lee. *Rehearsal for Reconstruction: The Port Royal Experiment.* Indianapolis, Ind.: Bobbs-Merrill, 1964.

Rosen, Hannah. *Terror in the Heart of Freedom: Citizenship, Sexual Violence, and the Meaning of Race in the Postemancipation South.* Chapel Hill: Univ. of North Carolina Press, 2009.

Rosenzweig, Roy, and David Thelen. *The Presence of the Past: Popular Uses of History in American Life.* New York: Columbia Univ. Press, 1998.

Ross, Michael A., and Leslie S. Rowland. "Adam Fairclough, John Burgess, and the Nettlesome Legacy of the 'Dunning School.'" *Journal of the Historical Society* 12 (Sept. 2012): 249-70.

Rothman, Adam. *Slavery, the Civil War, and Reconstruction.* Washington, D.C.: American Historical Association, 2012.

Rousey, Dennis C. Review of *Uncivil War: Five New Orleans Street Battles and the Rise and Fall of Radical Reconstruction*, by James K. Hogue. *Journal of Southern History* 73 (Nov. 2007): 928-29.

Rubin, Hyman S., III. *South Carolina Scalawags.* Columbia: Univ. of South Carolina Press, 2006.

Rugemer, Edward Bartlett. *The Problem of Emancipation: The Caribbean Roots of the American Civil War.* Baton Rouge: Louisiana State Univ. Press, 2008.

Rushdy, Ashraf. *American Lynching.* New Haven, Conn.: Yale Univ. Press, 2012.

Saunt, Claudio. "The Paradox of Freedom: Tribal Sovereignty and Emancipation during the Reconstruction of Indian Territory." *Journal of Southern History* 70 (Feb. 2004): 63-94.

Savage, Kirk. *Standing Soldiers, Kneeling Slaves: Race, War, and Monument in Nineteenth-Century America.* Princeton, N.J.: Princeton Univ. Press, 1997.

Saville, Julie. *The Work of Reconstruction: From Slave to Wage Laborer in South Carolina, 1860-1870.* New York: Cambridge Univ. Press, 1994.

Saxton, Alexander. *The Rise and Fall of the White Republic: Class Politics and Mass Culture in Nineteenth-Century America.* London: Verso, 2003.

Schachtman, Max. *Race and Revolution.* Edited by Christopher Phelps. New York: Verso, 2003.

Schantz, Mark S. *Awaiting the Heavenly Country: The Civil War and America's Culture of Death.* Ithaca, N.Y.: Cornell Univ. Press, 2008.

Schmidt, James D. *Free to Work: Labor Law, Emancipation, and Reconstruction, 1815-1880.* Athens: Univ. of Georgia Press, 1998.

Schwalm, Leslie A. *Emancipation's Diaspora: Race and Reconstruction in the Upper Midwest.* Chapel Hill: Univ. of North Carolina Press, 2009.

——. *A Hard Fight for We: Women's Transition from Slavery to Freedom in South Carolina.* Urbana: Univ. of Illinois Press, 1997.

Schwartz, Stuart B. *Slaves, Peasants, and Rebels: Reconsidering Brazilian Slavery.* Urbana: Univ. of Illinois Press, 1992.

Scott, Rebecca J. *Degrees of Freedom: Louisiana and Cuba after Slavery.* Cambridge, Mass.: The Belknap Press of Harvard Univ. Press, 2005.

Sellers, Charles. *The Market Revolution: Jacksonian America, 1815-1846.* New York: Oxford Univ. Press, 1991.

Sexton, Jay. *Debtor Diplomacy: Finance and American Foreign Relations in the Civil War Era, 1837-1873.* Oxford Historical Monographs. Oxford: Clarendon, 2005.

——. *The Monroe Doctrine: Empire and Nation in Nineteenth-Century America.* New York: Hill and Wang, 2011.

——. "Toward a Synthesis of Foreign Relations in the Civil War Era, 1848-77." *American Nineteenth Century History* 5 (Fall 2004): 50-73.

Shaffer, Donald R. *After the Glory: The Struggles of Black Civil War Veterans.* Lawrence: Univ. Press of Kansas, 2004.

Shofner, Jerrell H. *Nor Is It Over Yet: Florida in the Era of Reconstruction, 1863-1877.* Gainesville: Univ. Presses of Florida, 1974.

Silber, Nina. *The Romance of Reunion: Northerners and the South, 1865-1900.* Chapel Hill: Univ. of North Carolina Press, 1993.

Silby, Joel. *A Respectable Minority: The Democratic Party during the Civil War Era, 1860-1868.* New York: W. W. Norton, 1977.

Simkins, Francis B. "New Viewpoints of Southern Reconstruction." *Journal of Southern History* 5 (Feb. 1939): 49-61.

——, and Robert Woody. *South Carolina during Reconstruction.* Chapel Hill: Univ. of North Carolina Press, 1932.

Simpson, Brooks D. *The Reconstruction Presidents.* Lawrence: Univ. Press of Kansas, 1998.

Sipress, Joel M. Review of *A Dangerous Stir: Fear, Paranoia, and the Making of Reconstruction,* by Mark Wahlgren Summers. *History Teacher* 43 (May 2010): 471-72.

Sizer, Lyde Cullen. *The Political Work of Northern Women Writers and the Civil War, 1850-1872.* Chapel Hill: Univ. of North Carolina Press, 2000.

Slap, Andrew L. *The Doom of Reconstruction: The Liberal Republicans in the Civil War Era.* New York: Fordham Univ. Press, 2006.

———. Review of *Andrew Johnson's Civil War and Reconstruction*, by Paul H. Bergeron, and *Andrew Johnson*, by Annette Gordon-Reed. *Civil War History* 59 (June 2013): 254-57.

———, ed. *Reconstructing Appalachia: The Civil War's Aftermath.* Lexington: Univ. Press of Kentucky, 2010.

Smith, Claude. "Official Efforts of the State of Mississippi to Encourage Immigration, 1868-1886." *Journal of Mississippi History* 32 (Nov. 1970): 327-40.

Smith, Jean Edward. *Eisenhower: In War and Peace.* New York: Random House, 2013.

———. *Grant.* New York: Simon and Schuster, 2001.

Smith, John David. *An Old Creed for the New South: Proslavery Ideology and Historiography, 1865-1918.* 1985. Reprint, Carbondale: Southern Illinois Univ. Press, 2008.

———. *When Did Southern Segregation Begin?* Boston: Bedford/St. Martin's, 2002.

———, and J. Vincent Lowery, eds. *The Dunning School: Historians, Race, and the Meaning of Reconstruction.* Lexington: Univ. Press of Kentucky, 2013.

Smith, Stacey L. *Freedom's Frontier: California and the Struggle over Unfree Labor, Emancipation, and Reconstruction.* Chapel Hill: Univ. of North Carolina Press, 2013.

Snay, Mitchell. *Fenians, Freedmen, and Southern Whites: Race and Nationality in the Era of Reconstruction.* Baton Rouge: Louisiana State Univ. Press, 2007.

Sombart, Werner. *Warum gibt es in den Vereinigten Staaten keinen Sozialismus?* Tübingen, Germany: J. C. B. Mohr, 1906.

Sommerville, Diane Miller. Review of *Gendered Strife and Confusion: The Political Culture of Reconstruction*, by Laura F. Edwards. *Journal of Southern History* 64 (Aug. 1998): 566-68.

Sproat, John G. *"The Best Men": Liberal Reformers in the Gilded Age.* New York: Oxford Univ. Press, 1968.

Stagg, John W. "Race Problem in the South." *The Presbyterian Quarterly* 14 (July 1900): 317-48.

Stampp, Kenneth M. *The Era of Reconstruction, 1865-1877.* 1965. Reprint, New York: Vintage Books, 1967.

———. *The Peculiar Institution: Slavery in the Antebellum South.* New York: Knopf, 1956.

———, and Leon F. Litwack, eds. *Reconstruction: An Anthology of Revisionist Writings.* Baton Rouge: Louisiana State Univ. Press, 1969.

Stanley, Amy Dru. *From Bondage to Contract: Wage Labor, Marriage, and the Market in the Age of Slave Emancipation.* Cambridge: Cambridge Univ. Press, 1998.

Stein, Judith. *The World of Marcus Garvey: Race and Class in Modern Society.* Baton Rouge: Louisiana State Univ. Press, 1986.

Steinfeld, Robert J. *Coercion, Contract, and Free Labor in the Nineteenth Century.* New York: Cambridge Univ. Press, 2001.

———. *The Invention of Free Labor: The Employment Relation in English and American Law and Culture, 1350-1870.* Chapel Hill: Univ. of North Carolina Press, 1991.

Storey, Margaret M. *Loyalty and Loss: Alabama's Unionists in the Civil War and Reconstruction.* Baton Rouge: Louisiana State Univ. Press, 2004.

Stowe, Steven M. Review of *Reconstructing the Household: Families, Sex, and the Law in the Nineteenth-Century South,* by Peter W. Bardaglio. *Journal of American History* 83 (June 1996): 187-88.

Stowell, Daniel W. *Rebuilding Zion: The Religious Reconstruction of the South, 1863-1877.* Oxford: Oxford Univ. Press, 1988.

Summers, Mark Wahlgren. *A Dangerous Stir: Fear, Paranoia, and the Making of Reconstruction.* Chapel Hill: Univ. of North Carolina Press, 2009.

———. *The Era of Good Stealings.* New York: Oxford Univ. Press, 1993.

———. *The Ordeal of the Reunion: A New History of Reconstruction.* Chapel Hill: Univ. of North Carolina Press, 2014.

———. *The Press Gang: Newspapers and Politics, 1865-1878.* Chapel Hill: Univ. of North Carolina Press, 1994.

———. *Railroads, Reconstruction, and the Gospel of Prosperity: Aid under the Radical Republicans, 1865-1877.* Princeton, N.J.: Princeton Univ. Press, 1984.

———. "What Fresh Hell Is This? Revisiting Reconstruction." *Register of the Kentucky Historical Society* 110 (Summer-Autumn 2012): 559-74.

Sutherland, Daniel. *A Savage Conflict: The Decisive Role of Guerrillas in the Civil War.* Chapel Hill: Univ. of North Carolina Press, 2009.

Sweet, James H. *Domingos Álvares, African Healing, and the Intellectual History of the Atlantic World.* Chapel Hill: Univ. of North Carolina Press, 2011.

Taylor, Alrutheus A. "Historians of the Reconstruction." *Journal of Negro History* 23 (Jan. 1938): 16-34.

———. *The Negro in the Reconstruction of Virginia.* Washington, D.C.: Association for the Study of Negro Life and History, 1926.

———. *The Negro in South Carolina during the Reconstruction.* Washington, D.C.: Association for the Study of Negro Life and History, 1924.

———. *The Negro in Tennessee, 1865-1880.* Washington, D.C.: Association for the Study of Negro Life and History, 1941.

———. Review of *Black Reconstruction,* by W. E. Burghardt Du Bois. *New England Quarterly* 8 (Dec. 1935): 608-12.

Taylor, Joe Gray. *Louisiana Reconstructed, 1863-1877.* Baton Rouge: Louisiana State Univ. Press, 1974.

Thomas, David Y. *Arkansas in War and Reconstruction, 1861-1874.* Little Rock: Arkansas Division, United Daughters of the Confederacy, 1926.

———. Review of *The Reconstruction Period: The History of North America,* by Peter Joseph Hamilton. *American Political Science Review* 2 (May 1908): 490-92.

———. "The South and Her History." *American Monthly Review of Reviews* 26 (Oct. 1902): 461-64.

Thompson, E. P. *The Making of the English Working Class.* 1964. Reprint, New York: Vintage, 1966.

Thompson, Elizabeth Lee. *The Reconstruction of Southern Debtors: Bankruptcy after the Civil War.* Athens: Univ. of Georgia Press, 2004.

Thornton, J. Mills. "Class Conflict and Black Enfranchisement in Alabama." *Journal of the Historical Society* 12 (Sept. 2012): 238-40.

Thornton, John. *Africa and Africans in the Making of the Atlantic World, 1400-1800.* 2nd ed. New York: Cambridge Univ. Press, 1998.

Tindal, Retta D. "Reconstruction, 1865-1877." *UDC Magazine* 75 (Dec. 2012): 11-14.

Tindall, George Brown. *South Carolina Negroes, 1877-1900.* Columbia: Univ. of South Carolina Press, 1952.

Trefousse, Hans. *Andrew Johnson: A Biography.* New York: W. W. Norton, 1989.

———. *The Radical Republicans: Lincoln's Vanguard for Racial Justice.* New York: Knopf, 1969.

———. Review of *Reconstruction: After the Civil War,* by John Hope Franklin. *American Historical Review* 67 (Apr. 1962): 745-46.

Trelease, Allen W. *White Terror: The Ku Klux Klan Conspiracy and Southern Reconstruction.* 1971. Reprint, Baton Rouge: Louisiana State Univ. Press, 1995.

Trent, W. P. "A New South View of Reconstruction." *Sewanee Review* 9 (Jan. 1901): 13-29.

Tsesis, Alexander. *The Thirteenth Amendment and American Freedom: A Legal History.* New York: New York Univ. Press, 2004.

Tunnell, Ted. *Edge of the Sword: The Ordeal of Carpetbagger Marshall H. Twitchell in the Civil War and Reconstruction.* Baton Rouge: Louisiana State Univ. Press, 2001.

Turner, Mary, ed. *From Chattel Slaves to Wage Slaves: The Dynamics of Labour Bargaining in the Americas.* Bloomington: Indiana Univ. Press, 1995.

Varon, Elizabeth R. Review of *Gendered Strife and Confusion: The Political Culture of Reconstruction,* by Laura F. Edwards. *Journal of American History* 84 (Mar. 1998): 1517-18.

Vinson, Robert Trent. *The Americans Are Coming! Dreams of African American Liberation in Segregationist South Africa*. Athens: Ohio Univ. Press, 2012.

Vitalis, Robert. "The Noble American Science of Imperial Relations and Its Laws of Race Development." *Comparative Studies in Society and History* 52 (Oct. 2010): 909-38.

Vorenberg, Michael. *Final Freedom: The Civil War, the Abolition of Slavery, and the Thirteenth Amendment*. Cambridge: Cambridge Univ. Press, 2001.

W. A. D. Review of *The Reconstruction Period*, by Peter Joseph Hamilton, and *The Rise of the New South*, by Philip Alexander Bruce. *Political Science Quarterly* 23 (Mar. 1908): 129.

Waldrep, Christopher. Review of *Free to Work: Labor Law, Emancipation, and Reconstruction, 1815-1880*, by James D. Schmidt. *Journal of Southern History* 66 (Aug. 2000): 616-17.

———. *Roots of Disorder: Race and Criminal Justice in the American South, 1817-1880*. Champaign: Univ. of Illinois Press, 1998.

Wang, Xi. *The Trial of Democracy: Black Suffrage & Northern Republicans, 1860-1910*. Athens: Univ. of Georgia Press, 1997.

Waugh, Joan. *U. S. Grant: American Hero, American Myth*. Chapel Hill: Univ. of North Carolina Press, 2009.

Wehler, Hans Ulrich, ed. *Radikalismus, Sozialismus und bürgerliche Demokratie*. Frankfurt am Main, Federal Republic of Germany: Suhrkamp, 1969.

Weisberger, Bernard A. "The Dark and Bloody Ground of Reconstruction Historiography." *Journal of Southern History* 25 (Nov. 1959): 427-47.

Weissbuch, Theodore N. "Literary and Historical Attitudes toward Reconstruction following the Civil War." PhD diss., State Univ. of Iowa, 1964.

Wesley, Charles H. "Racial Propaganda and Historical Writing: The Emancipation of the Historian." *Opportunity: A Journal of Negro Life* 13 (Aug. 1935): 244-46, 254.

West, Elliott. *The Last Indian War: The Nez Perce Story*. New York: Oxford Univ. Press, 2009.

———. "Reconstructing Race." *Western Historical Quarterly* 34 (Mar. 2003): 6-26.

West, Stephen A. Review of *South Carolina Scalawags*, by Hyman Rubin III. *Journal of Southern History* 73 (Aug. 2007): 717.

Wetta, Frank J. *The Louisiana Scalawags: Politics, Race, and Terrorism during the Civil War and Reconstruction*. Baton Rouge: Louisiana State Univ. Press, 2013.

Wharton, Vernon Lane. *The Negro in Mississippi*. Chapel Hill: Univ. of North Carolina Press, 1947.

White, Richard. *Railroaded: The Transcontinentals and the Making of Modern America*. New York: W. W. Norton, 2011.

Wiener, Jon. "In Memoriam: Jack D. Foner." *AHA Perspectives* (Apr. 2000).

http://www.historians.org/publications-and-directories/perspectives-on-history/april-2000/in-memoriam-jack-d-foner (accessed Mar. 10, 2014).

Wiener, Jonathan M. "Class Structure and Economic Development in the American South, 1865-1955." *American Historical Review* 84 (Oct. 1979): 970-92.

Wiggins, Sarah Woolfolk. *The Scalawag in Alabama Politics, 1865-1881.* 1977. Reprint, Tuscaloosa: Univ. of Alabama Press, 1991.

Wilentz, Sean. *Chants Democratic: New York City and the Rise of the American Working Class, 1788-1850.* New York: Oxford Univ. Press, 1984.

Williams, George Washington. *A History of the African Race in America from 1619 to 1880.* 2 vols. New York: G. P. Putnam's Sons, 1883.

Williams, Kidada E. *They Left Great Marks on Me: African American Testimonies of Racial Violence from Emancipation to World War I.* New York: New York Univ. Press, 2012.

Williams, Lou Falkner. *The Great South Carolina Ku Klux Klan Trials, 1871-1872.* Athens: Univ. of Georgia Press, 1996.

Williams, T. Harry. *Lincoln and the Radicals.* Madison: Univ. of Wisconsin Press, 1941.

Williams, William Appleman. *The Tragedy of American Diplomacy.* 1959. Reprint, New York: W. W. Norton, 2009.

Williamson, Joel. *After Slavery: The Negro in South Carolina during Reconstruction.* Chapel Hill: Univ. of North Carolina Press, 1965.

Wilson, Mark. *The Business of Civil War: Military Mobilization and the State, 1861-1865.* Baltimore: Johns Hopkins Univ. Press, 2006.

Wilson, Woodrow. "The Reconstruction of the Southern States." *Atlantic Monthly* 87 (Jan. 1901): 1-15.

Wish, Harvey. *The American Historian: A Social-Intellectual History of the Writing of the American Past.* New York: Oxford Univ. Press, 1960.

Wood, Amy Louise. *Lynching and Spectacle: Witnessing Racial Violence in America, 1890-1940.* Chapel Hill: Univ. of North Carolina Press, 2009.

Woodman, Harold D. "'Class Structure and Economic Development in the American South, 1865-1955': Comments." *American Historical Review* 84 (Oct. 1979): 997-1001.

Woodward, C. Vann. *Origins of the New South, 1877-1913.* 1951. Rev. ed. Baton Rouge: Louisiana State Univ. Press, 1972.

———. *Reunion and Reaction: The Compromise of 1877 and the End of Reconstruction.* Boston: Little, Brown, 1951.

———. *The Strange Career of Jim Crow.* 1955. New York: Oxford Univ. Press, 1974.

Woodworth, Steven E., ed. *The Human Tradition in the Civil War and Reconstruction Era.* New York: Scholarly Resources, 1999.

Wormser, Richard. *The Rise and Fall of Jim Crow.* New York: St. Martins, 2003.

Wright, Gavin. *Old South, New South: Revolutions in the Southern Economy since the Civil War.* New York: Basic Books, 1986.

Zimmerman, Andrew. *Alabama in Africa: Booker T. Washington, the German Empire, and the Globalization of the New South.* Princeton, N.J.: Princeton Univ. Press, 2010.

———. "From the Rhine to the Mississippi: Property, Democracy, and Socialism in the American Civil War." *Journal of the Civil War Era* 5 (Mar. 2015): 3–37.

———, ed. *Marx, Engels, and the Civil War in the United States.* New York: International Publishers, forthcoming in 2016.

Zuczek, Richard. "The Government's Attack on the Ku Klux Klan: A Reassessment." *South Carolina Historical Magazine* 97 (Jan. 1996): 47–64.

———. "The Last Campaign of the Civil War: South Carolina and the Revolution of 1876." *Civil War History* 42 (Mar. 1996): 18–31.

———. *State of Rebellion: Reconstruction in South Carolina.* Columbia: Univ. of South Carolina Press, 1996.

Contributors

KEVIN ADAMS is Associate Professor of History at Kent State University. A specialist in the study of War and Society in the United States, he has published *Class and Race in the Frontier Army: Military Life in the West, 1870-1890* (2009). He served as Associate Editor of the journal *Civil War History* until the end of 2015. Adams currently is working on a series of projects that examines the U.S. Army's attempts to enforce federal power in the aftermath of the Civil War and Reconstruction.

EDWARD O. FRANTZ is Professor of History at the University of Indianapolis and Director of the Institute for Civic Leadership & Mayoral Archives. He is the editor of *Companion to the Reconstruction Presidents, 1865-1881* (2014) and the author of *The Door of Hope: Republican Presidents and the First Southern Strategy, 1877-1933* (2011).

R. BLAKESLEE GILPIN, Assistant Professor of History at Tulane University, won the Southern Historical Association's 2010 C. Vann Woodward Prize for the best dissertation in southern history. His first book, *John Brown Still Lives! America's Long Reckoning with Violence, Equality, and Change* (2011), was a finalist for the Gilder Lehrman Center's Frederick Douglass Prize. Gilpin also has edited (with Rose Styron) *Selected Letters of William Styron* (2012).

J. VINCENT LOWERY is Associate Professor of Humanistic Studies and History at the University of Wisconsin-Green Bay. He co-edited (with John David Smith) *The Dunning School: Historians, Race, and the Meaning of*

Reconstruction (2013) and contributed an essay on Paul Leland Haworth to that collection. The Historical Society of North Carolina awarded Lowery the R. D. W. Connor Award for his essay "The Transatlantic Dreams of the Port City Prophet: The Rural Reform Campaign of Hugh MacRae," which appeared in the *North Carolina Historical Review* in July 2013.

SHEPHERD W. MCKINLEY is Senior Lecturer of History at the University of North Carolina at Charlotte. He is the coauthor of *North Carolina: New Directions for an Old Land* (2006) and author of *Stinking Stones and Rocks of Gold: Phosphate, Fertilizer, and Industrialization in Postbellum South Carolina* (2014), winner of the 2014 George C. Rogers Jr. Book Award from the South Carolina Historical Society. He is also co-editor of *North Carolina during the First World War, 1914-1922* (forthcoming).

K. STEPHEN PRINCE is Assistant Professor of History at the University of South Florida. He is the author of *Stories of the South: Race and the Reconstruction of Southern Identity, 1865-1915* (2014) and *Radical Reconstruction: A Brief History with Documents* (2015). He is currently working on a study of Robert Charles and the 1900 New Orleans riot.

JOHN DAVID SMITH is the Charles H. Stone Distinguished Professor of American History at the University of North Carolina at Charlotte. He is the author or editor of many books including, most recently, *We Ask Only for Even-Handed Justice: Black Voices from Reconstruction, 1865-1877* (2014) and *Soldiering for Freedom: How the Union Army Recruited, Trained, and Deployed the U.S. Colored Troops* (2014, with Bob Luke). Smith received the Mayflower Society Award for Nonfiction for *Black Judas: William Hannibal Thomas and "The American Negro"* (2000).

ANDREW ZIMMERMAN is Professor of History at The George Washington University. He is the author of *Anthropology and Antihumanism in Imperial Germany* (2001) and *Alabama in Africa: Booker T. Washington, the German Empire, and the Globalization of the New South* (2010). He is also the editor of *Marx, Engels, and the Civil War in the United States* (forthcoming in 2016). Zimmerman is currently writing a history of the American Civil War as part of a transnational revolution against slave labor and wage labor.

Index

abolitionists, on colonization, 185-86
Africa, 171, 185-86
African Americans, 91, 181; agency of, 5, 21-22, 27, 31, 73, 75, 134; blamed for Reconstruction's failure, 19, 22-23; capabilities of, 18-19, 21, 186; changes effected by, 28, 143-44; changing attitudes about, 25, 95; citizenship of, 14, 18, 28, 32, 71, 74, 94, 99, 101-2, 141-42, 156, 157; commemorations and, 164-65; countermemory of Civil War and Reconstruction, 3, 82; Dunning School's contempt for, 20, 130; economic support for, 61, 77; fear of, 61, 79-80, 95; federal government and, 113-14, 117, 131-32; federal support for, 21, 26, 61, 80; free labor system and, 61, 117, 142; Freedmen's Bureau aid for, 4, 146-47; freedwomen, 140-42, 145-47; as historians, 3-4, 50-51, 72; historiography increasingly focused on, 28, 56-57, 74, 76, 96, 135; labor of, 22, 28, 30, 61, 78, 140; lack of land of, 7, 26, 38; leaving South after Redemption, 144-45; missions to Africa, 185-86; mobility of, 135-36; northerners' attitudes toward, 58-59, 61, 103, 159; northerners' weak commitment to, 75, 117; organizations and institutions of, 7, 28, 32, 136, 144; political participation of, 8, 19, 29, 33, 73, 79, 101-2, 122, 155; in politics, 29, 39, 101-2, 122, 155; power over white southerners, 18-20; presidents' support for, 123-24, 187; Radical Republicans advocating for, 4, 14, 70-71, 132; resisting efforts at control, 136-37; stereotypes of, 15, 18-19, 107n11, 164, 182; trying to acquire land, 7, 32, 135-36, 141; white southerners' treatment of, 13-14, 53, 133; withdrawing labor, 133-34, 176-77; women, 130, 133-34, 140-41, 144-45, 155-56; women working for and with, 61, 142-43; work ethics questioned, 80, 134-35. *See also* civil rights; suffrage

After Slavery Project, 147
After the Glory: The Struggles of Black Civil War Veterans (Shaffer), 163
The Age of Hate: Andrew Johnson and the Radicals (Milton), 20
agency, of African Americans, 5, 147; in Civil War and Reconstruction, 21-22; importance of understanding, 31, 73, 134; postvisionists minimizing, 27, 75; of slaves, 101-2; working-class, 72
agriculture, 85, 140, 173, 182; expansion of cotton growing, 184, 186; expansion of plantation system in, 184-85; globalization of, 184-85;

INDEX

agriculture (*cont.*)
    labor on sugar plantations, 138-39, 144; labor systems in, 29, 85, 131, 140-41, 171, 184; planters maintaining control of, 75, 135; planters trying to keep control of, 38, 134, 145, 174. *See also* plantation system
American Colonization Society (ACS), 185
American Mediterranean: Southern Slaveholders in the Age of Emancipation (Guterl), 158
American Negro Slavery (Phillips), 107n11
Anderson, Eric, 83
Andrew Johnson (Gordon-Reed), 100
Andrew Johnson: A Biography (Trefousse), 123
Andrew Johnson and Reconstruction (McKitrick), 51-53
Angels in the Machinery (Edwards), 121-22
"apprenticeship system" in British West Indies, 174
Archer, William, 2
Arenson, Adam, 157
Arkansas, overthrow of Reconstruction in, 13
Astor, Aaron, 35
At Freedom's Edge: Black Mobility and the Southern White Quest for Racial Control (Cohen), 135-36
Awaiting the Heavenly Country: The Civil War and America's Culture of Death (Schantz), 163

Baggett, James Alex, 78-79
Baker, Bruce E., 82, 147, 166
Baker, Ella, 122-23
Bardaglio, Peter W., 79-80
Barreyre, Nicholas, 119
Bassett, John Spencer, 3
Beale, Howard Kennedy, 4, 23, 72-73, 107n15, 131
Beard, Charles, 70

Beard, Mary, 70
Becoming Free in the Cotton South (O'Donovan), 35, 145, 154-55
Been in the Storm So Long: The Aftermath of Slavery (Litwack), 31, 96, 153-54
Before Jim Crow: The Politics of Race in Post-Emancipation Virginia (Dailey), 35
Belz, Herman, 26
Ben Tillman and the Reconstruction of White Supremacy (Kantrowitz), 160
Benedict, Michael Les, 5, 26, 74-75, 95, 100
Bennett, Lerone, Jr., 110n44
Bercaw, Nancy, 141, 156
Bergeron, Paul, 64n5
Berlin, Ira, 97
"The Best Men": Liberal Reformers in the Gilded Age (Sproat), 120
Beyond Redemption: Race, Violence, and the American South after the Civil War (Emberton), 155
biographies, 123-25, 160
The Birth of a Nation (Griffith film), 20, 91-92
Black Codes, 13-14, 53-54, 137, 145; defenders of, 20, 38, 50
Black Power U.S.A.: The Human Side of Reconstruction, 1867-1877 (Bennett), 110n44
Black Reconstruction: An Essay Towards a History of the Part Which Black Folk Played (Du Bois), 21-22, 51, 92-93, 113, 176-77
Blackmon, Douglas A., 104
Blaine, James G., 13-15
Blair, Frank, 114
Blair, William A., 61, 163-64
Blakeslee, George H., 183
Blight, David W., 5, 31-32, 116, 162, 182
Blum, Edward J., 35, 81
Blyden, E. W., 186
Boles, John B., 83, 95
Bourbons, 38, 115

Bowers, Claude G., 20, 50, 65n12, 65n13, 93
Bragg, William, 108n19
Branches without Roots: Genesis of the Black Working Class in the American South, 1862-1882 (Jaynes), 133-34
Brandwein, Pamela, 31, 78
Bright Radical Star: Black Freedom and White Supremacy on the Hawkeye Frontier (Dykstra), 30
Britain, 178, 186, 192n30
British West Indies, "apprenticeship system" in, 174
Brodie, Fawn, 94
Brophy, Alfred L., 39
Brown, Benjamin Gratz, 120
Brown, Thomas J., 84
Brown, William Garrott, 39n1
Bruce, Blanche K., 31
Bryan, William Jennings, 120
Bryce, James, 183
Burgess, John W., 12-13, 71, 107n11; influence of, 70, 130, 182-83
Burton, Vernon, 92, 95, 105, 110n49
Burying the Dead but Not the Past: Ladies' Memorial Associations and the Lost Cause (Janney), 164
business, liberals opposing limits on, 180-81
But There Was No Peace: The Role of Violence in the Politics of Reconstruction (Rable), 116
Butchart, Ronald E., 35
Butler, Benjamin, 138
Butler, Leslie, 151-52
By One Vote: The Disputed Presidential Election of 1876 (Holt), 31

Cain, Richard, 31
Calhoun, Charles C., 118-19
Capital (Marx), 178
capital, vs. labor, 159, 174
capitalism, 142, 171, 190n12; development of system, 174-75; industrial, 8, 29; lack of economic independence in, 175-76, 190n17; northern, 70, 156; owners vs. workers in, 159, 174
Capitol Men: The Epic Story of Reconstruction through the Lives of the First Black Congressmen (Dray), 31
Caribbean, imperialism in, 186-87
carpetbaggers, 70-71, 79; vilification of, 2, 15, 17-19, 23
Carter, Dan, 56, 101
Censer, Jane Turner, 160
Cheney, Matthew, 110n49
China, contract labor from, 139-40, 184
Cimbala, Paul, 35, 36
Cities of the Dead: Contesting the Memory of the Civil War in the South, 1865-1914 (Blair), 61, 164
citizenship, of African Americans, 32, 99, 156; demands for, 28, 141-42; expressions of, 101-2; fitness for, 18, 71, 94; meanings of, 74, 157; opposition to, 14, 101; social, 141-42
civic nationalism, 121
civil rights, 34, 71; blacks' ongoing struggle for, 30, 98; federal government and African Americans', 30, 38, 78, 113-14; Freedmen's Bureau protecting, 134, 135-36; freedpeople demanding, 141, 146, 181; Hayes's commitment to African Americans', 123-24; justifications for limiting African Americans', 71; northerners' lack of commitment to African Americans', 72, 74, 117, 142
Civil Rights acts, 20, 38, 49, 52, 59
Civil Rights Era (1960s), 4, 24, 26, 71
civil rights movement, 69, 82; linked to Reconstruction, 29, 34, 74, 122-23; Reconstruction as foundation for, 76, 98, 134; revisionism and, 71-72, 95; shortcomings of, 27, 74

Civil War, 178, 182; competing ideologies following, 61, 116; consequences of, 16, 60, 121; Democratic Party and, 61, 67n43; Dunning School's interpretations of, 3, 94, 107n11; effects of devastation of, 163-64; slavery as cause of, 13, 18; struggle to define meaning of, 162, 164-65; struggle to control memories of, 3, 161-62
Claiming the Union: Citizenship in the Post-Civil War South (Lee), 156
Clark, Kathleen Ann, 165
class, 23, 52; conflict and, 80, 82, 85; race and, 130, 179
Clinging to Memory: The Faithful Slave in Twentieth-Century America (McElya), 164
Clune, Erin Elizabeth, 140
Cohen, William, 135-36, 138
Colfax Massacre, 99
colonialism, 171, 182-85. See also imperialism
colonization, 185-86
Color-blind Justice: Albion Tourgée and the Quest for Racial Equality from the Civil War to Plessy v. Ferguson (Elliot), 160
Communism, 176-77
A Companion to the Civil War and Reconstruction (Ford), 84
Compromise of 1877, 114-15
Conceiving a New Republic: The Republican Party and the Southern Question, 1869-1900 (Calhoun), 118
Confederacy, Britain not aiding, 178
Confederates, 2-3, 16, 53, 61; Johnson's lenience toward, 14, 59, 135
Congress, 100, 130; 1884 elections to, 118-19; African Americans in, 8, 31, 39; Johnson *vs.*, 49, 56, 58-60
Congressional Reconstruction. See Radical Reconstruction
Conner, Frank, 37
conservatism: of Johnson, 48-49; of Reconstruction, 26-27, 69, 74-75; of Republicans, 96
Constitution, U.S., 49, 98
constitutional amendments (13th, 14th, and 15th), 31, 38, 74, 85, 98, 100, 114
constitutional conventions, southern, 55, 79
constitutions, state, 5-7, 24
contract ideology, 30
convict lease systems, 29
Coolies and Cane: Race, Labor, and Sugar in the Age of Emancipation (Jung), 139, 158
corruption, 3, 16, 112, 120; by black politicians, 21, 73; exaggerations of, 4, 24, 71; Radical Republicans accused of, 19-20, 73
Coulter, E. Merton, 23
court system, federal, 114
Cox, John H., 42n47, 73-75, 94
Cox, Karen L., 164
Cox, LaWanda, 42n47, 73-75, 94
Creating a Confederate Kentucky: The Lost Cause and Civil War Memory in a Border State (Marshall), 32, 163
criminal justice system, 30
Crooked Paths to Allotment: The Fight over Federal Indian Policy after the Civil War (Genetin-Pilawa), 157
cultural history, 151-53, 161, 166
Current, Richard N., 25

Dailey, Jane E., 35, 102
"The Dark and Bloody Ground of Reconstruction Historiography" (Weisberger), 23-24
Davis, David Brion, 8
Davis, Hugh, 33-34
Davis, Mike, 185
Davis, William W., 19
De Santis, Vincent J., 118
death and mourning, in memory studies, 163-64
The Death of Reconstruction: Race, Labor, and Politics in the Post-Civil

War North, 1865-1901 (Richardson), 30, 60-61, 103, 117, 142, 159
debt peonage, 29
Declaration of Dependence: The Long Reconstruction of Popular Politics in the South, 1861-1908 (Downs), 126, 160
Defining Moments: African American Commemoration and Political Culture in the South, 1863-1913 (Clark), 165
"Defining Reconstruction" (Burton, Herr, and Cheney), 110n49
Degler, Carl N., 20
Degrees of Freedom: Louisiana and Cuba after Slavery (Scott), 155
Delany, Martin, 185-86
democracy, 85, 161, 173; of postwar state governments, 24-25; Reconstruction as experiment in racial, 2-3, 7, 28; split of proletarian and bourgeois, 180-81
Democratic Party, 67n43, 114, 156; ascendancy as end of Reconstruction, 80, 144, 158-59; ideology after Civil War, 61-62; Redemption of, 61, 91; reintegration of national party, 61; southern, 16, 79-80, 122; strength of, 16, 118-19
disfranchisement: of African Americans, 3, 23, 82, 132; of former Confederates, 16
Dixie's Daughters: The United Daughters of the Confederacy and the Preservation of Confederate Culture (Cox), 164
Dixon, Thomas, 91-92
Dodd, William E., 17
Donald, David, 73
The Doom of Reconstruction: The Liberal Republicans in the Civil War Era (Slap), 31
The Door of Hope: Republican Presidents and the First Southern Strategy, 1877-1933 (Frantz), 117
Downs, Gregory P., 126, 160

Dray, Philip, 31, 100, 104
Du Bois, W. E. B., 73, 91; *Black Reconstruction* by, 51, 92-93; on effects of Reconstruction, 1, 21, 39; evaluation of arguments of, 22-23; influence of, 51, 72, 97, 113; on labor, 104, 130, 176-77; Marxism of, 21-22, 130-31; on racism, 93, 171-72
Dube, John, 186
Dunning, William Archibald, 2, 17, 65n12, 71, 82, 107n11; Foner discrediting, 97-98; influence of, 20, 24, 48, 97, 106n10, 130; on Johnson, 48-50, 65n8; racial hierarchy of, 18-19, 101-2, 182-83
Dunning School, 2-3, 86; assumptions and conclusions of, 70-71, 73, 130; biographies and history of, 83-84; discrediting of, 6, 23-25, 72, 74, 108n19; dissertations by, 19-20; influence of, 17, 93-94, 107n15; praise for, 73, 84-85; racism of, 70-72, 93-94, 98, 107n11; on Reconstruction as nightmare, 3-4, 69, 183; regional focus of, 10n8, 107n11; revisionists' criticisms of, 21, 24, 69, 72-73, 94, 131
The Dunning School: Historians, Race, and the Meaning of Reconstruction (Smith and Lowery), 83-84, 107n12, 166
Dutton, Faye E., 33
Dykstra, Robert R., 30

economics, 34-35, 133, 183-84
economy, 125, 133, 171; black efforts at independence in, 28, 32; global, 184-85; influence on political system, 119-20
education, 21, 26, 28, 74, 85
Edwards, Laura F., 33, 80, 102, 141, 156
Edwards, Rebecca, 121-22
Egerton, Douglas R., 1-2, 77, 104-5
elections, 114, 118-20

231

INDEX

Elliot, Mark, 160
Elliott, Robert Brown, 31
emancipation, 107n11, 158, 173, 185; historians' focus on, 97-98, 165; labor and, 139, 176-80; meanings of, 155, 174
"emancipationist vision," 32, 116, 162
Emancipation's Diaspora: Race and Reconstruction in the Upper Midwest (Schwalm), 35
Emberton, Carole, 155
empire. *See* imperialism
end, of Reconstruction, 7, 142, 172; dates of, 82, 115, 119, 158-59; effects of, 16, 18, 132
Enforcement Acts, 38
equality, racial, 6, 25; failure of, 1, 76; quest for, 21-22, 160
The Era of Reconstruction, 1865-1877 (Stampp), 24-25, 74, 131-32
Essays on the Civil War and Reconstruction (Dunning), 17-19, 71
Eudell, Demetrius L., 155
Europe, 171, 178-79, 182-83, 185
An Example for All the Land: Emancipation and the Struggle over Equality in Washington, D.C. (Masur), 155
Exodusters, 144

The Facts of Reconstruction: Essays in Honor of John Hope Franklin (Anderson), 83
failure, Reconstruction as, 17; blacks blamed for, 22-23; blamed on black suffrage, 18, 74, 84-85; blamed on conservatism, 25, 27; blamed on lack of land reform, 26, 132; blamed on political incompetence, 56, 115-16; contradictions of, 3-5; effects of, 28-29, 76; influences on opinion of, 20, 94; as missed opportunity *vs.*, 1-2, 37; northerners' responsibility for, 32-33, 82-83; other factors blamed for, 92-93, 130; partial, 37-38; problems as intractable,

7-8; revisions of conclusion of, 4-6; as tragedy *vs.*, 5-6, 25, 37
Fairclough, Adam, 84-86
families, African American, 102, 141-42, 146
Farmer-Kaiser, Mary, 146
Faulkner, Carol, 61, 142-43
"Fault Lines, Color Lines, and Party Lines: Race, Labor, and Collective Action in Louisiana and Cuba, 1862-1912" (Scott), 139
Faust, Drew Gilpin, 163
Feldman, Glenn, 83
Fenians, Freedmen, and Southern Whites (Snay), 121, 158
Festivals of Freedom: Memory and Meaning in African American Emancipation Celebrations, 1809-1915 (Kachun), 165
Fields, Barbara J., 34
Fifteenth Amendment, 15, 28. *See also* constitutional amendments (13th, 14th, and 15th)
Fighting Chance: The Struggle over Woman Suffrage and Black Suffrage in Reconstruction America (Dutton), 33
Final Freedom: The Civil War, the Abolition of Slavery, and the Thirteenth Amendment (Vorenberg), 31
First International, 178-80
Fitzgerald, Michael W., 5-8, 11n22, 24, 26, 29, 32, 35, 85
Fleming, Walter Lynwood, 19
Florida, redemption of, 159
Foner, Eric, 2-3, 24-25, 27, 60, 116, 134; on Dunning School, 20, 107n12; on effects of Reconstruction, 26, 28, 85, 135, 147; influence of, 97-99, 104, 154; integrating revisionism and postrevisionism, 69-70, 78; on lack of understanding of Reconstruction, 75, 105; on national politics, 113-14; providing best synthesis of Reconstruction historiography, 28, 59, 75-77,

232

85-86, 113, 134; *Reconstruction: America's Unfinished Revolution* by, 6-8, 47-48, 58-59
Ford, Lacy K., 84
Foreign Affairs, 183
Forever Free: The Story of Emancipation and Reconstruction (Foner), 29, 98
Foster, Gaines M., 81
Fourteenth Amendment, 28, 52, 180-81. *See also* constitutional amendments (13th, 14th, and 15th)
The Fourteenth Amendment: From Political Principle to Judicial Doctrine (Nelson), 31
Frankel, Noralee, 33
Franklin, John Hope, 4, 23, 27, 108n17, 132; Dunning School challenged by, 72, 74; influence of, 24, 97; synthesis by, 73, 94-95
Frantz, Edward, 117
Fredrickson, George M., 153
free labor, 78, 137, 153-54; transition from slavery to, 130, 147, 154-55
free labor ideology, 61, 117, 138, 142
Free Soil, Free Labor, Free Men: The Ideology of the Republican Party before the Civil War (Foner), 60
Free to Work: Labor Law, Emancipation, and Reconstruction, 1815-1880 (Schmidt), 34, 136-37
Freedmen's Bureau, 60, 80, 114; aid offered by, 4, 132, 134-37; end of, 38, 132; labor of black women and, 146-47, 156; seized by Radical Republicans, 133-34
The Freedmen's Bureau and Reconstruction: Reconsiderations (Cimbala and Miller), 35
Freedmen's Bureau Bill, Johnson's veto of, 49
freedom, 155, 176; contested meanings of, 147, 154, 157, 173. *See also* emancipation
Freedom: A Documentary History of Emancipation (Berlin), 97
Freedom National (Oakes), 64n3

Freedom's Frontier: California and the Struggle over Unfree Labor, Emancipation, and Reconstruction (Smith), 35, 157
Freedom's Women: Black Women and Families in Civil War Era Mississippi (Frankel), 33
freedpeople. *See* African Americans
Freedwomen and the Freedmen's Bureau: Race, Gender, and Public Policy in the Age of Emancipation (Farmer-Kaiser), 146
From Appomattox to Montmartre: Americans and the Paris Commune (Katz), 158
From Bloody Shirt to Full Dinner Pail: The Transformation of Politics and Governance in the Gilded Age (Calhoun), 118-19
From Bondage to Contract: Wage Labor, Marriage, and the Market in the Age of Slave Emancipation (Stanley), 155
From Slavery to Agrarian Capitalism in the Cotton Plantation South: Central Georgia, 1800-1880 (Reidy), 34-35
From Slavery to Freedom (Franklin), 108n17

Gannon, Barbara, 163
Garner, James W., 13, 19, 71
Garvey, Marcus, 122-23, 143-44, 186
gender, 102-3, 122, 130; Freedmen's Bureau struggling with conflicting assumptions of, 146-47; intellectual history and, 156-57; studies of, 33, 79, 156
gender roles, 121, 141-42, 160
Gendered Freedoms: Race, Rights, and the Politics of Household in the Delta, 1861-1875 (Bercaw), 141, 156
Gendered Strife and Confusion: The Political Culture of Reconstruction (Edwards), 33, 141, 156
Genetin-Pilawa, C. Joseph, 157
Georgia, labor issues in, 145
Gilded Age, 118-20, 159

Gillette, William, 5, 26, 31, 115-16
Gilmore, Glenda, 3, 102
Give Me Liberty! An American History (Foner), 98
global history. *See* transnational history
Glymph, Thavolia, 32, 145-46, 156
Gordon-Reed, Annette, 100
Gough, Jerry B., 79
government, citizens' relation to, 114, 118, 160
government, federal, 126, 186; African Americans' rights and, 38, 78, 113-14; effects of Reconstruction policies of, 28, 54-55; expanded powers of, 75-76, 114, 117; fear of African Americans' dependence on, 61, 159; influence of Reconstruction on, 12; lack of commitment to freedpeople, 21, 26, 131-32; Reconstruction's failure blamed on, 2, 38, 92-93; roles of, 69, 81, 143, 159; support for freedpeople by, 21, 80
government, local, 38, 77
government, state: Democrats retaking, 38, 80, 138; leadership of, 53, 56, 77; Reconstruction, 4-5, 74; Republican, 21, 24-25, 75, 80, 100, 144
Grant: A Biography (McFeely), 124
Grant, Ulysses S., 14, 163, 187; biographies of, 124-25; corruption under, 19, 120; Reconstruction policies of, 115-16
The Great Heart of the Republic: St. Louis and the Cultural Civil War (Arenson), 157
Great Migration, during WWI, 145
Greater Reconstruction, 62
Greeley, Horace, 120, 181
Green, Fletcher M., 24
Greeson, Jennifer Rae, 161
Griffith, D. W., 92
Guterl, Matthew Pratt, 158

Hahn, Steven, 32, 97, 104-5; on blacks' political participation, 101-2, 122; on expanded time frame for historiography, 143, 145, 147
Hale, Grace Elizabeth, 166
Hamilton, J. G. de Roulhac, 19
Hamilton, Peter Joseph, 13
Hands of Persons Unknown: The Lynching of Black America (Dray), 100
A Hard Fight for We: Women's Transition from Slavery to Freedom in South Carolina (Schwalm), 33, 140, 156
Harris, J. William, 101
Harris, William C., 30
Hart, Albert Bushnell, 21
Haworth, Paul L., 20, 71
Hayes, Rutherford B., 16, 112, 123-24
Hayford, J. E. Casely, 186
Help Me to Find My People (Williams), 102
Herr, David, 110n49
Hesseltine, William B., 53
Hirshson, Stanley P., 118
historians, 83, 105; focused on culture *vs.* politics, 57-58; influence of race of, 73, 94
historical profession, African Americans marginalized within, 50-51
historiography, of Reconstruction, 39n1, 135, 140; biases in, 24, 37-38, 92-93; biographies in, 51-53, 83, 123-25, 160; call for expanding time frame of, 102, 110n49; changes in, 26, 30, 95; changing focuses of, 56-57, 99, 147, 151; cultural history in, 166; Dunning School's dominance of, 17, 19, 94, 107n15; economics and labor in, 34-35, 133; effects of time passage on, 12-13; expanded geography of, 33-34, 77, 103, 157, 158; expanded populations in, 33, 77-80, 96, 157; expanded time frame of, 29-30, 36, 118, 121-22, 126, 143, 145, 147, 158-61; expanded topics

included in, 35; focus on African Americans, 56-57, 76; focus on complexity of Reconstruction, 6, 25, 36, 70, 78-79, 83, 86, 157; Foner's remaining main synthesis of, 77, 85-86, 98-99, 113, 134; future of, 8; gaps in, 25, 46, 112-13; gender in, 33; influence of current events and attitudes on, 71-72, 95; of intellectual life, 153; on national politics, 112-13, 127; need for synthesis in, 27, 28, 61, 73; ongoing reevaluations in, 85-86; partisanship of, 12-13, 21-23, 70, 92; Progressive, 65n12; regional analyses in, 34-35; revisionists' dominance of, 25-26, 74, 94-95; southern perspective in, 20, 92; syntheses in, 19, 75, 94, 104; transnational history in, 172, 187-88

history, as site of power, contestation, and debate, 161-62

History of the United States from the Compromise of 1850 (Rhodes), 17

Hobsbawm, Eric J., 1

Hogue, James K., 30, 82

Holt, Michael F., 31

home rule, as euphemism for white supremacy, 3, 19

Honoring the Civil War Dead: Commemoration and the Problem of Reconciliation (Neff), 164

Hoogenboom, Ari, 123-24

households, 80, 156

Howard, Oliver O., 135

Howard, Victor B., 80-81

Hume, Richard L., 79

Hunter, Tera, 102-3

Huntington, Collis P., 125

Hyman, Harold, 100

immigrants, 29, 139, 175-76, 178, 184

imperialism, 181-84, 186-87. *See also* colonialism

India, contract labor from, 184

industrialization, 171, 175

The Inner Civil War: Northern Intellectuals and the Crisis of the Union (Fredrickson), 153

intellectual history, 151-53, 155; gender and, 156-57, 160; memory in, 161-66

international history. *See* transnational history

Iron Confederacies: Southern Railways, Klan Violence, and Reconstruction (Nelson), 34, 156

Janney, Caroline E., 32, 162-63, 164

Jaynes, Gerald David, 133-34

Jim Crow laws, 24, 82, 102-3, 142; Dunning School justifying, 70-72; rise of, 38-39

Johnson, Andrew, 64n5, 65n13, 81, 100; biographies of, 51-53, 123; Congress and, 48, 56, 58-60, 73; goals of, 54, 59; lenience toward Confederates, 14, 135; personality and governing style of, 24, 48-49, 52, 73; Radical Republicans *vs.*, 2-3, 15, 48-50; Reconstruction plans of, 2-3, 19, 47, 53-56, 77; Republicans and, 48, 76; role in collapse of Presidential Reconstruction, 51-52, 59

Journal of Race Development, 183

Jung, Moon-Ho, 103-4, 139-40, 158

Kachun, Mitch, 165

Kantrowitz, Stephen, 32, 160

Katz, Philip M., 158

Kelly, Brian, 147

Kentucky, 163

Knights of Labor, 139

Ku Klux Klan, 14-15, 24, 92, 99, 158

labor, 28, 143, 157, 182; in agriculture, 144, 171; blacks withdrawing, 140-41, 146, 176-77; capital *vs.*,

INDEX

labor (*cont.*)
 159, 174; contested meanings of, 154, 155; contract, 184; control of, 133, 137-38, 142; domestic, 145-46; exploitation of, 29, 104; freedpeople's, 30, 133; freedpeople's work ethics questioned, 80, 134-35; freedwomen's, 140-41, 145-47, 156; immigrants', 139-40; limits on work days, 179-80; in manufacturing, 171, 190n14; mobility of, 135-38; planters trying to control, 135-36, 145, 154, 174; in Reconstruction historiography, 34-35, 155; slaves', 61, 139; task labor system in, 140-41; wage, 173, 175-76, 178-79
labor activism, 145, 158; freedwomen's, 140-41; northerners' fear of, 103, 142; on sugar plantations, 138-39
labor ideology, 60-61
labor law, 34, 136-37
labor movement, 29, 176-79, 180
labor relations, 32
land: freedpeople trying to acquire, 7, 32, 135-36, 141; lack of, 7, 26, 38
land reform: lack of, 6, 26, 75, 132; Republicans not promoting, 77, 136
The Last Indian War: The Nez Perce Story (West), 157
Lears, Jackson, 126
Lee, Susanna Michele, 156
legislatures, state, 8, 21-22. *See also* government, state
Let Us Have Peace: Ulysses S. Grant and the Politics of War and Reconstruction, 1861-1868 (Simpson), 124
Lewis, David Levering, 93
Liberal Republican Party, 181
Liberal Republicans, 120-21
liberals, 180-82
Liberia, 172, 185
Lincoln, Abraham, 19, 30, 52, 123
Lincoln and Reconstruction (Rodrigue), 30
Lincoln's Last Months (Harris), 30
Linebaugh, Peter, 172-73

Link, Arthur S., 83
Litwack, Leon F., 25-26, 31, 75, 96, 153-54
Logan, Rayford W., 118
Lost Cause perspective, 2, 124
Louisiana, 103-4, 138, 159
Love, Eric T., 187
Lowery, J. Vincent, 83-84, 107n12, 166
loyalty, southerners' claims of, 156
Lynch, John R., 72
lynching. *See* violence
Lynching and Spectacle: Witnessing Racial Violence in America, 1890-1940 (Wood), 166

Making Whiteness: The Culture of Segregation in the South, 1890-1940 (Hale), 166
manufacturing, free and slave labor in, 190n14
marriage, 79-80, 155
Marshall, Anne E., 32, 163
Marten, James, 163
Marx, Karl, 178-79
Marxism, of Du Bois, 92, 130-31, 177
Masters without Slaves (Roark), 96
Masur, Kate, 33, 155
McConnell, Stuart, 163
McElya, Micki, 164
McFeely, William S., 5, 26, 124
McKinley, William, 120
McKitrick, Eric, 51-53, 56, 59, 74-75, 94
memory: Civil War and Reconstruction in, 32, 82, 165-66; death and mourning in, 163-64; in intellectual history, 161-66; reconciliationist, emancipationist, or white supremacist, 116, 162
military governments, 20, 24, 60
military occupation of South by, 4, 14-15, 77, 172
Military Reconstruction Acts of 1867, 38
militias, suppressing black labor activism, 139
Miller, Randall M., 35-36

Index

Milton, George Fort, 20
"Mirror for Americans: A Century of Reconstruction History" (Franklin), 95
miscegenation, fear of, 79-80
monetary policy, 119-20
Moneyhon, Carl, 101
Montgomery, David, 179
monuments, 105, 164
A More Perfect Union (Hyman), 100
More Than Freedom: Fighting for Black Citizenship in a White Republic (Kantrowitz), 32

A Nation under Our Feet: Black Political Struggles in the Rural South from Slavery to the Great Migration (Hahn), 32, 101-2, 122, 143-44
National Association for the Advancement of Colored People (NAACP), 92
National Labor Reform Party, 179
National Labor Union (NLU), 179
nationalism, 126, 158, 161
Native Americans, 61-62, 157, 186
Nazi Germany, racial hierarchies in, 182
Neff, John R., 163-64
"Negro rule," Reconstruction imposing, 2
Nelson, Scott Reynolds, 34, 156
Nelson, William E., 31
Neo-Confederates, 37
New Orleans, 30, 82
Nolen, Evelyn Thomas, 83
North, 34, 49, 85, 130; attitude toward South in, 37-38, 53; attitudes toward Reconstruction in, 55-57, 82-83; economic and political changes in, 8, 28-29, 78; fear of labor activism in, 30, 142; labor laws in, 136-38
northerners, white, 19, 103, 161, 164; attitudes toward African Americans and labor, 61, 159; weak commitment to freedpeople, 32-33, 75, 117, 142

Nothing But Freedom: Emancipation and Its Legacy (Foner), 97

Oakes, James, 64n3
Oberholtzer, Ellis P., 17
O'Donovan, Susan Eva, 35, 145, 154-55
An Old Creed for the New South: Proslavery Ideology and Historiography, 1865-1918 (Smith), 165
One Kind of Freedom: The Economic Consequences of Emancipation (Ransom and Sutch), 133, 140
The Ordeal of the Reunion: A New History of Reconstruction (Summers), 35-36
Our South: Geographic Fantasy and the Rise of National Literature (Greeson), 161
Out of the House of Bondage: The Transformation of the Plantation Household (Glymph), 32, 145-46, 156

Pacific islands, 171, 186-87
Panic of 1873, 119-20, 185
Paris Commune of 1871, 158, 181
Parsons, Elaine Frantz, 166
"The Past as a Foreign Country: Reconstruction, Inside and Out" (Smith), 111n50
Patrick, Rembert W., 83
patronalism, 126
Payne, Charles, 128n20
The Peculiar Institution (Stampp), 51
Perman, Michael, 5-6, 10n8, 26, 77, 94-95, 115; on Johnson and Presidential Reconstruction, 53-56; on moderate Republicans, 74-75
Personal Memoirs of Ulysses S. Grant, 125
Phelps, Christopher, 21-22
Phillips, Ulrich Bonnell, 107n11
Pinchback, Pinckney B. S., 31
plantation system, 7; blacks' influence on, 28, 133; continuity of, 6, 29, 132; expansion of, 183-85
policy history, 47
political history, 155

237

INDEX

Political Language of Emancipation in the British Caribbean and the U.S. South (Eudell), 155
political parties, 115, 179. *See also specific parties*
political rights. *See* civil rights
Political Science Quarterly, 183
The Political Worlds of Slavery and Freedom (Hahn), 102
politics, 30, 82, 100, 180; African Americans in, 8, 19, 29, 39, 101-2, 122, 155; black organizations and institutions in, 28, 32; in Gilded Age, 118-19; historians focused on culture *vs.*, 57-58; influences on, 119-20, 125-26, 155; limits of moderate, 55-56; monetary policy in, 119-20; national, 113-14, 118-19, 121-22, 127; race in, 114, 171; Reconstruction-era, 112-13; religion's intersection with, 80-81; women's participation in, 33, 121-22
Poole, W. Scott, 81
population, black, 15
post-postrevisionists, 11n22, 38, 70
postrevisionists, 5-6, 57; critiques of, 8, 75, 86; questioning effectiveness of Reconstruction, 69, 134; on Reconstruction, 5-6; revisionists and, 26-27, 69-70, 74-76, 78
Presidential Reconstruction, 61-62; ignored by historians, 46, 57-58; Johnson's role in collapse of, 51-56, 59
presidents, 100; biographies of, 123-25; elections of, 119-20; of Reconstruction Era, 112, 117, 127
The Problem South: Region, Empire, and the New Liberal State, 1880-1930 (Ring), 161
Progressive Era, 65n12, 126
Prosser, Gabriel, 104

Rable, George, 99-100, 116
race, 164, 175; attitudes on, 25, 71, 79;

effects of color line, 171-72; in historiography, 26, 155; influence of historians', 73, 94; influence on economic practices, 183-84; meanings of, 157; in politics, 114, 182
Race and Reunion: The Civil War in American Memory (Blight), 31-32, 116, 162
race relations, southern, 50, 139
racism, 185; of Dunning School, 70, 71, 84, 98, 107n11, 183; historiography and, 92-95; Johnson's, 64n5, 73; post-slavery, 57, 124, 182; in U.S. imperialism, 186-87; of white working class, 175, 179
Radical Reconstruction, 46, 59, 70; conservatism of, 69, 74-75; influence of northern Christians on, 80-81; revisionists rehabilitating, 69, 73
Radical Republicans: accusations against, 2-3, 15-16, 73; character of, 4, 17, 73; civic, not economic, ideology, 76-77; corruption under, 19, 73; criticized as not radical enough, 26-27, 77; Dunning School denouncing, 20, 69; effects of policies, 15-16; Freedmen's Bureau seized by, 133-34; in historiography, 24, 56-57; influence of northern Christians in, 73, 80-81; Johnson *vs.*, 48-50, 52, 73; revised reputation of, 4, 69, 73, 132; state governments under, 21, 24-25, 75, 80, 100, 144. *See also* Republicans
Railroaded: The Transcontinentals and the Making of Modern America (White), 125
railroads, 125, 156
Rainey, Joseph H., 31
Ramsdell, Charles W., 19-20
Ransom, Roger L., 133, 140
Reading Southern History: Essays on Interpreters and Interpretations (Feldman), 83

Rebels on the Border: Civil War, Emancipation, and the Reconstruction of Kentucky and Missouri (Astor), 35
Rebirth of a Nation: The Making of Modern America (Lears), 126
Rebuilding Zion: The Religious Reconstruction of the South, 1863-1877 (Stowell), 35
reconciliation, 49, 182
"reconciliationist vision," 162
Reconstructing Reconstruction: The Supreme Court and the Production of Historical Truth (Brandwein), 31
Reconstruction. *See* Presidential Reconstruction; Radical Reconstruction
Reconstruction: After the Civil War (Franklin), 24, 73, 95
Reconstruction: America's Unfinished Revolution (Foner), 6-8, 47-48, 114, 154; as best synthesis, 75-76, 85-86, 113, 134; influence of, 97-98, 154
Reconstruction: New Perspectives on the Postbellum United States (Brown), 84
Reconstruction: Political and Economic, 1865-1877 (Dunning), 17, 19, 48, 71
Reconstruction in the Cane Fields: From Slavery to Free Labor in Louisiana's Sugar Parishes, 1862-1880 (Rodrigue), 35, 138, 154-55
The Reconstruction of Mississippi (Garner), 13
The Reconstruction of Southern Debtors: Bankruptcy after the Civil War (Thompson), 34
The Reconstruction of White Southern Womanhood (Censer), 160
The Reconstruction Period: The History of North America (Hamilton), 13
The Reconstruction Presidents (Simpson), 124
Redeemers, 73, 119
Redemption, 91, 138, 144-45, 159
Rediker, Marcus, 172-73

Reforging the White Republic: Race, Religion, and American Nationalism, 1865-1898 (Blum), 35, 161
regionalism, 119-20, 161
Regosin, Elizabeth A., 163
Rehearsal for Reconstruction: The Port Royal Experiment (Rose), 153
Reidy, Joseph P., 34-35
religion, and politics, 80-81
Remembering the Civil War: Reunion and the Limits of Reconciliation (Janney), 32, 162-63
republicanism, 118-21, 175
Republicans, 57, 60, 82, 117, 118, 136, 144; conservatism of, 7, 96; criticisms of, 7, 11n22, 42n47, 70, 118; Democrats retaking power from, 59, 80, 144; end of dominance of, 118-19; freedpeople and, 14, 72, 144; guiding Reconstruction, 74-75, 119, 142; Johnson *vs.*, 48, 52, 65n8, 76; northern, 72, 122, 142; postrevisionist historians on, 6, 57; southern, 30, 78-79 (*see also* scalawags). *See also* Radical Republicans
Retreat from Reconstruction (Gillette), 115-16
Reunion without Compromise: The South and Reconstruction, 1865-1868 (Perman), 53-56
Revels, Hiram R., 31
revisionists, 4, 42n35, 42n47, 53-55, 57, 86; civil rights movement and, 71-72, 74, 134; criticizing Dunning School, 17, 21, 24, 69, 72-73, 94-95, 131; dominating Reconstruction historiography, 22-26, 74; postrevisionists and, 69-70, 74-76, 78; postrevisionists on, 5-6, 26-27; rehabilitating Radical Republicans, 73, 132
Rhodes, James Ford, 17-19, 94
Richardson, Heather Cox, 30, 33-34, 103; on end of Reconstruction, 82,

Richardson, Heather Cox (*cont.*) 142; on free labor ideology, 60-61; on northerners' lack of commitment to African Americans' rights, 117, 159; on time frame for Reconstruction historiography, 159-60
The Right to Vote: Politics and the Passage of the Fifteenth Amendment (Gillette), 31
rights. *See* civil rights
Ring, Natalie J., 161
The Road to Redemption (Perman), 115-16
Roark, James L., 96, 104
Rodrigue, John C., 30, 35, 103, 138, 154-55
Roediger, David, 179
The Romance of Reunion: Northerners and the South, 1865-1900 (Silber), 164
Roots of Disorder: Race and Criminal Justice in the American South, 1817-1880 (Waldrep), 30
Roots of Southern Populism (Hahn), 101
Rose, Willie Lee, 153
Rosen, Hannah, 33, 102, 155-56
Ross, Michael A., 85
Rothman, Adam, 8
Rowland, Leslie S., 85
Rubin, Hyman, III, 79
rural areas, politics in, 122
Rutherford B. Hayes: Warrior and President (Hoogenboom), 123-24

Saunt, Claudio, 186
Savage, Kirk, 164
Saville, Julie, 35, 101, 136, 154-55
scalawags, 70-71, 78-79; vilification of, 2, 15, 17-19, 31. *See also* Republicans: southern
scandals, in Reconstruction-era politics, 112
Schantz, Mark A., 163
Schmidt, James D., 34, 78, 136-38
scholarship. *See* historiography

Schooling for the Freed People: Teaching, Learning, and the Struggle for Black Freedom (Butchart), 35
Schwalm, Leslie A., 33, 35, 140, 156
Scott, Rebecca, 139, 155
Scott, Tom, 125
Scramble for Africa, 185
secession, as crime, 14
Second Reconstruction. *See* civil rights movement
"second slavery," capitalist, 190n17
segregation, attachment to, 96
self-reconstruction, 54
Sellers, Charles, 190n12
sense history, 166
serfdom, agriculture shifting away from, 171
sexuality, fear of African Americans', 79-80
Seymour, Horatio, 114, 118
Shaffer, Donald, 163
sharecropping, 29; as benefit for African Americans, 85, 131; effects of, 133, 135; as global model, 177-78
A Short History of Reconstruction (Foner), 28, 97
Silber, Nina, 164
Simpkins, Francis Butler, 4, 23, 72-73, 131
Simpson, Brooks, 124
Slap, Andrew L., 31, 120-21
slavery, 94, 97, 165, 173; as cause of war, 13, 18; justifications for, 107n11, 182; opposition to, 172, 175-76; postwar forms of, 13-14, 29, 137; roots and legacies of, 104-5; similarity of other labor systems to, 131, 174-76, 184; transition to free labor from, 60, 130, 147, 154-55
Slavery and Freedom on the Middle Ground: Maryland during the Nineteenth Century (Fields), 34
Slavery by Another Name: The Re-Enslavement of Black Americans

Index

from the Civil War to World War II (Blackmon), 104
slaves, 164; agency of, 101-2; labor of, 61, 174, 176-77, 190n14
Smalls, Robert, 31
Smith, Jean Edward, 125
Smith, John David, 83-84, 107n12, 165, 166
Smith, Mark, 111n50
Smith, Stacey L., 35, 157
Snay, Mitchell, 121, 158
social history, 151, 154-55, 160
socialism, 173, 176, 178-80
Sombart, Werner, 180
South, 53, 122, 161, 164; African Americans leaving, 144-45; continuity in, 26, 29, 115-16, 134; Dunning School's sympathy with, 69, 130; effects of Reconstruction policies on, 13, 24, 28-29, 60, 77; imagined effects of enforced sectional peace on, 55-56; Johnson trying to champion, 54, 59; military occupation of, 4, 14-15, 71, 77; Old *vs.* New, 6, 26, 182; punishment of, 18, 37-38, 70; race relations in, 16, 50, 139; racial hierarchies in, 182
South Africa, racial hierarchies in, 182
South Carolina, 79, 101, 140-41, 159
South Carolina during Reconstruction (Simkins and Woody), 131
The South during Reconstruction (Coulter), 23
The South under Siege (Conner), 37
southerners, white, 4, 61, 70, 96, 139, 156; acting on race, not class interests, 85, 130, 161; black political participation and, 18-19, 85, 101; efforts to maintain control, 101, 136, 154, 174; freedmen and, 13-14, 74; maintaining control of agriculture, 75, 134-35, 174; political parties of, 16, 78-79; responses to Reconstruction, 2-3, 15-16, 53-55, 59, 71
Spanish American War, 16, 187

Splendid Failure: Postwar Reconstruction in the American South (Fitzgerald), 32
Sproat, John G., 120
Stagg, John W., 15
Stampp, Kenneth M., 4, 24-25, 51, 72, 74, 94-95, 97, 131-32
Standing Soldiers, Kneeling Slaves: Race, War, and Monument in Nineteenth-Century America (Savage), 164
Stanley, Amy Dru, 137, 140, 155
"state action doctrine," of Supreme Court, 30, 78
State of Rebellion (Zuczek), 101
states, 18, 54; historians examining Reconstruction in, 19-20, 101, 103-4, 107n11. *See also* government, state
states' rights, 2
Stevens, Thaddeus, 18-19, 50, 52, 70, 76
Stowell, Daniel W., 35, 81
successes, of Reconstruction, 7-8, 38, 82-83; Foner on, 28, 85; as foundation for civil rights movement, 4, 76
suffrage, for African Americans, 3, 8, 14, 16, 30; advocates for, 15, 143; benefits attributed to, 21-22, 85; blamed for Reconstruction's failure, 71, 74; disfranchisement, 82; Dunning School's criticism of, 71, 84-85, 130, 183; effects of, 85, 144; grim predictions for, 17-18; importance of, 6, 28; lack of commitment to, 72, 181; responses to, 57, 99-100
Summers, Mark Wahlgren, 7, 8, 11n22, 35-36, 82-83
Sumner, Charles, 19, 70
Supreme Court, 30, 78
Sutch, Richard, 133, 140

task labor system, 140-41
Taylor, Alrutheus A., 22, 106n7
tenant farming, 29

241

territorial expansion, 62. *See also* imperialism
Terror in the Heart of Freedom: Citizenship, Sexual Violence, and the Meaning of Race in the Postemancipation South (Rosen), 33, 155-56
They Left Great Marks on Me: African American Testimonies of Racial Violence From Emancipation to World War I (Williams), 165
Thirteenth Amendment, 28. *See also* constitutional amendments (13th, 14th, and 15th)
The Thirteenth Amendment and American Freedom: A Legal History (Tsesis), 31
This Republic of Suffering: Death and the American Civil War (Faust), 163
Thomas, David Yancey, 12-13
Thompson, C. Mildred, 20, 71
Thompson, Elizabeth Lee, 34
Thornton, J. Mills, 85
Tillman, Benjamin, 160
To Joy My Freedom (Hunter), 102-3
Toombs, Robert, 15
Tourgée, Albion W., 160
The Tragic Era: The Revolution after Lincoln (Bowers), 20, 50, 93
transnational history, 172-73, 187-88
Trefousse, Hans L., 123
Trelease, Allen, 99
Trent, William P., 15-16
The Trial of Democracy: Black Suffrage & Northern Republicans, 1860-1930 (Wang), 30
Tsesis, Alexander, 31
Tunnell, Ted, 79
Tuskegee Institute, 186
Twenty Years of Congress (Blaine), 13-15
Twitchell, Marshall H., 79

U. S. Grant: American Hero, American Myth (Waugh), 124, 163
Ulysses S. Grant: Triumph over Adversity, 1822-1865 (Simpson), 124
Uncivil War: Five New Orleans Street Battles and the Rise and Fall of Radical Reconstruction (Hogue), 30
Under the Guardianship of the Nation: The Freedmen's Bureau and the Reconstruction of Georgia, 1865-1870 (Cimbala), 35
Union, 162, 192n30; Confederate states rejoining, 18, 57; Johnson trying to restore, 49, 54; strengthened by Reconstruction policies, 28, 36
Union League, 158
The Union League Movement in the Deep South: Politics and Agricultural Change during Reconstruction (Fitzgerald), 29
Union Party, 65n8
Unionist narrative, 126
Unionists, 2, 5, 30, 53
Urban Emancipation: Popular Politics in Reconstruction Mobile, 1860-1890 (Fitzgerald), 35

vagrancy laws, 78, 137
Vale of Tears: New Essays on Religion and Reconstruction (Blum and Poole), 81
Vesey, Denmark, 104-5
veterans, 82, 163
Vietnam War, disillusionment from, 27
violence, 1, 50, 53, 81; effectiveness of, 116, 145, 155; in historiography, 92, 99-100; ongoing, 26, 29, 38; sexual, 33, 155-56
Voices of Emancipation: Understanding Slavery, the Civil War, and Reconstruction through the U.S. Pension Bureau (Shaffer and Regosin), 163
Vorenberg, Michael, 31, 100

Waite Court, 78
Waldrep, Christopher, 30
Wang, Xi, 30
warfare, Reconstruction as low-grade, 67n42

The Wars of Reconstruction: The Brief, Violent History of America's Most Progressive Era (Egerton), 1, 77, 104
Washington, Booker T., 3, 186
Waugh, Joan, 124, 163
We Will Be Satisfied with Nothing Less: The African American Struggle for Equal Rights in the North during Reconstruction (Davis), 34
Weisberger, Bernard A., 1-2, 73
Wesley, Charles H., 22
West, 34, 157
West, Elliot, 62, 157
West from Appomattox: The Reconstruction of America after the Civil War (Richardson), 33-34, 103, 159
Wharton, Vernon L., 20, 73
What Reconstruction Meant: Historical Memory in the American South (Baker), 166
When the War Was Over: The Failure of Self-Reconstruction in the South, 1865-1867 (Carter), 56, 101
Whigs, 115
White, Richard, 125
white supremacy, 16, 116, 182; effects of, 114, 171; home rule as euphemism for, 3, 19; memory used in maintenance of, 82, 162; violence in maintenance of, 99-100, 155-56
White Terror (Trelease), 99
Wiener, Jonathan, 135
Wiggins, Sarah Woolfolk, 37
Williams, Heather Andrea, 102
Williams, Kidada E., 165
Williams, T. Harry, 73
Wilson, Woodrow, 12, 91-92
With Charity for All: Lincoln and Restoration of the Union (Harris), 30
Wolfe, Thomas, 112
women, 103, 164; in black migrations, 144-45; divided by race and class biases, 143, 156; political participation of, 80, 121-22; sexual violence against black, 155-56; withdrawing labor, 133-34, 140-41; working for and with freedpeople, 61, 142-43
women's history, 160
Women's Radical Reconstruction: The Freedmen's Aid Movement (Faulkner), 61, 142-43
Wood, Amy Louise, 166
Woodman, Harold, 135
Woodward, C. Vann, 73, 106n10, 182
Woody, Robert H., 131
The Work of Reconstruction: From Slave to Wage Labor in South Carolina, 1860-1870 (Saville), 35, 136, 154-55
work-rent system, 141
working class, 175, 178-79, 192n30; black, 72, 133-34, 182; interracial, 139, 182
World War I, Great Migration during, 145
Wright, Gavin, 135

Zuczek, Richard, 101

www.ingramcontent.com/pod-product-compliance
Lightning Source LLC
Chambersburg PA
CBHW032021230426
43671CB00005B/165